Contents

OFFICE FOR STANDARDS
IN EDUCATION

Primary
1994-98 Education
A REVIEW OF PRIMARY SCHOOLS IN ENGLAND

Office for Standards in Education
Alexandra House
33 Kingsway
London WC2B 6SE

Telephone 0207-421 6800

ISBN 0 11 350106 4

INTRODUCTION

The last survey by Her Majesty's Inspectors of Schools (HMI) of primary education in England[1] was published in September 1978 by the Department of Education and Science. It was based on a random, stratified sample of 542 schools and it was conducted by a small team of HMI who made visits to all the schools in the sample.

The final section of the 1978 survey was entitled "Looking Forward" and concluded:

> Taking primary schools as a whole, the curriculum is probably wide enough to serve current educational needs. But the demands of society seem likely to continue to rise; literacy and numeracy will no doubt remain matters of great interest but priorities may well change within these areas and in other parts of the curriculum. The immediate aim, especially for the average and more able pupils, should probably be to take what is done to greater depth rather than to introduce content that is new to primary education. To do this it is important to make full use, on behalf of schools as a whole, of teachers' strengths and to build on the existing knowledge of individual teachers without losing the advantages that are associated with the class teacher system.

These concerns about the quality and standards of primary education were taken up in another well known report. In December 1991 the Secretary of State asked Professor Robin Alexander, Jim Rose HMI (Chief Inspector for Primary Education) and Chris Woodhead (Chief Executive of the National Curriculum Council) to "review available evidence about the delivery of education in primary schools" in order "to make recommendations about curriculum organisation, teaching methods and classroom practice appropriate for the successful implementation of the National Curriculum particularly in Key Stage 2".

The focus of the report, entitled *Curriculum Organisation and Classroom Practice in Primary Schools*,[2] was teaching: its quality; subject expertise, teaching roles and staff deployment; and initial training, induction and in-service training. In some respects the report anticipated changes to the organisation of the curriculum in primary schools:

> Over the last few decades the progress of primary pupils has been hampered by the influence of highly questionable dogmas which have led to excessively complex classroom practices and devalued the place of subjects in the curriculum. The resistance to subjects at the primary stage is no longer tenable. The subject is a necessary feature of the modern primary curriculum.

> There is clear evidence to show that much topic work has led to fragmentary and superficial teaching and learning. There is also ample evidence to show that teaching focused on single subjects benefits primary pupils.

A major issue addressed by the report was how to secure sufficient subject expertise in primary schools to keep pace with pupils' developing abilities and meet the expectations of the National Curriculum:

> The extent of subject knowledge required in order to teach the National Curriculum is more than can reasonably be expected of many class teachers, especially but not exclusively in the upper years of Key Stage 2.

> Every primary school should, in principle, have direct access to specialist expertise in all nine National Curriculum subjects and in religious education.

The report made recommendations about effective methods of teaching and of classroom organisation, and about the deployment of teachers beyond the traditional "one teacher one class" model:

> The organisational strategies of whole-class teaching, group work and individual teaching need to be used more selectively and flexibly. The criterion for choice must be fitness for purpose. In many schools the benefits of whole-class teaching have been insufficiently exploited.

> Primary teaching roles are currently too rigidly conceived and much greater flexibility in staff deployment is needed. We recommend the

---

[1] *Primary Education in England, A Survey by HM Inspectors of Schools.* DES, 1978.

[2] Alexander R, Rose A.J., and Woodhead C. (1992) *Curriculum Organisation and Classroom Practice in Primary Schools. A discussion paper.* DES.

introduction of semi-specialist and specialist teaching in primary schools to strengthen the existing roles of class teacher and consultant. There is a particular case for concentrating specialist teaching at the upper end of Key Stage 2.

Twenty years on from the review of primary education, and approaching a decade after the publication of the "Three Wise Men" report (the *Curriculum Organisation and Classroom Practice* report came out around Christmas 1992), OFSTED is in a strong position to comment on the strengths and weaknesses of the maintained primary schools in England and on the issues confronting them.

The four year review: the evidence base

Following the Education (Schools) Act 1992, the first cycle of inspections was completed in July 1998. By this time every primary school in England had been inspected and inspection reports, including a summary report for parents, had been published. This four-year review of primary education is based principally on the evidence from the inspections of primary schools carried out by registered inspectors and their teams. The number of primary schools inspected increased each year, reflecting the growth in the number of inspectors qualified to conduct inspections, and the involvement of many "Additional Inspectors"[3] employed by OFSTED between 1995 and 1997 on short-term secondments and trained to inspect by HMI.

The scale of the evidence base from these inspections – including individual lesson observation forms to the published inspection reports on over 18,000 primary schools – is colossal. Over the period of the first inspection cycle, about 200,000 pre-Key Stage 1 lessons were inspected, 400,000 at Key Stage 1 and over 650,000 lessons at Key Stage 2, a total of over 1,250,000 lessons inspected over the four-year period. This has created a unique record of primary school education in England at the end of the twentieth century.

This review also makes use of a wide range of other evidence available on the standards of achievement in English primary schools and the quality of education provided. It draws on the

National Curriculum test data for the four years, providing an increasingly accurate picture of standards in the core subjects of English, mathematics and science. It draws on the findings from HMI inspection surveys carried out during the same period, for example: the inspection of the teaching of reading in three local education authorities and the inspection of the teaching of number in three local education authorities; the evaluation reports on the National Numeracy and Literacy Projects; and surveys of aspects of pedagogy such as the use of specialist teachers at Key Stage 2 and the use of setting in primary schools.

The review also reports on the findings of the inspection of primary-phase initial teacher training, especially training to teach reading and number; and the progress made by schools identified as having serious weaknesses or requiring special measures. In other words, while the review draws principally on the extensive database released by the Section 9 and Section 10 statutory inspections, it also draws on a considerable range of other data and inspection evidence. Finally, it refers to research commissioned by OFSTED, such as that into international comparisons. Above all, it takes as its theme the drive to raise standards through school improvement.

---

[3] For further information see *The Additional Inspector Project.* OFSTED, 1997.

1 MAIN FINDINGS AND COMMENTARY

1.1 Main findings

- The quality of education in primary schools has improved over the four years of the inspection cycle. More pupils are achieving higher standards by the time they transfer to secondary school; the quality of teaching has improved; and headteachers, teachers and governors now give greater attention to raising standards and improving their schools. Nevertheless, there is room for improvement, particularly in literacy and numeracy, in most schools. About 3 per cent of schools fail to provide an acceptable standard of education, with a further 8 per cent having serious weaknesses.

- The proportion of pupils reaching the basic threshold of Level 2[4] in reading and writing at Key Stage 1 has remained at about 80 per cent over the four years. There has been a modest improvement in standards of mathematics, rising from 78 per cent at Level 2 in 1995 to 84 per cent in 1998. About one in five pupils, therefore, has not achieved the expected standards in the essential skills of literacy, numeracy and mathematics at transfer from Key Stage 1 to Key Stage 2.

- At Key Stage 2 there has been a substantial increase in the proportion of pupils achieving Level 4 in English and mathematics. This proportion has risen by about 15 percentage points over the four years. A similar improvement is needed over the next four years if government targets are to be met by the year 2002.

- While there has been some increase in the proportion of pupils achieving Level 3 or better,

about one in ten pupils leaves primary school without having achieved Level 3. These pupils are poorly equipped to face the demands of the secondary curriculum.

- More pupils reach the expected level of attainment in reading than in writing. It is a particular concern that there is a considerable gap between the achievement of girls and boys, particularly in writing, where in 1998 girls outperformed boys by 16 percentage points. There are few signs that this gap is narrowing.

- Progress varies as pupils move through school. They make good progress in the earlier years, but there is a dip in Years 3 and 4, the beginning of Key Stage 2. Progress then improves and is greatest in Year 6.

- Pupils make good progress in three in ten schools. In about six in ten schools they make satisfactory progress, although it is unlikely that this rate of progress will be sufficient to ensure that four out of five pupils will reach the national targets for English by 2002. There was substantial underachievement in one in 14 schools at Key Stage 1 and one in ten at Key Stage 2.

- Standards of achievement have improved in most subjects over the past four years. Nevertheless, serious problems remain with design and technology and are even more acute in information technology in over four in ten schools.

- The greatest challenges are faced by schools serving disadvantaged areas. The link between low attainment and disadvantage is strong and persistent. There are, however, schools which achieve well against the odds; and for any given level of socio-economic factors there is a wide variation between the performance of the best and worst schools.

- Over the four years of the inspection programme the quality of teaching has improved, with 1998 being the first year in which the teaching of the core subjects of English, mathematics and science was better than the teaching of all other subjects. The proportion of good teaching has risen at Key Stage 2 to over one-half, and that of overall unsatisfactory teaching has fallen to one in 14 schools. This improvement is striking, but there

[4] Level 2 is the level 'expected of seven-year-olds'. Level 4 is the level 'expected of eleven-year-olds'. Taken from: *Results of the 1997 NC assessments.* DfEE, 1997.

are still over a quarter of a million pupils in schools where the teaching is unsatisfactory.

- Several factors underpin this improvement. There has been an improvement in teachers' knowledge, skills and understanding of the subjects they teach. As teachers have become more familiar with the programmes of study, their planning has improved and learning objectives have been more precisely defined. Above all, there has been an increase in the amount of direct, whole-class teaching. This is not an easy option, however, and requires a secure subject knowledge, clear instructive teaching and skilled questioning.

- The quality of leadership and management is good or very good in just over half of schools; it is weak in about one in eight schools. There is a strong link between the quality of the leadership and management and the quality of the teaching. Important aspects of leadership are the sense of educational direction given by a headteacher, the extent and impact of the monitoring of the work of teachers, and the evaluation of curriculum initiatives. The weakest aspects of leadership and management have been the monitoring and evaluation of classroom practice.

- The role of governors has changed in recent years; the demands made of them are greater and their responsibilities are clearer. The overall picture is one of governors supporting their schools positively and effectively, and dealing with their duties with dedication. There is considerable variation in practice, however, and in about one-quarter of schools the governors are poorly placed to influence the education provided.

- Headteachers are particularly successful at establishing a positive ethos in their schools. This is one of the great strengths of English primary schools, and is illustrated by many positive indicators. The behaviour of pupils is good in four out of five primary schools, and poor in only 2 per cent of schools. Virtually all primary schools are orderly, safe communities in which children are taught to respect each other, their teachers, other adults and property.

- Attendance, too, is good in the vast majority of schools, falling below 90 per cent in only about 4 per cent of schools. Most schools work hard to ensure regular attendance and have effective procedures for monitoring and promoting good attendance.

- Most schools adapted well to implementing the National Curriculum by meeting the expectation that the curriculum should be broadly based, balanced and relevant. More recently, the strong emphasis on literacy and numeracy has meant that primary schools have had to review their priorities and to consider the balance between the essential basic skills of literacy and numeracy and the rest of the curriculum.

- Wide-ranging topic work, in which elements of several subjects were taught, has given way over the four years to work which focuses on a single subject. This has contributed strongly to the improvement in work in most subjects. At the same time it has helped pupils to apply or consolidate their skills, particularly in literacy and numeracy.

- Greater and more effective use of assessment data has helped schools to establish targets for improvement and to analyse more precisely the strengths and weaknesses in their teaching programmes. Not all schools make the best use of the data available, for example to analyse the performance of different groups of pupils.

- The quantity and quality of learning resources are inadequate in one in ten schools; resources for teaching English are a particular cause for concern, although there has recently been a significant reallocation of spending priorities towards literacy. Accommodation is good in less than half the schools, but there has been a significant move in recent years to make school grounds and buildings more secure. Most schools have sufficient qualified and experienced teachers to meet the demands of the curriculum, although the pupil–teacher ratio rose in each year of the inspection cycle.

- There has been, in recent years, a marked improvement in the attention given on initial teacher training courses to training in the teaching of reading and number work. Mental calculation and phonics are now given a greater and more appropriate priority.

- The main issues facing the training partnerships are how to ensure consistency in assessing the trainees; and how to ensure that trainees receive comparable training experiences of sufficiently high quality.

1.2 Commentary and recommendations

Primary schools are getting better. Taking primary education, pre-five to eleven plus, as a whole, while there is still too much unevenness in the system, it is irrefutable that more teachers are teaching more effectively than was the case four years ago. There is more good practice in every subject of the National Curriculum and in government-funded provision for under-fives. As a result, more children are getting a better primary education and the nation is receiving a better return for its £6.5 billion annual investment in our primary schools.

This overall picture of progress is drawn from an unprecedented amount of information about the performance of pupils and teachers in primary schools and about such important matters as the resources and management systems which support them. As a nation, we almost certainly lead the world in the amount of information we hold on school and pupil performance, particularly when the data from national tests are added to that of inspection.

Impressive though this information base may be, it is of little value unless it can be used to improve practice and raise standards. It is all too easy to become 'information-rich and action-poor'. What is at issue is how we make best use of this rich information about primary schools to accelerate the raising of standards, particularly in schools serving disadvantaged areas. Progress is being made, but it needs to be faster and more extensive if we are to meet the Government's targets for primary education for 2002.

The significance of those targets invites comment because they stand as a proxy for national concerns, as well as for national confidence in those who teach in our primary schools and those who provide for primary education. The targets recognise the priority that primary schools must give to raising standards of English and mathematics, at the heart of which are pupils' achievements in literacy and numeracy.

The widespread belief that standards of pupil

achievement in primary schools have been too low for far too long is strongly supported by this review. What most people have in mind when the issue of low standards of achievement is discussed are standards of reading, writing, number knowledge and the skills of calculation – the foundation work of primary schools. Whatever might be said about changes in the national tests and in the Framework for Inspection over this four-year period, there has been sufficient stability in both to indicate that standards in these crucially important areas in 1994 were woefully low. They are now much better, though not yet good enough if our children are to have the best chances of leading fulfilled lives and succeeding in a world economy where high educational standards will continue to be of paramount importance.

Perhaps the message that most needs to be heeded from the inspection of primary schools over the last four years is that the primary phase, which covers the greater part of statutory education, is not only important in its own right but also has a crucial "make or break" influence on what follows. Insofar as it is possible to make like-for-like comparisons, primary schools serving similar socio-economic populations can vary to the extent that over two years' difference can be made to a pupil's progress, depending on the school he or she attends. All of these points argue that we must continue to strive for much greater consistency in the quality of our primary schools.

Primary schools know full well that they must give top priority to making sure that their pupils are taught the "basic skills" as effectively as possible. Many schools, however, continue to struggle with the long-standing problem of providing a broad and balanced curriculum, of which the statutory National Curriculum and religious education are but a part, while giving sufficient attention to what has become an enlarged programme of basic skills. For example, the latter now includes information technology along with the traditional skills of literacy and numeracy. Schools have to decide how time is to be apportioned to these priorities, so that the curriculum does not become so narrow as to stultify pupils' wider progress in subjects such as art, music and physical education or so broad that little or nothing is taught very well. The most successful schools are efficient users of the time available for teaching and are imaginative in what they do to extend teaching and learning time through, for example, homework and extracurricular activities.

Of all the issues facing primary education over the last four years, the teaching of reading has almost certainly caused the greatest professional debate and public concern. Despite the introduction of a detailed framework for teaching reading and other key aspects of literacy within the National Literacy Strategy, how best to teach the early stages of reading remains a contentious issue, albeit from a much changed perspective about the central importance of teaching phonics. The professional debate has shifted markedly. Few, if any, now seriously disagree with the well researched position which insists that children must be taught essential phonic knowledge and skills from an early stage. The debate is no longer so much about whether to teach phonics, but rather about how to teach phonic knowledge and skills efficiently and effectively so that children can enjoy early success and read effortlessly. Inspection and test results show that the vast majority of children are capable of achieving these goals by the end of Key Stage 1.

Many teachers need to update considerably their knowledge of phonic work in order to teach it well. This reflects a period of neglect of this crucial aspect of reading in both initial and in-service teacher training. It is hardly surprising, therefore, that the phonic component, ie the "word level" work in the literacy hour of the Government's National Literacy Strategy, is often the weakest aspect of the teaching of reading and continues to need urgent attention in many schools.

The importance of phonic work attaches to more than reading. Over this four-year period it has become clear that children's writing skills also require more attention and are heavily dependent upon an understanding of phonics, the effective teaching of spelling and handwriting, and opportunities for wider reading.

Two serious problems in many primary schools, highlighted by HMCI's Annual Reports and by this review, are the considerably poorer literacy performance of boys in comparison with that of girls, and the dip in the overall performance of primary pupils which has occurred persistently in Year 3 and to a lesser extent in Year 4. Common sense suggests that each of these problems compounds the other. Given that differences in pupil achievement emerge at an early stage and

can widen alarmingly, the close monitoring of pupil performance deserves more attention. Although some schools consistently monitor pupil performance – for example, to address gender and ethnic concerns – for many this is not a well developed practice.

It is difficult to spell out exactly how the gender differences in achievement might be overcome. For boys, it is likely that more thorough teaching of the basic skills of reading to help them to achieve early success, accompanied by more appealing reading material and more challenging opportunities to write about interests other than fictional stories, would help to close the gap. The national initiatives to encourage parents to do more to support reading at home, combined with schools' efforts to enlist the help of parents, are also showing promising results.

The dip in the performance of certain year groups of pupils, most often Years 3 and 4, goes unheeded in too many schools. Whatever the reasons for this uneven pattern of performance by year group, the problem needs to be taken seriously because many Year 3 and Year 4 pupils, especially boys, are often at a critical stage in consolidating hard-won skills of reading and writing. Headteachers should be wary of deploying the least experienced or the weakest teachers in a particular year group such as Year 3 in the hope that any ground lost by the pupils in these year groups can be made up later.

Schools must also address two other important variables that influence pupil performance, which are different but often overlapping: ethnicity and poverty. Over the period of this review, some primary schools have amply demonstrated that it is possible to raise pupils' achievement despite distinctly unpromising social and economic home backgrounds. In the case of schools containing pupils from ethnic minorities, many of whom have to learn English as an additional language, there have been some spectacular successes, showing how focused, well-structured teaching can accelerate learning so that pupils achieve good standards of literacy and numeracy, and much else, by the age of eleven. The attitude which prevails in these successful schools is a powerful intolerance of underachievement and a refusal to accept variables related to pupils' home backgrounds as an excuse for a lack of progress. All that said, it must be acknowledged that teachers in these circumstances often face problems which many others simply do not have to tackle to anything like the same extent. These conditions are certainly sufficient to justify additional resources, for example to allow schools to employ teaching assistants. Indeed, inspection shows that well-trained teaching assistants are a key resource and are used very effectively in many primary schools. More importantly, there is a clear case for assuring better pupil–teacher ratios in schools serving areas of social and economic disadvantage, especially at Key Stage 1.

In one sense this review provides a glance in the rear-view mirror to make sure we are not overtaken by the mistakes of the past and are better prepared for what lies ahead. We would do well to remember that primary schools have been through a period of considerable turbulence. Primary school teachers, for example, bore the brunt of curricular reform. The National Curriculum and its assessment were introduced first into primary schools, closely followed by a new inspection regime. They had to accommodate other major reforms, such as more open enrolment and an enlarged responsibility for managing their budgets. In many respects these reforms have been welcome, and indeed essential. However, there has hardly been a breathing space for primary schools since the 1988 Education Reform Act, let alone over the last four years, during which one reform has had the time to settle down before others have followed, or changes have been made to those already introduced. All of this suggests that primary schools would benefit from a period of greater stability in which to consolidate and build upon what, arguably, has been the most extensive programme of educational reform in living memory.

Primary teachers, and particularly primary headteachers, have had to become much more management-minded as responsibilities for devolved budgets and school resources, including staffing, have grown. The most effective headteachers are good managers but are not infected with "managerialism", as if management existed to serve itself. They understand the difference between leadership and management. In order to reduce bureaucracy, to focus upon monitoring and raising standards of pupil achievement, and to create a context for teachers to give of their best, they challenge themselves with such questions as, "What am I managing for?"

and "How will proposed changes benefit the pupils and improve what exists already?"

Primary schools, because they are relatively small institutions, have to manage both the benefits and the obstacles arising from their size. On the one hand they gain from a keen sense of teamwork, in which the whole staff can communicate easily and, given good leadership, respond swiftly to agreed changes in policy and practice. On the other hand, it is clear that their expertise, for example in providing consistently high-quality teaching in all the subjects and aspects of the curriculum, is often fully stretched. The average-sized primary school is rarely able to employ sufficient teachers to have a one-to-one co-ordinator for each subject, or time for subject co-ordinators to carry out important aspects of their role, such as monitoring teaching, during the school day.

The use of topic work, whereby several subjects are integrated under a common theme such as "ourselves" or "buildings", which many teachers found difficult to manage and which led to much superficial work for many pupils, is now far less common. Teachers are focusing more rigorously upon the programmes of study for each subject and planning lessons accordingly. The demise of broadly based topic work and the stronger emphasis on subject teaching, encouraged by the National Curriculum, have required a greater command of subject knowledge on the part of primary teachers. To expect class teachers to teach every subject to pupils who may well, by the end of Key Stage 2, be achieving beyond Level 4 in the core subjects, is a tall order.

Over the last four years some primary schools have begun to take steps to organise pupils and teachers in different ways, so as to make better use of the subject expertise available in the school. In many schools there is now a greater use of teachers with particular expertise to teach classes other than their own. Music and physical education have long been treated in this way, but the approach now often encompasses other subjects.

The wider use of specialist teaching has been accompanied by an increase in grouping pupils by ability for some subjects, particularly English and mathematics at Key Stage 2. This has often been done by creating ability sets from more than one class, thus making it easier for the teacher to plan and match the work to the developing abilities of the pupils and the requirements of the National Curriculum. While these arrangements for deploying teachers and organising pupils do not in themselves guarantee success, they offer considerable potential for good teaching to be made available to more children than may be the case where, typically, one class teacher teaches all the curriculum to the same class for at least one school year.

Given the clear link between teaching quality and pupil achievement, the availability of teachers with sufficient subject expertise remains a key issue for primary schools. Because they have a thorough grasp of the subject matter that they are required to teach, good teachers are not only able to set high expectations but they also understand the incremental steps, ie the progression, that pupils have to make to fulfil curricular expectations. They are thus well equipped to promote both continuity and progression in the primary curriculum. Unfortunately, all too often the subject expertise available within a school remains underused because the teachers concerned are confined to working with their own class.

By one means or another, primary schools have had to build expertise to keep pace with the fast-growing field of information and communication technology as well as teaching the programme of study for information technology. Information technology remains the weakest subject in the primary curriculum overall, although there is evidence of high attainments and exemplary work by many pupils in a few schools. We are thus unwittingly developing two populations of pupils, with those who are able to benefit from IT-literate homes and from schools where information technology is well taught rapidly outpacing those where neither of these conditions applies.

Primary education is essentially a person-to-person service in which teachers and pupils alike benefit from constructive feedback about the strengths and weaknesses of their work, together with clear guidance about what they need to do to improve. Sadly, however, the appraisal of teaching remains a seriously weak feature in primary schools, as in schools in general. Despite – or perhaps because of – the close teamwork that is a feature of many primary schools, there seems to be a reluctance rigorously to appraise teachers, including headteachers, with the intention of managing performance to raise pupil achievement.

It is by no means unusual, however, for headteachers, teachers and governors to press for more feedback about their work from inspectors. There is, it seems, an unresolved tension between the reluctance to tackle school-based appraisal and the appetite for more and better feedback, particularly about teaching, from inspection. Some progress might be made on resolving this tension were more schools to consider using the OFSTED Framework and Guidance for Inspection to align their appraisal requirements more closely with the inspection criteria for judging teaching quality. The issues of performance management will be thrown into sharp relief as a result of developments stemming from the recent Green Paper.[5]

Surveys of parents' views conducted by OFSTED over this four-year period show that they are concerned about their children's achievement and what they often describe as their children's "happiness" at school. Many, for example, suggest that homework ought to feature more strongly in the programme for older primary pupils and would like clearer information about their children's progress. High on their list of concerns, of course, are children's safety and welfare. They seek reassurance that bullying and racial discrimination will not be tolerated. Inspection shows that the great majority of primary schools are safe and orderly communities in which children are taught to respect each other, their teachers, other adults and property. Norms of good behaviour, fairness and an understanding of right and wrong actions are generally well established in primary schools. Attendance rates are generally good.

Insidious harassment and bullying are difficult for schools to deal with and call for constant vigilance, clear policies and decisive action, including the creation of a climate which makes it easy for children to tell their teachers about these problems rather than suffer in silence. While overt bullying, discrimination and harassment are not tolerated, and the vast majority of primary schools rightly take a stand on these issues, it is difficult for them always to hold the line against poor relationships which may exist in the neighbourhood. Although pupils may behave well in school, the school cannot so easily inoculate them, for example, from prejudice which may persist outside its

---

[5] *Teachers Meeting the Challenge of Change*, DfEE, 1999.

gates. Clearly, a greater all-round effort must be made to support schools in these respects, drawing upon the experience of the most successful local networks which some schools enjoy.

Though a cliché, the picture which emerges from this four-year review is one of cautious optimism. Primary schools are much more focused than ever before on raising standards of pupil achievement and less willing to tolerate professional weaknesses and ideologies that depress pupils' progress. They need to build on their successes through the relentless pursuit of better-quality teaching consistently applied in all year groups.

It follows that the temptation to pour more educational quarts into primary pint pots should be resisted in order to give primary schools the opportunity they need to develop the quality of their work and capitalise on the reforms set in place.

The Government is making a determined effort to raise standards of pupil achievement through a broad range of policy initiatives and reforms that are either in place or in the pipeline. The findings of this four-year review point to four main recommendations for the continued improvement of primary education and the achievement of the ambitious national targets. These recommendations are not, of course, exhaustive, but all those involved with primary education should:

- provide a period of stability for primary schools to implement fully and consolidate the extensive programme of reforms, rather than introduce more that is new to an already stretched system;

- make sure that the expectations and priorities for primary schools are clearly understood, manageable and adequately resourced;

- give top priority to supporting the work of teachers in their classrooms. This will require far more robust teacher-appraisal arrangements than presently exist, linked to targeted training and close monitoring of the applications and outcomes of that training, in order to determine how well it advances pupils' progress;

- audit the use of the considerable resources that the Government has put into, and plans to put into, primary education, so as to make sure those resources support the priorities for which they are intended.

2
PRIMARY EDUCATION IN ENGLAND

2.1 The schools, the pupils and the teachers

In 1994 there were 18,679 maintained primary schools providing full-time education for 3,944,635 pupils. In 1998 the number of schools had fallen to 18,230 (a fall of 2.4 per cent) and the number of full-time pupils had risen to 4,109,624 (a rise of 4.2 per cent). There were about 83,000 more boys than girls receiving full-time primary education in 1998. The number of pupils receiving part-time education, almost always in nursery schools or as pupils under the age of five in nursery or reception classes in primary schools, rose from 267,385 in 1994 to 317,193 in 1998 (a rise of 18.6 per cent).

The number of pupils aged between five and ten attending independent schools rose from 185,200 in 1994 to 198,300 in 1998. In percentage terms this has remained virtually static, at around 5 per cent of the pupil population. OFSTED has some statutory responsibilities for inspecting independent schools, but this review does not report on this work. There are also relatively small numbers of pupils outside of the traditional school system, generally referred to as pupils "educated otherwise", perhaps being taught at home by their parents. In addition, there are excluded pupils, pupils in referral units, pupils for whom home tuition is provided, and pupils being educated in hospital schools or by social services. It is hard to establish a precise figure for the number of pupils falling into these categories, but it is probably about 8,000.

While the large majority of pupils are educated in local education authority maintained, non-denominational, combined infant and junior schools, there is some variation in the types of school.

As illustrated in Chart 1, 9 per cent of primary schools are first schools, with pupils usually

Chart 1
Types of school as at 1998
(percentage of schools)

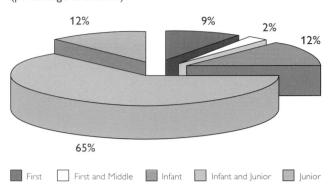

First ◼ | First and Middle ◻ | Infant ◼ | Infant and Junior ◼ | Junior ◼

Chart 2
Denomination as at 1998
(percentage of schools)

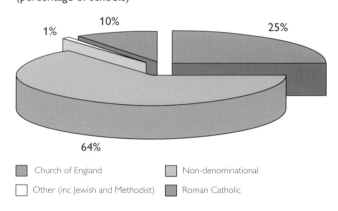

Church of England ◼ | Non-denominational ◻
Other (inc Jewish and Methodist) ◻ | Roman Catholic ◼

Chart 3
Types of control of schools as at 1998
(percentage of schools)

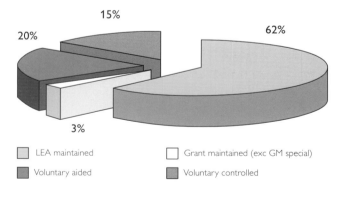

LEA maintained ◻ | Grant maintained (exc GM special) ◻
Voluntary aided ◼ | Voluntary controlled ◼

transferring at eight or nine (the end of Year 3 or Year 4). Twelve per cent of schools are infant schools, with pupils transferring to junior schools at the end of Year 2. There are now only 191 middle "deemed primary" schools, with pupils transferring after Year 7.

Chart 2 shows that one in four schools (including grant maintained schools) has denominational links (either LEA controlled or voluntary aided status) with the Church of England; just under one in ten schools is Roman Catholic.

As indicated in Chart 3, 62 per cent of schools are LEA maintained, and under 3 per cent are grant maintained. Of the schools with denominational links, 57 per cent are voluntary aided, 43 per cent voluntary controlled. In terms of the numbers of pupils, 64 per cent are in through primary (infant and junior combined) schools, and 10 per cent are in first or middle schools. Seventy-two per cent of pupils are in non-denominational schools, 17 per cent in schools with Church of England status and 10 per cent in Roman Catholic schools. Seventy per cent of pupils are in LEA maintained schools, 3 per cent in grant maintained schools, 17 per cent in voluntary aided schools and 10 per cent in voluntary controlled schools.

Chart 4 illustrates the considerable variation in the size of primary schools; 3.3 per cent of schools have less than 50 pupils on roll.

For just under 7 per cent of the pupil population English is an additional language (EAL); these pupils attend in any significant numbers about one-quarter of schools. Four-fifths of primary schools have less than 5 per cent of EAL pupils; 6 per cent of schools have over 40 per cent of EAL pupils.

In 1998 the percentage of pupils identified by schools as having special educational needs, and included on their registers of special educational needs, was 19.9. Over the period of the review, the percentage of pupils in mainstream primary schools with Statements of Special Educational Need has risen slightly, from 1.2 per cent in 1994

to 1.5 per cent in 1998. Roughly twice as many pupils in junior schools have Statements of Special Educational Need than in infant schools.

The percentage of pupils eligible for free school meals has remained relatively steady, averaging about 24 per cent of the pupil population. The percentage has been slightly higher in infant schools than primary schools. By the end of the four-year period, there had been an increase of six percentage points in the number of schools with up to 10 per cent free school meals; the changes are illustrated in Chart 5.

The proportion of pupils eligible for free school meals is not, of course, evenly distributed throughout primary schools. For example, 41 per cent of schools have 10 per cent or less of their pupils eligible for free school meals, whereas around 11 per cent of schools have over 40 per cent of their pupils eligible for free school meals.

The number of full-time equivalent qualified teachers remained virtually unchanged over the period 1994 to 1998, reaching 181,394 in 1998. Ten per cent of these teachers are headteachers. There are considerably more women teachers than men teachers: 152,764 women in 1998, compared with 28,630 men. In other words, only 16 per cent of teachers in primary schools are men. Furthermore, the number of male teachers has fallen by 2,000 over the four years, and continues to decline as a proportion of the teaching force.

Over the four-year period there has been a significant change in the balance between men and women headteachers. In 1994 there were nearly equal numbers of men and women headteachers:

Chart 4
Numbers on roll in primary schools (January 1998)
(percentage of schools)

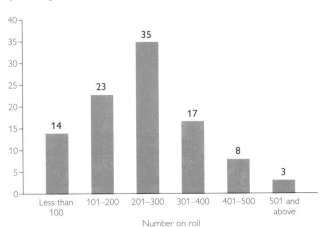

Number on roll

Chart 5
Primary schools banded by number of pupils eligible for free school meals, 1995 and 1998
(percentage of schools)

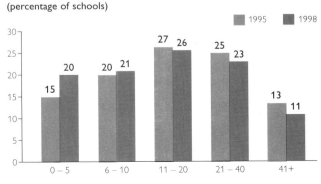

Percentage of pupils eligible for free school meals

9,247 men, 9,435 women. By 1998, however, the number and proportion of women headteachers had risen considerably: 7,951 men, 10,362 women. As a proportion, about 57 per cent of headteachers are women, compared with 50.5 per cent in 1994.

The major change in staffing over the four years has been in education support staff. Numbers have increased significantly, by about 40 per cent, from 41,117 in 1994 to 58,055 in 1998. There have been increases in the numbers of most categories of education support staff; there are now 29 per cent more nursery assistants, and 52 per cent more special needs support staff. The numbers of support staff for minority ethnic pupils have risen by 35 per cent over the last two years. There has also been a rise of about 13 per cent in the number of administrative or clerical staff, reaching a total of 19,565 in 1998, of which the majority were secretaries, but an increasing number (about 1,500) were bursars.

English primary schools, then, are extremely diverse: in size, age range, location, population; in buildings, resources, staffing and traditions; and in links with churches and local authorities. While it is possible to construct a statistically average primary school, it is misleading to assume that there is such a thing as a typical primary school.

3 EDUCATIONAL STANDARDS ACHIEVED BY PUPILS: AN OVERVIEW

3.1 National Curriculum test results

Since 1995 all maintained schools have been required to test pupils at the end of Key Stages 1 and 2, and the national figures have been reported annually by the DfEE. Devising annual tests with different test items that set the same standard each year poses very considerable challenges. Despite these, the tests are now firmly established in primary schools and provide an increasingly reliable picture of attainment in the core subjects of English, mathematics and science. Test results are used to identify the National Curriculum level that pupils have achieved. They are also used by inspectors as one of the key criteria against which to judge pupils' progress and a school's effectiveness.

Initially, Level 2 at Key Stage 1 and Level 4 at Key Stage 2 were the levels that "average pupils" were expected to reach at the end of the respective key stage. The proportion of "average pupils" who should achieve these levels was not identified, but in 1995 and 1996 these levels were reported as the levels expected of the "typical pupil". Then, in 1998, the Government set national targets for English and mathematics, to be achieved by the year 2002. These targets identified the proportions of pupils to achieve Level 4 at the end of Key Stage 2: 80 per cent in English, and 75 per cent in mathematics. These figures are much higher than those previously achieved, and present a formidable challenge for schools. However, the importance to be given to literacy and numeracy is reflected in these targets. The basic skills of literacy and numeracy are so vital to the continuing education of pupils that in future the large majority of pupils should achieve what was expected of "average pupils" only five years ago.

Standards at Key Stage 1

Charts 6, 7 and 8 show pupils' performance in the Key Stage 1 tests over the past four years. The percentage of pupils reaching Level 2 (the level expected of seven-year-olds) has remained constant at about 80 per cent in reading and writing. In spelling, in 1995 and 1998, the proportion of pupils reaching Level 2 was 66 per cent, significantly lower than the proportions for

Chart 6

Percentage of pupils achieving each level in the Key Stage 1 National Curriculum test/task (English: reading) 1995–98

(percentage of pupils)

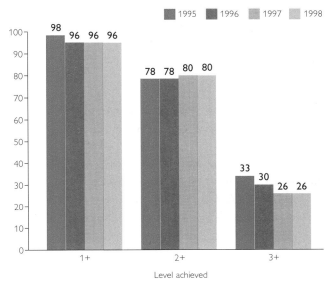

Chart 7

Percentage of pupils achieving each level in the Key Stage 1 National Curriculum test/task (English: writing) 1995–98

(percentage of pupils)

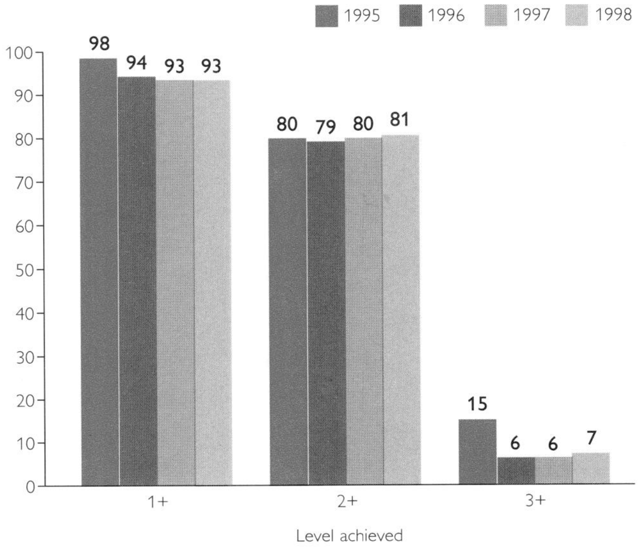

Chart 8
Percentage of pupils achieving each level in the Key Stage 1 National Curriculum test/task (mathematics) 1995–98
(percentage of pupils)

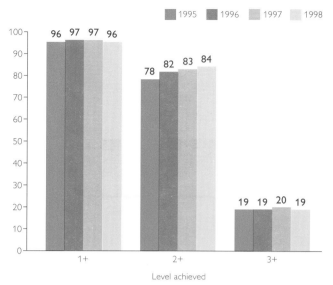

Chart 9
Percentage of pupils achieving each level in the Key Stage 2 National Curriculum test (English) 1995–98
(percentage of pupils)

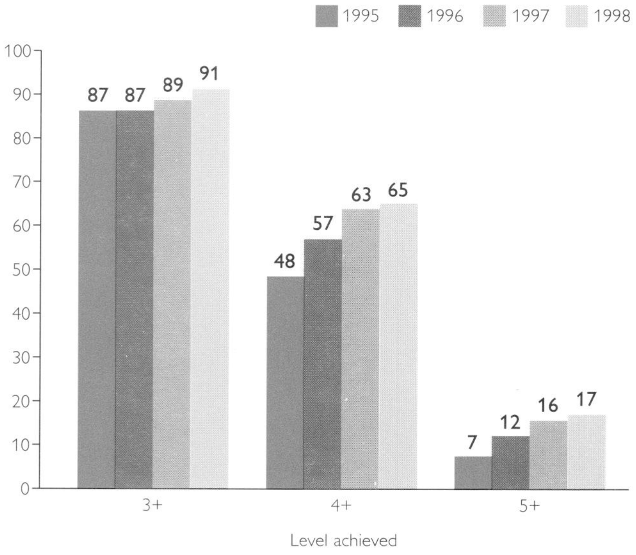

reading and writing. In mathematics, the proportion of pupils reaching Level 2 has increased steadily but not greatly, reaching 84 per cent in 1998. There is little difference in the performance of boys and girls in mathematics, but in reading, writing and spelling at Key Stage 1, girls do substantially better. The difference in the number of girls and boys reaching Level 2 is about 10 percentage points, and this gap shows no signs of narrowing. It indicates that the underachievement of boys in literacy begins in the first few years of their education, and eventually this leads to many boys transferring to secondary schools with weak literacy skills that are often insufficient to cope with the demands of the secondary curriculum.

While the fact that four in five pupils reach Level 2 is in many ways encouraging, three points need to be made. First, one in five pupils does not reach this basic threshold. Second, Level 2 covers a wide range of attainment. It is subdivided into three grades, namely 2A, 2B and 2C, with 2A being the most demanding. However, many of the pupils who reach Level 2C at Key Stage 1 do not go on to reach Level 4 at the end of Key Stage 2; the QCA has recently recommended that schools should look on grade 2B as the expected level of attainment for most children at the end of Key Stage 1. In 1998, the proportion of pupils achieving Level 2B or above was comparable to that of pupils reaching Level 4+ at the end of Key

Chart 10
Percentage of pupils achieving each level in the Key Stage 2 National Curriculum test (mathematics) 1995–98
(percentage of pupils)

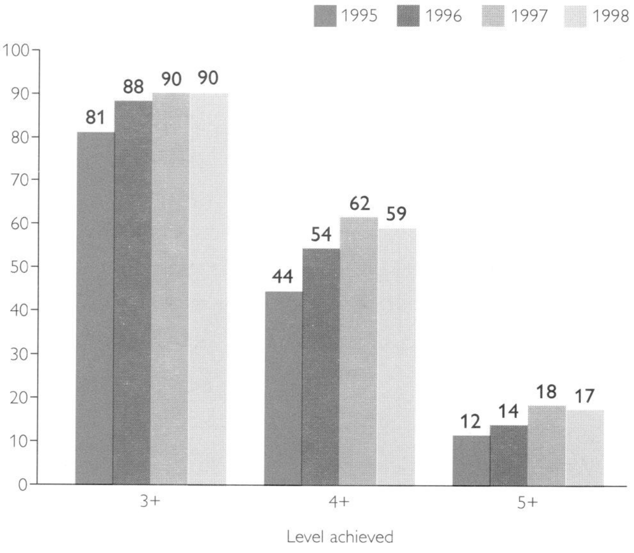

Stage 2. Third, there has been no appreciable improvement in standards in English at Key Stage 1, as measured by the national tests, over the last four years; many schools with Key Stage 1 pupils are not affected by the national targets because they are Key Stage 1 schools only.

Standards at Key Stage 2

Charts 9, 10 and 11 show pupils' performance in the Key Stage 2 tests in English, mathematics and science. A number of key points stand out. There

Chart 11
Percentage of pupils achieving each level in the Key Stage 2 National Curriculum test (science) 1995–98
(percentage of pupils)

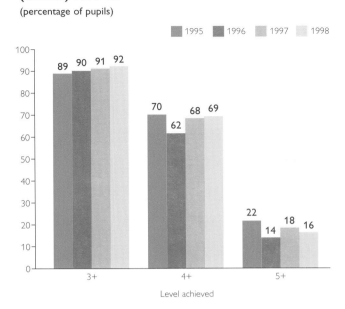

Chart 12
1998 Key Stage 2 test results for reading
(percentage of pupils)

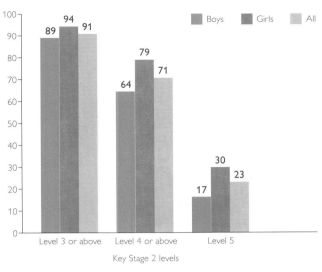

Chart 13
1998 Key Stage 2 test results for writing
(percentage of pupils)

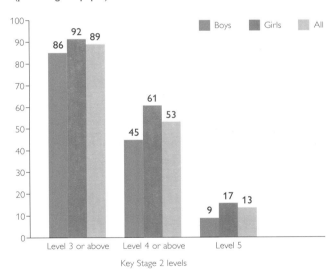

has been a substantial increase in the proportion of pupils achieving Level 4 in mathematics and English. This proportion has increased by about 15 percentage points over the four years: a similar improvement is needed over the next four-year period if Government targets are to be met by the year 2002. It is a matter of concern that the trend of improvement has weakened in 1998. This is particularly the case in mathematics, where the proportion reaching Level 4 fell in 1998, in part due to the additional demands of the new mental arithmetic test. There has also been some increase in the proportion of pupils achieving Level 3 or better, but about one in ten pupils still leaves primary school without having achieved Level 3.

Within English, there are considerable differences in test results for reading and writing at Key Stage 2. Writing is significantly weaker. Information on these components of English has only been available for the last two years, but in 1998 71 per cent of pupils achieved Level 4 for reading but only 53 per cent for writing. The gap between the attainment of boys and girls in English is wider than at Key Stage 1, and this gap has not reduced over the last four years. The differential achievement of boys and girls in the Key Stage 2 English tests is illustrated, for 1998, in Charts 12 and 13. Boys' achievement in writing is particularly weak, with only 45 per cent reaching Level 4 in Key Stage 2. This pulls down the overall performance of eleven-year-old pupils. It follows

that the improvement of boys' writing will be of crucial importance if the Government's targets for English are to be achieved.

3.2 Inspection evidence on achievement

Inspection also provides evidence of improvement in the standards achieved by pupils over the last four years, although changes in the inspection Framework make direct comparisons difficult. In 1994/95 inspectors judged that standards of achievement, taking account of pupils' capabilities, were unsatisfactory or poor, and that there was therefore substantial underachievement, in one in ten schools at Key Stage 1 and one in six at Key Stage 2. In the revised Framework used since 1996, the judgement that is closest to standards taking account of pupils' capabilities is the judgement of progress. In 1997/98 inspectors judged that pupils made good overall progress and achieved well in three in ten schools at both Key Stage 1 and Key Stage 2. In about six in ten schools pupils made satisfactory progress, but there was substantial underachievement in one in 14 schools at Key Stage 1 and one in ten at Key Stage 2.

Charts 14 and 15 illustrate that pupils are learning more in lessons. Chart 14 shows the progress made in lessons for 1997/98. Chart 15 shows the

Chart 14
Lessons in primary schools 1997/98: progress
(percentage of lessons)

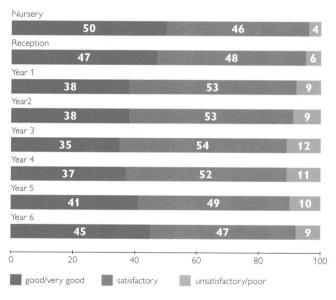

These figures have been rounded and may not add up to 100 per cent

Chart 15
Percentage of lessons with good or better progress, comparing 1996/97 and 1997/98

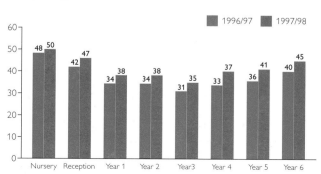

Chart 16
Progress in Key Stage 1 in 1997/98
(percentage of schools)

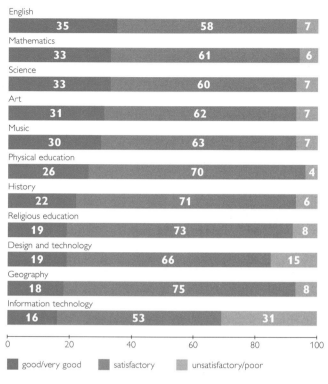

These figures have been rounded and may not add up to 100 per cent

Chart 17
Progress in Key Stage 2 in 1997/98
(percentage of schools)

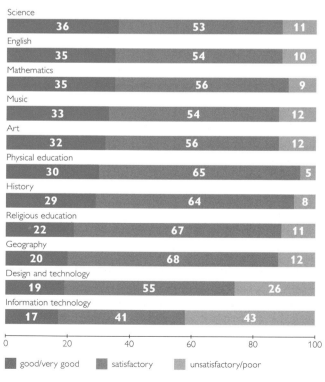

These figures have been rounded and may not add up to 100 per cent

Chart 18

Average level achieved by pupils in 1998 Key Stage 2 tests against eligibility for free school meals for a random selection of primary schools

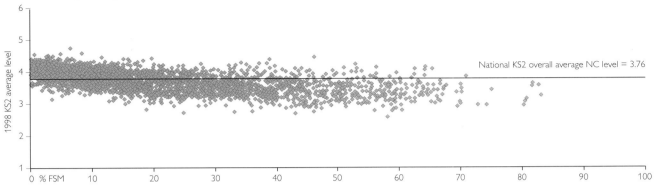

proportion of lessons in which progress was judged to be good in the last two years of the review period. Two points stand out. First, progress varies as pupils move through the different years in a primary school. Pupils make good progress in the earlier years, but there is a dip in Years 3 and 4, the beginning of Key Stage 2. Progress then improves and is greatest in Year 6, perhaps because this is where primary schools often deploy their strongest teachers and where the National Curriculum tests now provide a sharp focus for the work. The second point is that, across all years, pupils made more progress in 1997/98 than in 1996/97.

The rate of progress made by pupils varies considerably between subjects. Charts 16 and 17 show progress for both key stages in the National Curriculum subjects and religious education for 1997/98. Pupils are now making the most progress in the core subjects, reflecting the high and appropriate priority that schools are now giving to these subjects. Despite this additional attention to the core subjects, there is no evidence of a decline in the non-core subjects, with the exception of information technology. Inspectors report that standards achieved by pupils have risen gradually in most subjects over the last four years. Nevertheless, problems clearly remain with the rates of progress in some subjects. There is, for example, substantial underachievement at Key Stage 2 in design and technology in over one in four schools and in information technology in over four in ten schools. Progress in religious education and geography is good in less than one-quarter of the schools.

3.3 Variation in the results achieved by primary schools

The variation in the results achieved by different primary schools is striking, and is illustrated in Chart 18. The average National Curriculum level for a sample of primary schools has been plotted against eligibility for free school meals, which remains a useful indicator of the level of disadvantage in a school. The chart shows that as disadvantage increases, the achievement of pupils reduces significantly. However, for any particular level of eligibility for free school meals the achievement of pupils varies considerably, by about one National Curriculum level overall. Given that pupils are expected to progress at about one level every two years, this means that pupils in low-achieving schools are about two years behind pupils in schools with similar levels of disadvantage that achieve well.

A further analysis of similar schools confirms this variation. Chart 19 shows a group of schools with

Chart 19

Percentage of pupils achieving Level 4 or above at Key Stage 2 English in 1998 in a sample of 13 schools with similar characteristics

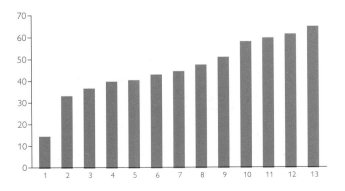

similar characteristics across a number of indicators: number on roll; eligibility for free school meals; proportion of pupils identified as having special educational needs; and the proportion of pupils with English as an additional language. For this group of schools the proportion of pupils reaching Level 4 ranged from about 16 per cent to 65 per cent.

3.4 Schools serving disadvantaged areas

Few schools with high levels of disadvantage achieve results which are above the national average. The link between low attainment and disadvantage remains strong and persistent. However, as Chart 20 shows, between 1995 and 1998 schools with high levels of disadvantage have made a significantly larger increase than other schools in the proportion of pupils reaching Level 4 at Key Stage 2. While these schools have had considerable scope for improvement and many have a long way to go before they reach the national average, it is encouraging that their results are rising, and rising faster than results in more advantaged schools.

Chart 20
Difference between 1995 and 1998 Key Stage 2 English Level 4+ results by average free school meal bands
(percentage improvement in 1995–8 KS2 English Level 4+)

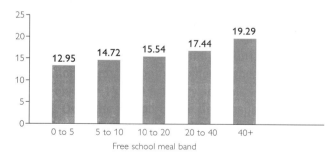

Free school meal band

3.5 The achievement of pupils from ethnic minorities

The standards achieved by pupils from ethnic minorities have improved over the last four years. Although the performance of Bangladeshi and Pakistani pupils in the early years of schooling remains depressed, once they become proficient in the English language their attainment often

matches or exceeds that of English first language pupils from similar backgrounds. For example, the OFSTED report on the teaching of reading in 45 inner-London primary schools[6] showed that Bangladeshi pupils achieved lower standards in Year 2 than any other minority ethnic group, but that they made good progress and by the end of Key Stage 2 their performance was very similar to other groups. White pupils from disadvantaged backgrounds performed less well overall than any other group. More recent evidence from the National Literacy Project showed that no ethnic minority group had a significantly lower performance than the average. Black Caribbean pupils, who often underachieve in secondary schools, generally make a sound start in primary schools.

In some areas, there are specific concerns about the underachievement of other ethnic minority groups, such as pupils of Turkish and Somali origin. Sometimes this is part of a more general anxiety about the underachievement of refugee pupils. Gypsy Traveller pupils are frequently hampered by poor attendance and are the group most at risk in the education system. Not surprisingly, when they are able to benefit from a settled period in a primary school, their progress improves, sometimes markedly.

3.6 International comparisons

An important impetus to the drive to "raise standards" has been given by the increasing availability of international comparisons of educational attainment, and by the increasing awareness of different approaches to teaching across the world. Significantly different systems of education appear to yield significantly different outcomes in terms of academic achievement.

Approaches observed in other countries have sometimes been tried in England. The approach to teaching reading known as "Reading Recovery" was developed in New Zealand and received some UK Government funding for a pilot project in England. The Gatsby Mathematics Project used in Barking and Dagenham is based on a system followed in Swiss primary schools. Furthermore,

[6] *The Teaching of Reading in 45 Inner London Primary Schools.* OFSTED, 1996.

several study visits have been made by HMI, for example to Hungary, the Czech Republic and Holland, and a review of international surveys of educational achievement was commissioned by OFSTED from David Reynolds and Shaun Farrell.[7]

Reynolds and Farrell acknowledged the difficulties in making international comparisons. It is not easy to compare the performance in different countries of similarly aged pupils in the same skills, bodies of knowledge or tests. It is also not easy to disentangle the relative impact of a range of non-educational influences on the achievement of pupils: social, cultural, economic and familial factors are of major importance in explaining performance. Reynolds and Farrell focused on mathematics and science, subjects on which wider, cultural influences might be assumed to be least marked. They concluded that the educational systems of different societies are key factors in determining their educational achievement. For England, the comparative studies suggest[8] that:

- performance in science is rather better than that in mathematics;

- overall performance in mathematics in England is relatively weak, with strengths in data handling and geometry, and considerable weaknesses in arithmetic and number operations;

- this performance deteriorated relative to other countries between the mid-1960s and the mid-1980s;

- English children show a very wide range of

achievement, with a greater proportion of low-achieving pupils than many of our economic counterparts.

Despite all the problems of comparability, the conclusion remains that the performance of English children, at the ages of nine and thirteen in important aspects of the core subjects, excluding science, is disappointing when compared with that of children of the same age in many other countries, particularly some on the Pacific Rim (China, Korea, Taiwan) but also some closer to home (Switzerland, the former USSR, Hungary).

It is also a feature of the English system that formal education, including the teaching of computation, reading and writing, starts earlier than in most other societies, and that English students spend longer in compulsory schooling than is often the case elsewhere.

Evidence from this review of international surveys is supported by the Third International Mathematics and Science Study (TIMSS)[9] of pupil performance, which again points to long-standing weaknesses in the performance of English nine- and thirteen-year-olds, particularly in number. This growing weight of evidence has been to a large extent behind the increased focus on numeracy, underpinned by, for example, surveys such as The Teaching of Number in Three Inner-urban LEAs[10] by HMI.

Inevitably much debate has been prompted by such international comparisons, seeking answers to questions such as:

- what are the reasons for the superior performance of Pacific Rim countries?

- what are the reasons for the superior performance of certain European countries as against England?

- what are the reasons for poor performance that relate to the nature of the English educational system?

It is widely agreed that there are a variety of factors responsible for the high achievement scores of Pacific Rim pupils. Among the cultural factors suggested are the high status of teachers,

---

[7] Reynolds, D and Farrell, S (1996) *Worlds Apart? A review of international surveys of educational achievement involving England*. London: HMSO

[8] Mathematical studies:
1964 *The IEA First International Mathematical Study* (FIMS)
1982–83 *The IEA Second International Mathematics Study* (SIMS)
1988 *The IAEP First International Assessment of Mathematics* (IAEPM 1)
1990 *The IAEP Second International Assessment of Mathematics* (IAEPM 2)

Science studies:
1970–72 *The IEA First International Science Study* (FISS)
1983–85 *The IEA Second International Science Study* (SISS)
1988 *The IAEP First International Assessment of Science* (IAEPS 1)
1990 *The IAEP Second International Assessment of Science* (IAEPS 2)

[9] *Third International Mathematics and Science Study.* NFER, 1996 and 1997.

[10] *The Teaching of Number in Three Inner-urban LEAs.* OFSTED, 1997.

the emphasis on effort and working hard, the high aspirations of parents for their children, the high calibre of newly trained teachers and the high level of commitment from children keen to do well.

Among the **systemic** factors thought to be important are the higher quantities of school time (for example, the school years in Korea and Taiwan have 222 days, compared with 190 in England); greater emphasis on homework; the prevalent belief that all children are able to acquire certain core skills in core subjects, and that there should be no "trailing edge" of low-performing pupils; and a concentration on a small number of attainable academic goals.

Important **school** factors are the use of mixed-ability classes in the early years at school ("basic skills in an egalitarian setting"[11]); the use of specialist teachers; the possibility of teachers working collaboratively with each other, frequent testing of students' skills in core subjects; and direct quality monitoring of the work of the teachers by the principal.

Key **classroom** factors include mechanisms to ensure that things are taught thoroughly and learned first time round; the use of the same textbooks by all children, channelling teachers' energies into classroom instruction and the marking of homework; and a "well ordered rhythm to the school day",[12] with frequent breaks and well managed lessons.

While some of the factors described above have been outside the immediate control of those responsible for shaping educational policy and practice, some are not. It is relatively easy to learn from school and classroom practice, and visits by educationalists – including HMI – to observe successful practice in some European countries are influencing developments such as the National Literacy and Numeracy Strategies. For example, from Switzerland[13] is noted the high proportion of high-quality, interactive, whole-class teaching; the use of textbooks linked to substantial teachers' manuals; the coherent planning of work; and a concentration in primary schools upon basic number work. From Hungary[14] is noted more formal classroom teaching, with more teacher direction, and more whole-class interactive instruction; high expectations and greater lesson pace; and national guidelines that expect teachers to move to advanced topics quickly.

---

[11] Reynolds and Farrell, ibid, p 55.

[12] Reynolds and Farrell, ibid, p 55.

[13] Bierhoff, H J, (1996) *Laying the Foundation of Numeracy: A Comparison of Primary School Textbooks in Britain, Germany and Switzerland.* London: National Institute for Economic and Social Research.

[14] Burghes, D, "Britain gets a minus in maths", *Sunday Times*, 14 May 1995.

4
THE QUALITY OF TEACHING

4.1 The quality and impact of teaching

Since the Education Reform Act 1988, primary schools have had to respond to a climate that has become far more focused on outcomes in terms of pupil achievement than ever before. The present Government's "standards agenda" has strongly reinforced the need to combat underachievement. Inspection findings for primary schools over the last four years clearly show that the most important input within the control of the school for promoting high achievement is the quality of the teaching. Indeed, the fact that the vast majority of that teaching for a given class is in the hands of one teacher for all or nearly all of a school year places a considerable responsibility upon the primary school class teacher.

Good teaching in primary schools makes a very significant difference. For example, in schools with the lowest proportion of good teaching, about 10 per cent fewer pupils reached Level 4 compared with pupils in a matched sample of schools in similar socio-economic circumstances and an above-average proportion of good teaching.

The 1978 report[15] contrasted "traditional" with "progressive", and "formal" with "informal" styles of teaching. Teaching styles were defined as either "mainly didactic" or "mainly exploratory". By 1994 the task of the primary school classroom teacher had been redefined, driven largely by the implementation of the subject-based National Curriculum. The curriculum had been defined in terms of the content, skills and concepts to be learned and taught, the National Curriculum being a common curriculum for everyone, "from Penrith to Penzance" in the words of the then Secretary of State. The consequences have been demanding of teachers' time and expertise and have led to an increased emphasis on planning, to ensure that the specified programmes of study are covered; an increased focus on separate subjects rather than topics which encompass elements of several

subjects; greater precision to assessment; and a greater willingness to consider what form of teaching is likely to be the most appropriate for a given objective or group of pupils.

The language used to describe teaching has changed too. There are now fewer references to the "exploratory work" and "extended studies" arising from "spontaneous incidents", which featured in inspection reports of 20 years ago. Inspection reports now make explicit references to features of teaching such as "demonstration" and "instruction". The curriculum is quite clearly now being "taught". This, in turn, has raised the importance of considering how a subject is best taught, reinforcing the crucial role of effective teaching in achieving high standards across a broad and balanced curriculum.

Since the publication of the first Handbook for the Inspection of Schools[16] the central importance of teachers and their teaching has been recognised, and the criteria which summarise the key components of the quality of teaching have been defined and published:

> *Teaching quality is to be judged by whether clear goals are set for the group and for individuals, by the extent to which activities are well-planned and presented in a range of ways, have suitable content, and engage and motivate all pupils enabling them to make progress at an appropriate pace, and by the extent of arrangements to improve teaching quality.*[17]

The guidance provided in the first inspection Handbook set out the evaluation criteria, amplified to illustrate features of good and unsatisfactory teaching. Good teaching was described in these terms:

> *Where teaching is good pupils acquire knowledge, skills and understanding progressively and at a good pace. The lessons have clear aims and purposes. They cater appropriately for the learning of pupils of differing abilities and interests, and ensure the full participation of all. The teaching methods suit the topic or subject as well as the pupils; the conduct of the lessons signals high expectations of all pupils and sets high but*

---

[15] *Primary Education in England, A Survey by HM Inspectors of Schools.* DES, 1978.

[16] *Handbook for the Inspection of Schools.* OFSTED, 1992.

[17] ibid, p 11.

attainable challenges. There is regular feedback which helps pupils to make progress, both through thoughtful marking and discussion of work with pupils. Relationships are positive and promote pupils' motivation. National Curriculum attainment targets and programmes of study are taken fully into account. Where appropriate, homework which extends or complements the work done in lessons, is set regularly.[18]

The current Guidance on the Inspection of Nursery and Primary Schools[19] is even more clear in its emphasis on the importance of teaching:

Teaching is the major factor contributing to pupils' attainment, progress and response. Evaluation of the quality and impact of teaching is central to inspection.[20]

The Handbook requires inspectors to judge[21] the extent to which teachers:

- have a secure knowledge and understanding of the subjects or areas that they teach;

- set high expectations so as to challenge pupils and deepen the pupils' knowledge and understanding;

- plan effectively;

- employ methods and organisational strategies which match curricular objectives and the needs of all pupils;

- manage pupils well and achieve high standards of discipline;

- use time and resources effectively;

- assess pupils' work thoroughly and constructively, and use assessments to inform teaching;

- use homework effectively to reinforce and/or extend what is learned in school.

4.2 The quality of teaching: inspection evidence

Notwithstanding changes to the grading system and adjustments to the evaluation criteria, it is clear that over the four years of the inspection programme the quality of teaching has improved. In 1994/95, in around two in five lessons the teaching was good or very good, in two in five lessons the teaching was sound, and in one in five lessons the teaching was unsatisfactory or poor. Teaching was poorer in Key Stage 2 than in Key Stage 1, and the weakest teaching of all was in Years 3 and 4, where 22 per cent of the teaching was unsatisfactory.

Chart 21 shows that by 1997/98 the picture had changed; the proportion of good teaching had risen at Key Stage 2 to over one-half (53 per cent) and that of unsatisfactory teaching had fallen to one in 14 primary schools (7 per cent). This improvement is striking: nevertheless, the figures suggest that there are still over a quarter of a million pupils in schools where the teaching is unsatisfactory, and around two million pupils in schools where the teaching is no better than sound. Given that the Government's targets for English and mathematics for 2002 are demanding and that most schools have some way to go before these are met, it is clear that there can be no relaxation in the drive to raise standards by improving the quality of teaching. It is unlikely that the "sound" teaching seen in many schools will be sufficient to enable them to achieve the ambitious targets which have been set.

Chart 21
Teaching in primary schools 1996/97 and 1997/98
(percentage of schools)

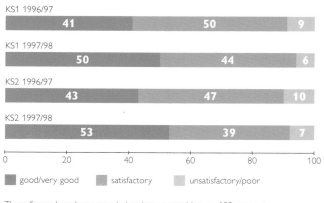

These figures have been rounded and may not add up to 100 per cent

---

[18] ibid, Guidance, p 21.

[19] *The OFSTED Handbook. Guidance on the Inspection of Nursery and Primary Schools.* OFSTED, 1995.

[20] ibid, p 67.

[21] ibid, p 66.

The quality of teaching in subjects

Charts 22 and 23 illustrate that the overall improvement in the quality of teaching applies to the teaching of almost all subjects.

For the first time, in 1997/98 the quality of the teaching of the three core subjects was better than the teaching of any other subjects, and the quality of the teaching of English and mathematics was better than that of science, at both key stages. The teaching of English and mathematics is now good in just over half the schools at Key Stage 2. This reflects a significant improvement since 1994/95, when the teaching of mathematics and English was good in only just over one-third of schools and was poor in one in five schools.

Several other features stand out. First, despite a general concern being voiced about the teaching of the arts and physical education in state schools, the quality of the teaching of music, art and physical education is very rarely weak and is better than the teaching of geography, history and religious education. Second, the quality of the teaching of religious education has improved over the four-year period, assisted considerably by the new style of Agreed Syllabus, recognisably in line in many cases with the format of the National Curriculum, with attainment targets and levels to be achieved. Third, the teaching of technology, whether design and technology or information technology, remains weaker than any other subject. If anything, the quality of the teaching of technology is deteriorating. In many schools other priorities are seen as more pressing, or the demands of increasingly sophisticated technology overwhelm or are ignored by teachers without sufficient training and support in the subject.

The quality of teaching by year group

Charts 24 and 25 illustrate that the four-year period has seen not only an improvement in the teaching of most subjects, but also an improvement within all year groups. The proportion of poor teaching has fallen throughout primary schools and the proportion of good teaching has risen. The best teaching is reported, throughout the period, in nursery classes and classes with reception-age pupils, and in Year 6. The weakest teaching remains in Years 3 and 4, although the percentage of weak lessons seen in these year groups has halved.

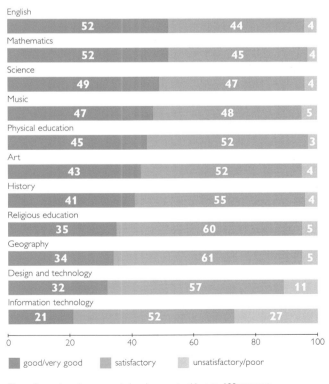

Chart 22
Quality of teaching by subject: 1994/95
(percentage of schools)

Subject	good/very good	satisfactory	unsatisfactory/poor
Music	48	35	17
Science	41	39	20
Physical education	41	39	20
History	40	41	19
English	39	43	19
Geography	39	42	19
Religious education	38	43	19
Mathematics	37	43	20
Design and technology	37	41	22
Art	36	42	22
Information technology	29	50	21

These figures have been rounded and may not add up to 100 per cent

Chart 23
Quality of teaching by subject: 1997/98
(percentage of schools)

Subject	good/very good	satisfactory	unsatisfactory/poor
English	52	44	4
Mathematics	52	45	4
Science	49	47	4
Music	47	48	5
Physical education	45	52	3
Art	43	52	4
History	41	55	4
Religious education	35	60	5
Geography	34	61	5
Design and technology	32	57	11
Information technology	21	52	27

These figures have been rounded and may not add up to 100 per cent

Chart 24
Quality of teaching by year group 1994/95
(percentage of lessons)

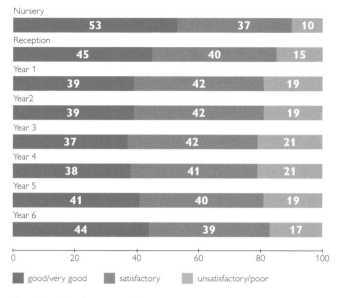

Nursery
53 | 37 | 10

Reception
45 | 40 | 15

Year 1
39 | 42 | 19

Year2
39 | 42 | 19

Year 3
37 | 42 | 21

Year 4
38 | 41 | 21

Year 5
41 | 40 | 19

Year 6
44 | 39 | 17

0 20 40 60 80 100

■ good/very good   ■ satisfactory   ■ unsatisfactory/poor

These figures have been rounded and may not add up to 100 per cent

The quality of the teaching of newly qualified teachers

Chart 26 shows the difference between qualified teachers who have taught for more than one year and newly qualified teachers. As expected, more experienced teachers teach better than newly qualified teachers. The gap in performance is similar across all subjects and encouragingly small.

Chart 26
Quality of teaching in primary schools: qualified teachers with more than one year's experience and newly qualified teachers
(percentage of lessons)

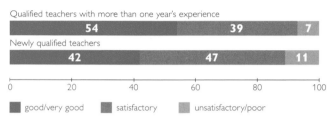

Qualified teachers with more than one year's experience
54 | 39 | 7

Newly qualified teachers
42 | 47 | 11

0 20 40 60 80 100

■ good/very good   ■ satisfactory   ■ unsatisfactory/poor

These figures have been rounded and may not add up to 100 per cent

Chart 25
Quality of teaching by year group 1997/98
(percentage of lessons)

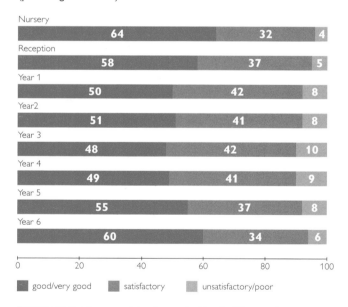

Nursery
64 | 32 | 4

Reception
58 | 37 | 5

Year 1
50 | 42 | 8

Year2
51 | 41 | 8

Year 3
48 | 42 | 10

Year 4
49 | 41 | 9

Year 5
55 | 37 | 8

Year 6
60 | 34 | 6

0 20 40 60 80 100

■ good/very good   ■ satisfactory   ■ unsatisfactory/poor

These figures have been rounded and may not add up to 100 per cent

4.3 The teaching of minority ethnic pupils[22]

Annual Reports over the past four years have generally reported positively on the provision for pupils for whom English is an additional language, and on the impact of the extra support provided under Section 11 of the Local Government Act 1966. For example, from 1996/97:

When Section 11 staff are well deployed they have an important and positive impact on the quality of pupils' learning. The work of bilingual assistants and teachers continues to be greatly valued by schools, especially in three areas: the support of young or early stage learners of English; the improvement of home/school relationships; and the advice they can give in the investigation of bilingual pupils thought to have special educational needs.

Most schools are engaged in a wide range of initiatives to improve provision and raise attainment, but few monitor the impact of these activities systematically and rarely do they have a specific ethnic focus. Most schools have equal

---

22 Much of the material in this section is taken from the HMI report, *Raising the Attainment of Minority Ethnic Pupils.* OFSTED, 1999.

opportunities policies and, especially in inner-city schools, policies on education for diversity. There is, however, too much variation in the way they are implemented and how they influence the work of the school. Sound intentions are not always translated into effective day-to-day practice. Saying that prejudice is unacceptable is not helpful unless it is backed up by agreed procedures for dealing with racist behaviour. Schools with Gypsy Traveller or Pakistani pupils seem particularly slow to underpin policies with systems to translate them into action.

In order to identify underachievement, diagnose need and take action, schools need accurate information about aspects of pupils' performance. Very few primary schools currently make effective use of the increasing amounts of data available to raise the attainment of minority ethnic pupils. Understandably, there is some fear of reducing expectations held by teachers of pupils of some ethnic minority groups; there are also some difficulties in establishing appropriate ethnic group categories.

Increasingly, local education authorities are providing their schools with an analysis of their National Curriculum assessment results, but the nature of this analysis varies considerably, with only a minority (mostly in urban and metropolitan areas) including ethnic data. Even where schools do receive good-quality data analysed by ethnicity, few make constructive use of it. There is a need for further training and guidance on how to analyse and respond to such information.

A majority of schools, when pressed to comment on the attainment of pupils from different ethnic backgrounds, rely on "hunches" or "general impressions"; when tested, however, these were sometimes proved wrong and revealed the presence of unhelpful stereotypes.

At a time of considerable educational change, involving for many schools a change of approach to the teaching of literacy and numeracy, many primary schools are implementing strategies designed to raise the attainment of all pupils irrespective of their ethnicity. Schools will need to evaluate how effective these strategies are for particular groups of pupils, for example those with low or even non-existent levels of spoken English. They will need to consider with even more care than in the past how to deploy their specialist

bilingual and Section 11 staff in order to make the most effective use of their skills.

Three important messages emerge from inspection evidence. First, there is a need to analyse data about attainment, attendance and behaviour and to respond precisely to the outcomes of the analysis; second, there is a need to evaluate the effectiveness of strategies for improving the attainment of different groups of pupils; and, third, given that the attainment of bilingual pupils is measurably improved when they have attained fluency in the English language, teaching pupils to be literate in English should be given the highest priority in all schools.

4.4 Taught time

The total teaching time per week varies markedly from school to school. This feature inevitably begs the question of what is the relationship between the amount of taught time and the quality and standards of pupils' work. The overall number of lesson hours is not prescribed, although guidance is given.[23] It is suggested that governing bodies of all maintained schools should take as a general rule to good practice:

- 21 hours for pupils aged five to seven;

- 23.5 hours for pupils aged eight to eleven.

Data provided by schools about the amount of taught time per week is not always based on immediately comparable data, as schools interpret the phrase "taught time" in a number of different ways. There is often uncertainty about what should be included or excluded in the statistics: for example, acts of worship, registration time, movement between classes, and so on.

Charts 27 and 28 show the extent of the variation in 1997/98. The charts suggest that almost one in five schools at Key Stage 1 and three-fifths of the schools at Key Stage 2 teach less than the suggested number of hours each week. There are signs, however, that for some pupils in some schools the length of the school day is being extended through regular homework and "homework clubs", after-school supported study and, in addition, summer schools.

Few schools have a clear rationale for the

---

[23] DES Circular 7/90.

Chart 27
Total teaching time per week for Key Stage 1 (1997/98)
(percentage of schools)

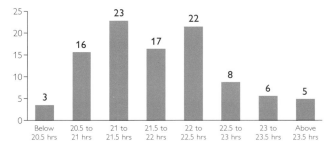

Chart 28
Total teaching time per week for Key Stage 2 (1997/98)
(percentage of schools)

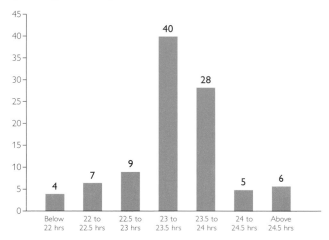

allocation of time to subjects. In a survey into taught time conducted by HMI,[24] only one in ten schools had attempted to prescribe how much time should be spent teaching each subject and none had monitored actual practice. It seems likely that schools will now be in a better position to report how time is allocated, assisted by the move to teach subjects discretely and the more precise identification of the time spent teaching literacy and numeracy.

In all of the primary schools surveyed, the reported time spent on teaching the core subjects averaged 57 per cent of the taught time, but varied from 40 per cent to 75 per cent. Schools found it particularly difficult to define how much time was spent teaching English; often they felt that much of the work in other subjects was contributing directly to progress in English. During Key Stage 2, two-thirds of schools spent between 4.5 and 6.0 hours on English; between 4.0 and 5.1 hours on

---

[24] *Taught Time.* OFSTED, 1994.

mathematics; and between 2.6 and 3.6 hours on science.

The time spent on non-teaching activities varied considerably; on average, over two hours each week were spent on registration and movement around school. While time for this is clearly necessary, schools need to ensure that it is not excessive, since the opportunity costs are considerable and teachers feel under pressure to "fit in" all the subject requirements.

There is little clear relationship between the total amount of taught time and overall achievement in terms of test results in the core subjects; inspection evidence suggests that the critical factor is how effectively time is used within the school day. Where the amount of taught time was relatively low, however, schools were more likely to allocate insufficient time to some subjects and to have imbalances within and between subjects.

Despite inconclusive evidence about the relationship between the length of taught time and pupils' educational achievement, it is clear that an adequate amount of time for a given subject is a necessary but not sufficient condition for producing work of quality. It is equally clear that where taught time is well below the recommended minima, schools often give their pupils short change in terms of the breadth, depth and balance of the curriculum provided.

4.5 The characteristics of good teaching

The principal themes of this section are the characteristics of good teaching, the features of which are the most important variables within the control of a school. The current inspection Framework sets out the criteria by which teaching is to be judged. Chart 29 shows the overall strengths and weaknesses of the teaching at Key Stages 1 and 2, and the changes – usually improvements – over the last two years.

The changes are striking, particularly over the past two years. In overall terms there is now less poor teaching and more good teaching than in 1996/97. Teachers' planning has improved considerably, more so at Key Stage 2 than at Key Stage 1; expectations are higher; and there have also been considerable improvements in the management of pupils, in the choice of methods and organisation, and in the use of time and resources. Although still weak, teachers' day-to-day assessment and their use of homework have also improved, although there is a long way to go before these aspects of teaching are handled as competently as the rest.

In schools where the teaching is judged to be good or very good overall, it is clear that inspectors are making this judgement on the basis of a combination of strengths which together promote

Chart 29
Quality of teaching 1996/97 and 1997/98:
Key Stages 1 and 2
(percentage of schools)

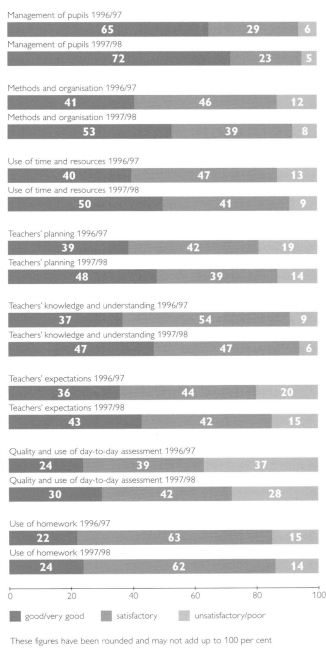

Management of pupils 1996/97
65 | 29 | 6
Management of pupils 1997/98
72 | 23 | 5

Methods and organisation 1996/97
41 | 46 | 12
Methods and organisation 1997/98
53 | 39 | 8

Use of time and resources 1996/97
40 | 47 | 13
Use of time and resources 1997/98
50 | 41 | 9

Teachers' planning 1996/97
39 | 42 | 19
Teachers' planning 1997/98
48 | 39 | 14

Teachers' knowledge and understanding 1996/97
37 | 54 | 9
Teachers' knowledge and understanding 1997/98
47 | 47 | 6

Teachers' expectations 1996/97
36 | 44 | 20
Teachers' expectations 1997/98
43 | 42 | 15

Quality and use of day-to-day assessment 1996/97
24 | 39 | 37
Quality and use of day-to-day assessment 1997/98
30 | 42 | 28

Use of homework 1996/97
22 | 63 | 15
Use of homework 1997/98
24 | 62 | 14

0   20   40   60   80   100

■ good/very good   ■ satisfactory   □ unsatisfactory/poor

These figures have been rounded and may not add up to 100 per cent

high standards. Typically, there is a consistently, high quality throughout the school. For example, **Wellesley First School** in Norwich:

Teaching is a strength of the school. It has several effective features:

- teachers and headteacher have high expectations;

- the whole staff plan the year's programme together. As a result their individual lesson planning benefits, helping to create a clear pattern of development and progress for the children;

- teachers assess their own teaching and the work of individual children in each lesson so they may plan future work better. They keep very good records of what children achieve. Effective assessment makes them aware of what the children know, understand and can already do;

- lessons have a clear structure, which the children understand and can follow;

- teachers have good knowledge in most subjects and support each other in subjects in which they feel less qualified;

- teachers explain very carefully to classroom assistants and volunteer adults what they are expected to do, especially in relation to children with special educational needs;

- teachers interact well with the children's learning and have good relationships with them;

- the whole school sets children the values and standards required and encourages effort in them.

Subject knowledge

Teachers' subject knowledge is strongly associated with high standards of pupils' achievement. In virtually all of the lessons where standards are good or very good, teachers' subject knowledge is judged to be satisfactory or good. Where teachers have good subject knowledge, they are more confident in planning and implementing work, more skilled at asking relevant questions, providing explanations and using the National Curriculum programmes of study, and more successful in providing demanding work for the more able pupils. They also have a good range of analogies and alternatives for presenting and illustrating knowledge so that pupils can understand the content of the subject. Inspection evidence indicates that in over two-fifths of the unsatisfactory and in half of the poor lessons, teachers' weak knowledge of the subject is a significant factor in pupils' low attainment. In these lessons, the teachers often have only a limited familiarity with the programmes of study, concentrate on the transmission of factual information and focus their work on too narrow a range of National Curriculum levels. In the worst examples, incorrect information is given to pupils.[25]

The issues of subject expertise, teaching roles and staff deployment were highlighted in *Curriculum Organisation and Classroom Practice in Primary Schools*,[26] which proposed that every primary school should, in principle, have direct access to specialist expertise in all National Curriculum subjects and in religious education. It concluded that:

> *Primary teaching roles are currently too rigidly conceived and much greater flexibility in staff deployment is needed. We recommend the introduction of semi-specialist and specialist teaching to primary schools to strengthen the existing role of class teacher and consultant. There is a particular case for concentrating specialist teaching at the upper end of Key Stage 2.*

This does, of course, run counter to the deep-seated commitment in English primary schools to the "one teacher, one class" organisation in which the pastoral role and the security of continuous contact with a single teacher are given a very high priority.

The demands placed on primary school teachers, particularly at Key Stage 2, in teaching ten subjects[27] and religious education have been recognised and considered by inspectors throughout the four-year period. Primary school classes almost always contain pupils with a wide range of attainment and often have pupils from more than one year group. It is usual for attainment towards the end of Key Stage 2 to range over three or four National Curriculum levels in the core subjects and to cover work as high as Level 5 and sometimes Level 6. The class teacher in a primary school has to meet far wider curricular requirements than subject teachers in secondary schools, usually without the support

structures of a subject department, and with much less non-contact time.

These pressures have been reported in each of the last four Annual Reports from HMCI, for example:

> *In over half of the schools, the teachers have a good command of the subjects they teach. The demands of subject knowledge do, however, become greater as pupils get older, and by Key Stage 2 teachers in one in eight schools have insufficient subject expertise, particularly in information technology, design and technology, mathematics, science and religious education. This prevents them from teaching key aspects of the subjects in sufficient depth.*[28]

> *A lack of subject knowledge often limits teachers' objectives and the challenge for pupils. Some teachers, for example, steer away from more complex topics in science in which abler pupils could flourish. In teaching geography there is sometimes a reluctance to organise investigations of features of the local area. In religious education, when the teacher lacks sufficient knowledge of the beliefs and practices of the major religions, work often fails to convey the significance of religious belief for everyday life.*[29]

Inspection has shown a steady improvement in teachers' knowledge and understanding of the

Chart 30
Teachers' knowledge and understanding, 1997/98
(percentage of schools)

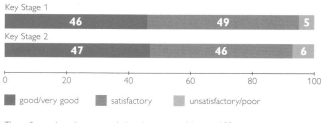

These figures have been rounded and may not add up to 100 per cent

---

[25] *Primary Matters. A discussion on teaching and learning in primary schools.* OFSTED, 1994.

[26] London, DES 1992.

[27] On the advice of the School Curriculum and Assessment Authority (now Qualifications and Curriculum Authority), information technology and design and technology are now treated as separate subjects.

[28] *The Annual Report of Her Majesty's Chief Inspector of Schools, 1995/96.* OFSTED, 1997.

[29] *The Annual Report of Her Majesty's Chief Inspector of Schools, 1994/95.* OFSTED, 1996.

subjects they teach. As Chart 30 illustrates, by 1997/98, while the proportion of primary schools in which subject knowledge was good remained at about one-half of the schools, subject knowledge was judged to be weak in around one in 20 schools.

Not surprisingly, teachers' knowledge and understanding varies from subject to subject; the extent of this is illustrated in Charts 31 and 32. Encouragingly, class teachers' subject knowledge of English, mathematics and science is at least satisfactory in most schools, although the preparatory training courses for the National Literacy Project revealed a considerable need for teachers to receive more training in the teaching of reading, particularly phonological awareness. Modern languages are frequently taught by teachers with good knowledge of the chosen language, but the sample is small. The weaknesses of subject knowledge in design and technology, and above all in information technology, stand out starkly: in only one in five primary schools is there good subject expertise in information technology at Key Stage 2; in Key Stage 1 the figure is even lower, at around one in six.

The case is strongly made, therefore, that the attainment of high standards by pupils requires teaching by teachers who have a good grasp of the subject itself, fully understand the requirements of the National Curriculum, and know how to teach the subject effectively. Two further elements of subject expertise play their part. First, in primary schools subject expertise is often acquired through personal effort, interest and enthusiasm, rather than studying for a formal qualification. Second, the best teaching brings with it more than just subject expertise. For example, it remains the case that there are some teachers with good academic qualifications in a subject (they "know their stuff") but fail to teach it well. In other words, subject knowledge is a necessary but not sufficient condition of good teaching. The most successful teachers have a contagious enthusiasm for their subject.

Schools secure good subject expertise in a range of ways. For example, they identify strengths and weaknesses and seek to support teachers with gaps in their subject expertise through in-service training. They provide curricular support through detailed schemes of work which help teachers to secure progression in a subject. They conduct an

Chart 31

Teachers' knowledge and understanding: KS1, 1997/98
(percentage of schools)

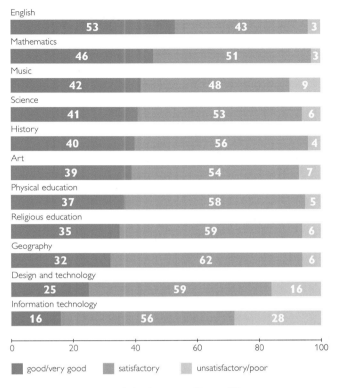

These figures have been rounded and may not add up to 100 per cent

Chart 32

Teachers' knowledge and understanding: KS2, 1997/98
(percentage of schools)

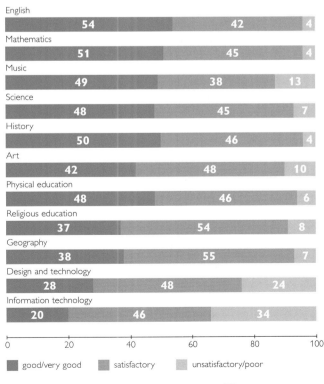

These figures have been rounded and may not add up to 100 per cent

audit of staff expertise and make as much use as they can of new appointments to fill gaps in particular subjects. They also seek to make the best use of the expertise at their disposal.

Using subject specialists to promote high standards at Key Stage 2

A feature of the last four years has been a growing recognition of the considerable professional expertise to which schools have access, and the development of a range of strategies to make use of this expertise. It has, however, been one thing to acknowledge the expertise available; it is another to make the best use of it. In 1996/97 HMI were asked to investigate how schools approach these issues;[30] some schools are clearly more successful than others in using specialist knowledge to promote high standards throughout the school rather than just in the class taught by the particular expert.

In summary, HMI found that

- the quality of the teaching of subject specialists was almost always better than that of non-specialists;

- features of the best teaching by specialists were a confident command of the subject, a driving pace to lessons and extremely ambitious and unusually high expectations, invariably met by pupils;

- the most successful approaches to using subject expertise involved a combination of direct subject teaching by a specialist, with strategies to enable the specialist to influence the work of the school as a whole;

- the most successful approaches were carefully managed and did not rely on ad hoc arrangements between staff;

- small schools were able to arrange for exchange of expertise with relative ease. They also recognised the telling impact which the use of a specialist could make in a short space of time;

- large schools were more likely to have teachers who did not have full-time class responsibilities,

allowing for greater scope for deploying expertise; and they had greater access to a wider range of expertise;

- it was often the medium-sized schools, with around ten teachers, which found it most difficult to make effective use of subject specialists;

- the lack of non-contact time was the most significant constraint on the effective use of subject expertise – in half the schools in the survey, no non-contact time at all was available for subject co-ordinators;

- the exchange of classes between teachers sometimes had an adverse effect, when pupils in the class of a skilled and sought-after subject specialist teacher suffered through receiving teaching of variable quality from other teachers.

There were notable exceptions, but the overall picture was disappointing and indicated a considerable underuse of talent: for example, physical education specialists limited in their contribution beyond their own class to some after-school games clubs; the theology graduate teaching religious education only to her own class; and teachers back from 20-day mathematics or science courses with little opportunity to influence practice in their subject beyond ordering and organising resources or writing guidelines.

Expectations

A recurrent theme of Annual Reports is that of the need to raise teachers' expectations. For example, from 1994/95:[31]

Teachers should expect more of their pupils in all key stages. They set the right pace and degree of challenge and motivation in only a little over half of schools. Intellectual challenge is commonly weak in Key Stage 2 and Key Stage 3. In many primary schools, teachers' expectations decline through the key stages. In Key Stage 2 they are too low in over a half of schools. In design and technology, for example, pupils are rarely called upon to use knowledge and understanding from other subjects, including science. The technical vocabulary and design suggestions that Key Stage 2 pupils can deploy far exceed teachers' expectations.

There are signs that expectations are rising.

---

[30] *Using Subject Specialists to Promote High Standards at Key Stage 2.* OFSTED, 1997.

[31] *Annual Report of Her Majesty's Chief Inspector of Schools, 1994/95.* OFSTED, 1996.

Nevertheless, by 1997/98 expectations were high in only two schools in five and were poor in one school in six at Key Stage 2. The raising of expectations remains one of the key issues still to be addressed properly. HMI inspection of the National Literacy Project revealed that the Framework for the teaching of reading and writing was helping teachers to raise their sights:

> *In the vast majority of schools, the use of the Framework is producing a more consistent, whole-school approach to the planning and organisation of the Literacy Hour and has raised teachers' expectations of what pupils can achieve.*[32]

Likewise, the National Numeracy Project has not only increased the enthusiasm that many teachers had for the teaching of mathematics, especially oral and mental work, but it also helped raise their expectations of what pupils could achieve.

Chart 33
Teachers' expectations in primary schools 1996/97 and 1997/98
(percentage of schools)

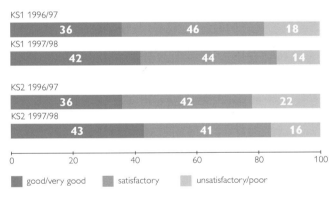

These figures have been rounded and may not add up to 100 per cent

Good teachers set high expectations because they have a good knowledge of the subject they are teaching. They know how to plan sequences of work to a sufficient depth and how to match the content to what the pupils already know. Good teachers also make their expectations explicit. For example, in **Elliston Infant School**, Cleethorpes:

> *Teachers signal high expectations both of achievement and behaviour. They make it clear to the pupils what is expected of them, how much time is available and emphasise the importance of concentration on the task in hand.*

32 *The National Literacy Project: an HMI evaluation.* OFSTED, 1998.

The themes of pace and challenge run through inspection reports when the teaching is predominantly good. For example, **Kea County Primary School** in Truro:

> *In the best lessons the teachers have enthusiasm, a high expectation of the pupils and a good knowledge of the subject. In these lessons teachers use time very effectively and the emphasis is on pupils working hard but also having fun. Excellent lessons are well thought out and planning is clear, producing work that is interesting and purposeful. Pupils enjoy the quick pace and intellectual challenges of these lessons. In one particularly good science lesson in Key Stage 2, pupils made very good progress in designing their own experiments to measure the effects of exercise on heart rate and in their understanding of the reactions of the body. In many lessons there are good links to other subjects and pupils are challenged, extending their knowledge and understanding.*

While the pace of work expected of the pupils is a common theme in inspection reports when the teaching is good, an important factor about the pace of a good lesson is that it is determined by the teachers and not the pupils. There is more to expectations than just the setting of a lively pace. Pace and intellectual challenge, moreover, are not the same thing. The two usually go together, however, and generally contribute to the sustaining of interest in a subject and to the good use of time.

A demanding and fast pace is the characteristic of challenge most frequently commented upon, but the most effective teachers are able to vary the pace and adapt it according to the requirements of the lesson and the response from the pupils. Good teachers are prepared to slow down the pace of lessons to allow for pupils to respond, but are not afraid to accelerate it, for example during a period of direct instruction. One lesson note commented: "teacher managed pace well, at times injecting dramatic speed and then slowing it down to give the pupils opportunities to reflect on video and discuss with partner".

Setting

One response of schools to the need to match work to levels of prior attainment has been to group pupils in sets for certain subjects. The grouping of pupils with similar attainment levels into sets is increasing. This is seen particularly in mathematics and English in Years 5 and 6. Setting reduces the range of attainment within a teaching group and consequently can help teachers to plan work more precisely and select appropriate teaching methods. Where inspectors refer to setting, their comments tend to be brief but in almost every case they are positive. For example, from **Christ Church CE Junior School**, Wolverhampton:

In Year 6 pupils are set, according to ability, for English and mathematics. Setting, together with further differentiation for each group, results in work being finely matched to challenge pupils of all ability levels, including those with special educational needs.

A radical solution to the questions of how to raise standards from an already high level has been taken at **Priory School**, Slough. The school serves an area of some social deprivation, including inner-city overspill. Standards are very high, well above average at both key stages, but the school believed there was scope for further improvement and brought in an external consultant to offer advice on what the school should do next. The developments have been radical, and have involved the use of setting and streaming, linked to the deployment of subject specialists throughout the school:[33]

From Key Stage 1 onwards the pupils are streamed according to attainment, and each class is set demanding academic targets. At Key Stage 1, with the exception of music which is taught by specialists throughout, the classes are taught all subjects by their class teacher. In Years 5 and 6, pupils work in mixed-ability classes for some subjects, but for the core subjects they are taught in attainment-related sets. The largest sets are the "top" sets, with the lower sets having smaller numbers. Extra staffing enables the three classes per year to be split into four sets for the core subjects.

In the core subjects the top sets are taught by subject specialists. This enables the most able pupils to be taught by subject specialists who can handle not only the technical understanding required by the more complex programmes of study, but also can answer the challenging questions from these able groups. The quality of the teaching in these sets is very high. It is not unusual to see pupils working at Level 6.

The school is frustrated but not overwhelmed by constraints. For example, it would like to extend the use of subject specialist teaching and setting to Years 3 and 4, and would like to tackle the teaching of history and geography in the same way as the core subjects.

HMI conducted a survey of setting in primary schools in 1997/98.[34] This showed that the incidence of setting has been increasing, that most schools use setting in Years 5 and 6 only, and that the higher the number on roll, the more likely the school is to use setting in one or more year groups. It appears that about six out of ten schools at Key Stage 2 set for at least one subject, principally mathematics and English. Virtually all schools that set did so with the explicit intention of raising standards. Setting was regarded by most of the headteachers in the survey schools as a way of catering for the needs of all pupils. It was seen as a means of challenging the most able and moving them beyond the national expectation, as well as a way of providing smaller, more focused teaching groups for the least able. Setting was also popular with the teachers, because the narrower range of attainment in sets enabled them to focus more easily on specific learning objectives, better matched to the needs of their pupils, and allowing more direct teaching to be used.

The most common reasons for not setting were practical ones: the small size of the school; the uneven composition of year groups; and the lack of either spare accommodation or additional staff, both of which are necessary if extra sets are to be formed. Very few schools avoided setting because of ideological objections such as preferring to maintain the tradition of one teacher to one class, or to teach the core subjects through integrated topics.

A very large proportion of the schools inspected demonstrated a clear trend of rising standards for pupils of all abilities once the use of setting had become established. All but a handful of the schools visited by HMI achieved higher scores in national tests in setted subjects in 1997 than they did in 1996, and most headteachers ascribed a good deal of the credit for improvements in standards to setting. Setting does not, by itself,

---

[33] *Using Subject Specialists to Promote High Standards at Key Stage 2*. OFSTED, 1997.

[34] *Setting in Primary Schools*. OFSTED, 1998.

guarantee success in raising standards, nor can it compensate for poor teaching. Safeguards need to be built in to avoid low self-esteem and the negative labelling of pupils which can occur in lower sets.

Setting tended to polarise the quality of the teaching: it was frequently either very good or poor, depending on whether or not the teachers had taken advantage of the opportunity to engage in focused, direct teaching with pupils of similar attainment levels. Without these teaching strategies in setted lessons, the characteristics of weak teaching became more pronounced and the potential advantages of setting were not achieved.

The quality of teaching in mathematics and English was highest in the "top sets" in all age groups, reflecting the fact that upper sets were frequently taken by subject co-ordinators or specialists. In mathematics, the least effective teaching was seen in the lower sets, while in English and science the weakest teaching was found in middle sets where three or more sets had been formed. The relatively better quality of lower-set teaching in English compared with mathematics is consistent with the frequent deployment of the special educational needs co-ordinators to lower English sets.

Schools usually went to great length to avoid labelling pupils as either high or low attainers through the sets to which they were allocated. However, pupils were found almost invariably to have a very good idea of the relative ranking of the sets that they were in. Nevertheless, in discussion, the vast majority of the pupils saw advantages to setting, accepted the purpose and fairness of their allocation to a particular set and liked having more than one teacher. They saw this, towards the end of Key Stage 2, as a good preparation for secondary school. Very few examples of either elitism or negative self-image were found, although evidence suggests that there were more boys than girls in lower sets, particularly in English.

HMI evidence, therefore, endorses the Government's view, set out in the White Paper, *Excellence in Schools*, that schools should not be wedded entirely to mixed-ability teaching and that setting "is worth considering in primary schools". Where teachers understand its potential and modify their teaching techniques accordingly,

setting can be a very successful way of organising teaching groups; carefully implemented and properly managed, setting facilitates direct, whole-class teaching and provides a powerful lever for raising standards.

Planning and preparation

At the beginning of the four-year cycle, inadequate planning as a factor associated with weaker teaching was highlighted as a concern in the Annual Report. Since then, there have been improvements in teachers' planning and, although planning was still weak in one in five schools in 1996/97, in 1997/98 this proportion had fallen to one in seven schools.

Several factors seem likely to have contributed to this improvement in planning. First, the Handbook for Inspection sets out clearly the characteristics of good planning:[35]

Good planning means that the teaching in a lesson, or sequence of lessons has clear objectives for what pupils are to learn and how these objectives will be achieved.

Second, increasingly schools are following schemes of work, either produced commercially or within the school, which set out progressively the objectives for subjects and which can be built directly into teachers' plans. Third, projects such as those for literacy and numeracy have been influential in setting out in some detail the objectives on a termly basis for each year group.

In the 10 per cent of primary schools with the highest percentage of good teaching, the good quality of the planning was a positive feature highlighted in every report. Where planning was most effective, it identified objectives (sometimes described as targets, aims or goals) for individual lessons. A feature of the best teaching was the sharing of the objectives by the teacher with the pupils; they knew what they were going to do and why. For example, **Morpeth County First School**, Northumberland:

There are many characteristics of the effective teaching, but the most significant is the sharing of the lesson aims and purposes with the children at the start of every lesson. This, together with a clear indication of how pupils

---

35 *The OFSTED Handbook. Guidance on the Inspection of Nursery and Primary Schools.* OFSTED, 1995, p 68.

could measure their own success within their learning, focuses teaching specifically on identified learning tasks and helps pupils to know what is expected of them.

And **Fair Oak Junior School**, Hampshire:

The quality of the teachers' planning is good. Due attention is paid to the National Curriculum programmes of study and to religious education. A particular strength is the planning which takes place within year groups and in the subject groups which include teachers from all year groups. The teachers' objectives and high expectations are usually made very clear and they are shared with the pupils. The planning makes clear what resources will be needed and what the pupils are expected to do.

There are increasing numbers of schools with **schemes of work** which set out for every subject what is to be taught to which year group at which point of the year. The following example is taken from the scheme of work for music, spring term, Year 6 at **Priory School**, Slough. It offers sufficient detail to show a teacher what objectives should be set, what National Curriculum links can be made, and what activities the pupils should actually undertake:

Objectives: by the end of Term 2 in Year 6 the children:

- will have continued to learn an instrument in a small group;

- will have listened to a variety of popular music composed in Britain from 1930 to the present day;

- will have continued to work with, and learn about, chords, keys and intervals;

- will have composed a tune for a song to be played over a chord sequence;

- will have continued to sing in a variety of groups focusing on learning to sight sing.

NC refs	Activities
1a, b	1. Continue to work with instrumental teachers in small groups.
2e, f, g	2. Focus on folk songs written in Great Britain, learn and sing the songs, perform some of them from memory and perform them with accompaniments from music and chord symbols.
3a, b	3. Compose a melody for a set of words to an unknown folk song. The melody must fit to a chord sequence. Although the work is an individual task, it can be discussed in groups.
4a, b, c, d, e, f	4. Rehearse the songs in groups and record them using staff notation and audio-visual equipment.
5a, b, c, d, e, f, h	5. Listen to different performers' versions of a famous folk song, eg *Scarborough Fair*, and discuss the differences and similarities.
6a, c, d, e	6. Listen to the original recordings of the words their compositions were based on, and discuss similarities and differences.
	7. Listen to a variety of popular music written in Great Britain from about 1930, starting with war songs and moving on to rock and roll, big band, jive, music from the 1960s and 1970s, punk and up to the 1980s and 1990s.
	8. Focus on the music of prominent groups from this time, for example Abba, The Beatles, Elvis and Queen.
	9. Study the effect electronic equipment has had on the popular music and learn how to use a keyboard.
	10. Continue to sing a variety of music and learn how to sight sing.

Most teachers prepare for most lessons well. A feature of the well organised primary classroom is the availability and accessibility of appropriate basic resources, the tools of everyday classroom life: papers, pens, pencils, crayons, scissors, glues and so on. Individual lessons are usually prepared well – often a time-consuming task but one that can make all the difference to the quality of a lesson.

While many primary school teachers have made extensive use of published schemes for mathematics and aspects of English, there has been a general reticence about the use of textbooks on a regular basis, although with careful selection and imaginative use these can provide valuable and informed background material. There has, however, been a steady growth in recent years, supported by the increasing availability of photocopiers, of the use of worksheets. As with textbooks, these can play a useful role, but there are dangers: too often the tasks require little more than completing sentences or lists of words;

storage of completed worksheets can be a problem; and, at worst, they can be little more than low-level holding activities contributing nothing to progress – colouring-in exercises and wordsearches, for example.

Methods and organisation

Chart 34
Methods and organisation in primary schools
(percentage of schools)

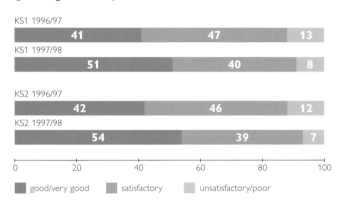

KS1 1996/97
41 | 47 | 13

KS1 1997/98
51 | 40 | 8

KS2 1996/97
42 | 46 | 12

KS2 1997/98
54 | 39 | 7

0   20   40   60   80   100

■ good/very good   ■ satisfactory   ■ unsatisfactory/poor

These figures have been rounded and may not add up to 100 per cent

In the last two years of the review period, inspectors reported a significant improvement in the selection by teachers of the most appropriate teaching methods (see Chart 34), and reports indicate that the feature which makes the most difference is the extent of **direct, whole-class teaching**. There is an assumption, however, that this appears to be something new. It is not. Good teachers have always recognised the place of good direct teaching and HMI have always commented on its impact and the need for its inclusion as part of the teacher's repertoire. On the other hand, a feature of much unsatisfactory teaching is the inability of the teacher to get the balance right between individual, group and whole-class work.

> *Some teachers did little or no direct teaching but acted largely as servicers or supervisors of the pupils' tasks... The most common organisational weaknesses stemmed from the teachers' failure to vary their favoured grouping strategies – which resulted in too much, or too little, time spent on whole class teaching or on individual work or on group work.*[36]

Recognition of the value of good, direct whole-class teaching may not be new, but inspection and international comparisons indicate that there is, or

[36] *Primary Matters.* OFSTED, 1994.

has been, a reluctance in English primary schools to teach a whole class, and a preference for individual work or group activity in an attempt to meet perceived differences in pupils' rates of learning.

The National Literacy Strategy and the National Numeracy Strategy set out to build on the experiences of the literacy and numeracy projects, in which direct teaching to either the whole-class or to small groups was a key element of the methodology. The influence of the projects has spread beyond the project schools and local education authorities. Inspectors are already reporting the occurrence of more frequent, regular and sustained daily sessions of whole-class teaching, aimed especially at raising standards of literacy and numeracy. In mathematics, for example, there is greater attention to the rapid and accurate recall of number facts and to the learning by heart of multiplication tables through whole-class methods. Daily sessions, brisk and sharply focused, in which number facts are taught, practised and used, are becoming more widespread.

Even before the introduction of the National Literacy Strategy in September 1998, many primary schools had anticipated the strategy by introducing a daily **Literacy Hour** which required carefully planned and timed elements of direct teaching to the whole class, some group work with the teacher directly teaching one or two groups, and a closing plenary in which the teacher checks that what has been covered is understood and requires pupils to share their work with each other. For example, **Christ Church CE Junior School**, Wolverhampton:

> *In most lessons, whole class teaching is used effectively to introduce the lesson. In many lessons this introduction is stimulating and motivates pupils to make the appropriate links between previous learning and the work currently to be undertaken. Most lessons have a good structure, with opportunities for individual or collaborative work focused appropriately to specific abilities to maintain interest and ensure a brisk pace of learning. Review time at the end of the lesson is used well to check, consolidate and extend pupils' knowledge and understanding.*

It is, however, very clear that teaching the class

together for part of a lesson is not an easy option and requires a secure understanding by the teacher of what is to be taught, clear instructive teaching, skilled questioning and discussion if all pupils are to make consistent progress. Without these features in place, inspectors report overextended introductions to lessons and teachers spending far too long simply talking to the class.

Questioning

Skilled questioning is a key competence of the good teacher. Good questioning is at the heart of good whole-class teaching of pupils with a range of abilities, including pupils with special educational needs, EAL and very able pupils. It was, for example, identified as the most significant aspect (highlighted in 58 per cent of the good or very good lessons) of pedagogy by HMI in Primary Matters, essential to assessing pupils' knowledge and to challenging their thinking. For example, in the inspection survey of the Teaching of Number in Three Inner-urban LEAs,[37]

Good teaching took place in just over a third of the lessons. In these lessons the pupils listened carefully as the teacher emphasised key aspects in the work and they responded eagerly when questioned or challenged to explain in their own words. In one lesson involving a class with a high proportion of pupils who were learning English as an additional language, the teacher began by teaching the whole class. They worked on the addition and subtraction of two numbers to make a sum or difference of 12. Pupils were encouraged to say what they thought would happen as the two numbers increased or decreased and to justify their answers – "Why did you do that?" They willingly provided alternatives, and corrected errors, responding positively to the high expectations set for them.

In schools in which the teaching was good or very good, questioning was the aspect of successful teaching most frequently mentioned. It is used by teachers for a number of reasons. The first is as a form of assessment, that is to test pupils' understanding of a subject. This is increasingly seen by teachers of the Literacy Hour as a part of the initial whole-class teaching; the teacher can use questions to gauge whether the whole class

has understood a particular issue or instruction, and to pinpoint with individual pupils just what has been learned and what needs further work. Second, questioning helps teachers to reinforce learning. Third, it is used to develop and probe understanding, and to move pupils' minds and imaginations forward, often linked to an object or a story... "What do you think lies under the stone?"... "I wonder what we shall see when I turn the page." Finally, questioning can be used to encourage reticent or reluctant pupils to participate in lessons.

Management of pupils and discipline

The management of pupils and the achievement of high standards of discipline are at least satisfactory in the large majority of schools; in only one school in 20 were these aspects weak in 1997/98. Nevertheless, the impact of poor behaviour – often by a small minority of pupils – on the quality of the education within a school can be considerable; the poor behaviour of a few affects the learning of everyone. There are several examples of inspection reports in which this serious issue is spelt out quite clearly. For example,

There is a clear difference between the consistently good attitudes and behaviour of the under-fives and of the pupils at Key Stage 1, the mostly satisfactory behaviour seen in Years 3 and 4, and the frequently poor, unacceptable behaviour by a small minority of pupils in Years 5 and 6. This unruly behaviour, usually by two or three boys in the upper classes, has serious implications for the work of the school. It affects adversely the attitudes, behaviour and personal development of the other pupils, and often prevents learning from taking place. It also affects staff morale and is of great concern to parents.

An outcome of the introduction of the National Literacy or Numeracy Projects was a positive impact on the behaviour of the pupils and on their attitudes to their work. The vast majority of pupils responded well to the Literacy Hour with its familiar organisation and structure. In nearly nine lessons in ten, pupils from Reception to Year 6 applied themselves well and showed improved confidence and positive attitudes to their work. In general, the interest in reading and writing and levels of motivation were high. The structure of the

---

[37] *The Teaching of Number in Three Inner-urban LEAs.* OFSTED, 1997, pp 19 and 20.

Literacy Hour meant that pupils were clear about basic routines, particularly when undertaking group work, and this aided class control and promoted good behaviour. Where there were examples of pupils having negative attitudes to literacy, these were strongly associated with slow-paced teaching and ineffective classroom management, often resulting in boredom, disinterest and an inability to work independently.

It is easy to overlook that one of the essential preconditions of good teaching is the appropriate **organisation** of the classroom. Some of the most effective feedback to teachers from headteachers, inspectors and advisers has been related to classroom organisation. If there is to be whole-class teaching using a whiteboard, can everyone see the board easily? Are seating arrangements comfortable and do they ensure immediate eye contact with the teacher? What are the benefits of pupils sitting on a carpeted floor rather than on chairs at their tables? If a 'big book' is used, is the text large enough for everyone to read it? Can everyone hear the teacher?

The quality and use of day-to-day assessment

Chart 35
Quality and use of day-to-day assessment in primary schools
(percentage of schools)

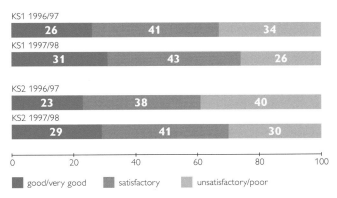

KS1 1996/97: 26 | 41 | 34
KS1 1997/98: 31 | 43 | 26
KS2 1996/97: 23 | 38 | 40
KS2 1997/98: 29 | 41 | 30

■ good/very good ■ satisfactory ■ unsatisfactory/poor

These figures have been rounded and may not add up to 100 per cent

It is difficult for teachers to gauge the level at which work should be set without a clear knowledge of what pupils already know. Primary schools cope rather better with the statutory requirements for assessment than the less formal day-to-day assessment of pupils. Although there has been some improvement in the use of day-to-day assessment, as illustrated in Chart 35, it is still a weakness in almost one-third of schools. Schools have quite understandably moved away from the

huge quantity of checksheets and ticklists which characterised much of the early assessment work related to the National Curriculum, but they are much less clear about what should replace them. There is, however, a strong association between good teaching and good assessment.

Examples of good practice can be found. Often the school which is successful at its day-to-day assessment is one which is also successful in its more formal assessment arrangements; the distinction between formative and summative assessment fades in these schools. Even in schools with successful assessment approaches, the issue of an unacceptable workload, or one which does not yet justify the time and effort spent, remains. Note, for example, the final sentence of the "assessment" section of the report on **Ramsden Infant School**, Barrow-in-Furness:

Procedures for the assessment of work and progress are a strength of the school. There is a timetabled programme for review and assessment throughout the key stage, which is consistently used by all staff. This enables changes in pupils' attainments to be closely monitored and effective steps planned to meet specific needs. Targets are set and reviewed carefully within the set timespan. In their planning, teachers use information gathered very effectively to promote pupils' development. Records of progress and achievement are maintained in both the core and foundation subjects. The development plans in each subject indicate that strategies are in hand to address this, such as collecting moderated examples of pupils' work in portfolios. Record keeping is related to coverage of the programmes of study and there is a useful record of achievement.

Pupils' work is marked regularly and conscientiously. Pupils receive feedback during lessons orally and written in their books, including appropriate praise, encouragement and suggestions for improvement. Staff are consistent in advising pupils how they can improve their work and in expecting high standards. In English and mathematics there is consistency between teacher assessment and results of National Curriculum tests. The amount of work undertaken in assessment is considerable and the school has rightly planned to review and evaluate all assessment procedures.

An important feature of schools in which the implementation of the National Literacy Project was successful was the detailed assessment of what pupils knew, in order for the teacher to plan accurately a structured programme for the teaching of reading.

Homework

Only one-quarter of schools make good use of homework. Reading scheme books are taken home by pupils in most schools, and many teachers ask pupils to learn and practise spellings and multiplication tables at home. However, practice is often inconsistent from one class to the next, and this is frequently raised as a concern by parents in their response to inspection questionnaires and at parents' meetings. In the completion of questionnaires prior to an OFSTED inspection, parents are more likely to express disquiet about homework than any other issue. In a recent scrutiny of over 1,500 primary schools from which data was obtained from parents' questionnaires, in just over half (51.42 per cent) of the schools parents registered a "significant" level of dissatisfaction with the homework that their child is expected to do.

A small but growing number of schools hold regular "homework clubs" after school. These schools are often in disadvantaged areas where some pupils find it hard to get the necessary support or facilities for working at home. Despite the voluntary nature of attendance at these sessions, schools have often been surprised at their popularity. Typically, a very good working atmosphere is established and pupils are able to continue with or complete work started in lessons, and receive extra help with areas in which they are having some difficulties. Year 6 pupils are sometimes given opportunities to revise issues likely to be encountered in the National Curriculum tests.

The place and value of homework have been debated widely in recent years, often in the context of concerns about the amount of time children spend watching television or playing computer games rather than reading or doing "school work". The Government's White Paper, *Excellence in Schools,* recognises the valuable role which well organised homework could play in raising standards, and proposed that national guidelines on homework should be drawn up for schools. A

survey conducted by HMI[38] in 1994 concluded that:

- *where staff, pupils and parents treat it seriously, homework has the potential to raise standards, extend coverage of the curriculum, allow more effective use to be made of lesson times and improve pupils' study skills and attitudes to learning;*

- *in general, many pupils and their parents saw work done at home as a valuable and essential part of school work, and as helping to create a partnership between home and school;*

- *there was little systematic and regular monitoring of the implementation of homework policies by the schools and, consequently, there was little knowledge of their impact or effectiveness.*

Although, from the HMI survey quoted above, it is impossible to provide firm evidence of any improvement in standards, many teachers and parents believed that homework had a direct effect in enhancing pupils' knowledge and understanding. They felt that where the school had a well-devised and systematic homework policy, the attendant sense of purpose encouraged pupils to respond maturely. Most Year 6 pupils valued the opportunity to become accustomed to homework in preparation for entry to secondary school, which, they felt, would be "a much more demanding regime".[39]

4.6 The characteristics of schools with good teaching

Of the primary teachers observed by inspectors on five or more occasions during inspections in 1997/98, 67 per cent taught no lesson where the teaching was unsatisfactory and 50 per cent of teachers taught mostly good lessons. In other words, poor teachers are rare. There were only 3.2 per cent of teachers, equivalent to about 6,000 teachers, whose teaching was unsatisfactory in over half of the lessons observed.

It is exceedingly unusual for a school to have no good teaching. For example, of the 2,682 schools

[38] *Homework in Primary and Secondary Schools.* OFSTED, 1995.

[39] ibid, pp 9 and 10.

(primary and secondary) inspected in the academic year 1997/98, only one school was reported as having no examples of good teaching. Chart 36 shows the proportion of good teaching found in the schools inspected in 1997/98. In over half the schools inspected, over half of the teaching is good. In only 3 per cent of schools is less than one-quarter of the teaching good.

Chart 36
The proportion of good teaching in the schools inspected in 1997/98

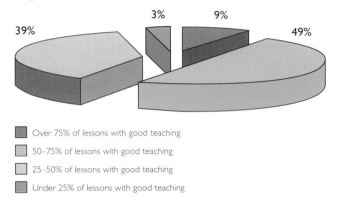

- Over 75% of lessons with good teaching
- 50–75% of lessons with good teaching
- 25–50% of lessons with good teaching
- Under 25% of lessons with good teaching

5
MANAGEMENT AND EFFICIENCY OF THE SCHOOL

5.1 Management

The Education Reform Act 1988 reallocated responsibilities and authority for managing schools from local education authorities to the headteacher and governors of individual schools. This inevitably shifted a much greater responsibility for decision making to school level. Strategic planning, usually summarised in the school development plan, now requires greater attention to be given to the monitoring of quality and efficiency. Much of the day-to-day responsibility for this new work has fallen to the headteacher, usually assisted by an administrative officer, bursar or secretary. The roles and responsibilities of governors have also changed dramatically. Unlike their counterparts in secondary schools, few primary headteachers have deputy headteachers or other members of a senior management team without full-time teaching responsibilities. Indeed, many headteachers, particularly those of small primary schools, take on considerable teaching commitments as well as the responsibilities for management and leadership.

The discussion paper, *Curriculum Organisation and Classroom Practice in Primary Schools,*[40] is unequivocal about where the responsibilities of headship should lie:

> There is a view at present in England that the introduction of LMS means that the primary head must become an administrator or chief executive. We reject this view absolutely. The task of implementing the National Curriculum and its assessment arrangements requires headteachers, more than ever, to retain and develop the role of educational leader. Primary

schools exist to provide a curriculum which fosters the development of their pupils. Headteachers must take the leading role in ensuring the quality of curricular provision and they cannot do this without involving themselves directly and centrally in the planning, transaction and evaluation of the curriculum.

> Headteachers are uniquely placed to look across the whole school for the purpose of judging its strengths and weaknesses, spotting incipient problems, drawing attention to work of distinction and to aspects of work which call for improvement.

The OFSTED Handbook *Guidance on the Inspection of Nursery and Primary Schools*[41] accepts that the role of the headteacher is one of the central contributors to an effective school. Inspectors are required to judge the extent to which:

- *strong leadership provides clear educational direction for the work of the school;*

- *teaching and curriculum development are monitored, evaluated and supported;*

- *the school has aims, values and policies which are reflected through all its work;*

- *the school, through its development planning, identifies relevant priorities and targets, takes the necessary action, and monitors and evaluates its progress towards them;*

- *there is a positive ethos, which reflects the school's commitment to high achievement, an effective learning environment, good relationships and equality of opportunity for all pupils;*

- *statutory requirements are met.*

5.2 Leadership: informed decision making

Given this recognition of the central importance of the headteacher of a primary school, it is disappointing to report that by 1997/98 the quality of the **leadership** and management was judged to be good or very good in only just over half of schools inspected. It was sound in one-third of schools, and was weak in around one in eight

---

[40] *Curriculum Organisation and Classroom Practice in Primary Schools,* Alexander R, Rose A J, and Woodhead C. DES, 1992

[41] *The OFSTED Handbook. Guidance on the Inspection of Nursery and Primary Schools.* OFSTED, 1995.

schools. The leadership and management of infant schools was stronger than that of any other type of school, being good in almost two-thirds of schools and weak in less than one school in ten.

Effective schools invariably have a clear set of aims, which is agreed and implemented by everyone. Typical comments on the **implementation of aims, values and policies** in good schools are like those from **Christ the King Junior School**, Coventry:

> *The school's mission statement and aims have been clearly identified by staff and governors and are fully described in the school brochure. The aims reflect the nature of the school, the promotion of personal and social values, and the provision of a curriculum which promotes children's learning. These aims are well met by the school.*

From **St John's CE Combined School**, Lacey Green, Buckinghamshire:

> *The school achieves its purpose as set out in its mission statement through an approach which enables pupils to achieve their full potential in a caring, Christian environment. The school's aims are in common with parents' wishes for the pupils and the school receives a large measure of support from them.*

Two sets of criticisms are levelled at the aims of some schools: first, that they give insufficient attention to achieving high and improving standards; and, second, that they are too bland and general.

The overwhelming majority of headteachers are successful at creating a positive ethos in their schools. They establish a welcoming atmosphere, provide good pastoral support, manage behaviour well and forge effective links with parents. This is clearly a great strength of English primary schools. Even schools with serious weaknesses in other aspects of their work frequently receive positive inspection reports for their ethos. In other areas of management, however, the quality varies considerably. To some extent this reflects the changing role of headship itself; but rather too many headteachers are slow or reluctant to take on their new responsibilities. Chart 37 indicates the variation in the key components of the leadership and management of primary schools.

5.3 Leadership, management and the quality of teaching

There is a strong correlation between the overall quality of teaching in a school and the quality of the leadership and management. In the 10 per cent of primary schools with the highest percentage of good teaching, the leadership and management were judged to be good in over nine out of ten schools. The feature of leadership which correlates most strongly to the quality of the teaching is the sense of **educational direction** provided by the headteacher, but a sample of quotations from a selection of reports on schools where there is good teaching and strong leadership indicates a wider range of factors, notably the **monitoring and evaluation** of the work of teachers. For example:

> *The headteacher provides very effective leadership and a clear direction for the work of the school... Planning and priority setting involve teachers, non-teaching staff and governors. The procedures are very effective. All teachers manage and lead the implementation of policies. Staff have a clear understanding of their roles and carry them out very effectively. Subject co-ordinators work alongside colleagues on planning. Last year they were released to monitor developments and this had positive effects on whole school planning and subject management.*

Chart 37
Leadership and management of primary schools 1997/98
(percentage of schools)

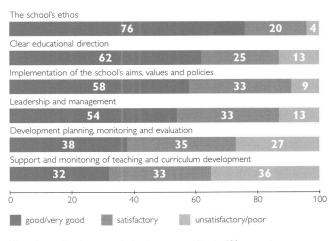

These figures have been rounded and may not add up to 100 per cent

St John's CE Combined School, Lacey Green, Buckinghamshire:

A clear sense of purpose has been established by the headteacher, the staff and the governing body through the well structured process for drawing up the school development plan. This is a comprehensive document with priorities for development, timescales and action plans for individual teachers. The progress against targets is effectively monitored and long-term objectives are identified as part of forward planning... Subject co-ordinators positively exercise leadership skills in influencing curriculum planning. Effective procedures for monitoring and evaluating curriculum provision across all key stages are secure in most subjects.

St John's CE Primary School, Sandown, Isle of Wight:

The school has recognised the importance of monitoring and evaluating its work. The management plan is reviewed annually before being revised. All teaching staff have specific responsibilities in relation to areas of the curriculum. This includes a commitment to supporting colleagues in their areas. The headteacher monitors the quality of work through her regular teaching commitment with each class and through monitoring planning. There is a very effective team approach to management.

Those schools with the best teaching have effective systems of monitoring, and although a range of approaches to monitoring the work of teachers emerges, characteristics generally include:

- lesson observation and feedback by the headteacher;
- scrutiny of pupils' work;
- scrutiny of teachers' planning;
- scrutiny of assessment data;
- assistance with the setting of objectives;
- assistance with planning.

A cluster of these approaches features in most schools with successful approaches to monitoring the work of teachers. For example, at **The Oaks County Infant School**, Sittingbourne:

The policy gives clear guidelines for the monitoring of teaching and the curriculum. It includes scrutiny of pupils' work through "book looks", scrutiny of teaching plans, classroom observations, joint planning sessions and joint agreement by staff of levels of attainment in pupils' work.

Three-fifths of schools are well led in the sense that their headteachers and governors provide clear **educational direction**. **Development planning, monitoring and evaluation**, although improving, remain areas of weakness in over one-quarter of schools. This overall judgement conceals growing confidence in development planning but considerable uncertainty about how to monitor and evaluate the work of a school. In successful practice the two aspects of management are inextricably linked. For example, **Milecastle First School**, Newcastle upon Tyne:

Central to the school's improvement is its good development plan. The headteacher draws out the main areas for progress in any one year, and all with management roles are involved in its compilation. The role of the subject co-ordinator is the key to much that is achieved in curriculum development. The model, which is now well established, serves the school well and has a clear and important impact on standards. Co-ordinators review the previous year's progress in their own subjects and set new targets as finance and whole-school priorities allow. The resulting plan gives clear guidance on growth, with targets clearly linked to responsibilities, available finance and success criteria. The development planning and the monitoring and evaluation of targets are further strengths of the school.

Good procedures are in place to monitor the quality of the teaching and to use the results to effect improvements. The teachers are regularly observed by the headteacher and the results discussed and acted upon. The teachers' plans are regularly scrutinised and the pupils' exercise books are analysed on a termly basis. Similar measures are used to monitor the curriculum. All co-ordinators have some non-contact time to work alongside colleagues and to see their own subjects being taught throughout the school. Staff are given real responsibility for their subjects, and this impacts well on their motivation and effectiveness as leaders.

Schools are increasingly focusing their attention on the standards achieved by pupils, with a view to raising these standards. Schools can rarely have had available to them as much performance data as at present; indeed, the amount and its range can make data handling a problem, and local education authorities are increasingly helping schools with the analysis of their statistics. This is likely to become more important because, from September 1998, schools have been required to set academic targets for their Year 6 pupils and will need to monitor progress towards these targets. There are signs, therefore, that schools are giving greater attention to monitoring the standards achieved and evaluating the quality of the teaching and the curriculum. They are, for example:

- analysing indicators such as National Curriculum assessment results;

- analysing the scores from standardised tests;

- undertaking the structured scrutiny of pupils' work;

- and, above all else, undertaking classroom observation using the inspection Framework evaluation criteria.

Just occasionally, pupils are involved formally in the decision-making process in their schools. Usually the schools are those with good arrangements for consulting with a wide range of people. For example, **Rowlands Gill County Junior School**, Tyne and Wear:

Responsibilities are appropriately delegated to teaching and non-teaching staff, and all staff are fully involved in consultation and discussion regarding whole school issues. Pupils are actively involved in the decision making process in the school. A school council meets regularly to consider issues raised by the children; their views are taken very seriously by the staff and are used to inform school management decisions. Different pupils attend the council meetings each time to ensure that all pupils have the opportunity to participate in the process. In addition, a suggestion box provides an effective and regular communication system between pupils, staff and governors.

5.4 Subject management

Schools are also, with variable success, seeking to develop **the role of the subject co-ordinator** or "subject manager". A critical constraint on this is the lack of non-contact time. In the majority of schools, this is the most serious obstacle to the development of the role of the subject co-ordinator; co-ordinators can rarely get into classes other than their own to influence the work or to monitor and evaluate what is going on. In most schools, short-term arrangements can be made to enable a co-ordinator to complete a particular task, such as preparing a new set of documentation or reorganising the library. Some schools are able to give a bit of time to a subject when it becomes a priority in the development plan, but they find it impossible to sustain the impetus beyond this.

For a sustained impact on the work of a subject, non-contact time is necessary, and schools rarely have sufficient staff to enable this to happen. In a survey by HMI,[42] co-ordinators in half the schools in the survey had no non-contact time in which to co-ordinate or manage their subject; at best, they relied on the occasional lesson in which the headteacher would take their class in order to release them.

Broadclyst Primary School, Devon, is an example of a school attempting to extend the role of the "subject manager".[43]

When the school moved to a subject-based curriculum the decision was taken to promote the quality of work in each subject by giving "subject managers" responsibility for their subjects. The first step was to define roles; the role of the senior management team, with its emphasis on the achievement of goals and quality assurance, was separated from that of subject manager. The subject manager is responsible for seeking to ensure that his or her subject is properly covered in every class, and for providing clear leadership in the subject.

The role is defined in terms of curriculum management, teaching and learning, and professional development. An important aspect

---

[42] *Using Subject Specialists to Promote High Standards at Key Stage 2.* OFSTED, 1997.

[43] ibid, p 24.

of the role is that of establishing the "health of the subject" by ensuring that both the teaching and the learning are successful. The subject manager is therefore asked to:

i. monitor and evaluate the teaching and learning in the subject;

ii. review, overall, the "health of the subject";

iii. provide feedback to staff, headteacher and governors.

Criteria based on knowledge, skills and understanding are established by subject managers for monitoring each subject. These are a combination of elements of the National Curriculum and the school's own priorities and plans.

A programme is set up twice a year to enable, at least, each subject manager to teach classes in Years 2, 4 and 6 and to monitor standards, provision and progression in their subject. The manager of the core subjects visits every year group. Following the visit, a brief report is provided for the senior management team and the governors, usually covering issues such as planning, teaching and learning, and standards. Recommendations are made; some refer to resources needs (eg "more sets of atlases"), and some refer to the need for changes in what is taught (eg "more opportunity for an investigative approach, using historical artefacts and pictures").

This approach is in its early stages of development, and the quality of both the criteria and the reports vary, but the school is convinced of the potential benefits of the model and is confident it is already having an impact. The school has acknowledged the waste in developing subject expertise without giving opportunities for subject managers to make use of it. It has also recognised that for subject managers to have a real impact at a time of severe financial constraints, their approach must be carefully planned and properly managed.

5.5 Governing bodies

The **role of the governing body** has also changed out of all recognition in recent years; the demands made on governors are greater than ever before

and their responsibilities are increasingly clear. Not surprisingly, inspection reports comment on difficulties in appointing and retaining governors, but the overall picture is one of governors supporting the school's professional staff positively and knowing their schools well. In about one-quarter of schools, governors are poorly placed to know about and influence the education provided. The proportion of ineffective governing bodies is twice as high in disadvantaged areas as in advantaged areas.

Nevertheless, the majority of governors deal with their many duties in a dedicated and usually effective manner. Inspection reports illustrate the range of responsibilities and governors' commitment to them. For example, **Alburgh with Denton VC First School**, Norfolk:

Governors are highly committed to the school. Regular meetings are held, including sub-groups for finance, curriculum and staffing. They are involved appropriately in many areas of the school's work, providing very good support for the headteacher in the financial management of the school, approving and reviewing policies, and monitoring the curriculum. The reports prepared by governors following visits to classrooms are very informative and worthwhile. Governors have taken a good strategic long-term view, considering how the number of children on roll can be raised in order to safeguard the future of the school. They have raised substantial funds successfully, both through village events and a grant from the National Lottery, to provide accommodation for pre-school provision on the school premises.

Typically, inspection reports refer to change and development in the role of a governing body, not least in the area of monitoring the work of the school. For example, **Bluehouse County Junior School**, Basildon:

The school has previously experienced difficulties in recruiting governors but is now fortunate in being supported by an enthusiastic governing body who have a clear understanding of the aims and priorities of the school. Governors are very aware of their responsibilities, have formed appropriate committees to support efficient working practices and have developed their own action plan. They use the experiences and expertise of individual governors wisely and are keen to develop professionally through appropriate in-service training. They are beginning to monitor curriculum development and, through focus visits, are planning to become more involved in monitoring aspects of teaching and learning. Significant achievements have been made by the governing body during the short time that they have worked together. The continuing development of their monitoring role is needed to ensure a positive contribution to the effective management of the school.

Finally, from **Fair Oak Junior School**, Eastleigh, Hampshire:

The excellent leadership of the headteacher, supported by the deputy headteacher, governing body and the staff, provides clear educational direction for the school. The governing body is very well informed in carrying out its duties. The chair of governors visits regularly and other governors attend whenever time permits. A register is kept of governors' visits. Governors visit for a variety of reasons: for example, they visit the classrooms to see work in progress, they attend professional in-service training, and they monitor the provision for pupils with special educational needs. Governors report back to the main governing body when appropriate. On occasions subject co-ordinators address governors' meetings and senior members of the teaching staff, as well as the teacher governors, regularly attend. The various committees are capably led; they meet regularly and contribute effectively to the management of the school. The governing body must take great credit for the impressive development of the school building.

The examples of good practice quoted above indicate the range of ways in which effective governing bodies work. They get to know their schools and are supportive of them, not least in the run up to, during and after Section 10 inspections. They have set up committee structures which help to share the load and make best use of expertise. They identify individual governors to take the lead on important matters such as special educational needs or literacy. However, workloads are demanding and contributions are unpaid and voluntary; not all employers are prepared to release governors during the working day to visit their school or attend meetings or interviews.

There remains considerable variation, therefore, in practice, and some weaknesses emerge, particularly where the strategic role of the governors is not defined with sufficient clarity. The quality and capability of governing bodies vary considerably and many governors remain uneasy about the breadth of their responsibilities. In such circumstances the governing body can be ineffective, unsure of what, if any, contribution it has to make; or, conversely, it can involve itself too closely in the day-to-day running of the school. In a small but worrying proportion of schools, governors have been unprepared to deal with serious weaknesses, particularly those where the leadership shown by the headteacher or the quality of the teaching in the school is poor.

Aspects relating to the **statutory responsibilities** of governors, often of a technical nature, are frequently raised in inspection reports. In particular, governors are sometimes unaware of the full range of information which must be provided for parents in the governors' annual report to parents, such as a record of the authorised and unauthorised absences of pupils or the inclusion of a record of staff development. They are also not always clear about which policies they are required to have in place, for instance a policy on sex education in line with Circular 5/94. On the other hand, governors are frequently very alert and active over health and safety matters, and it has often been governors who have taken the lead in pushing for greater school security in the light of recent tragic cases of violence in primary schools.

A second area of hesitancy in the role of governors is in relation to pay. Many governors are uneasy about their financial responsibilities, and are unsure about how to carry out their role in establishing **pay policies** and monitoring their impact. Pay policies tend to be rudimentary documents which are not linked to other documents defining aspects of management. Guidance provided by the DfEE is frequently neglected. Few schools have written their pay policies with the specific objective of raising standards. Discretionary points continue to be given almost exclusively for additional responsibility and to support good management. The climate in schools continues, at least at headteacher level, to be hostile to the notion of "excellence points".

In a survey conducted by HMI, two-thirds of the schools visited had used their discretion to increase the pay of the headteacher above the annual pay award. However, the management of this process is frequently unsatisfactory, and most schools visited were failing to comply with the Circular. The 1995/96 Annual Report of Her Majesty's Chief Inspector of Schools concluded:[44]

> *Many governing bodies are a long way from setting the clear and relevant performance indicators for headteachers which are needed if reliable judgements are to be made about the salary of the headteacher. Governors generally need to be better prepared for this task.*

5.6 The efficiency of the school

Chart 38
The efficiency of schools 1997/98
(percentage of schools)

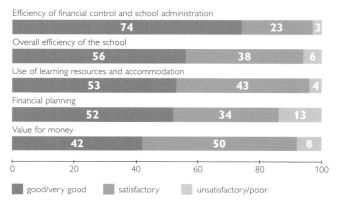

Efficiency of financial control and school administration
74 | 23 | 3
Overall efficiency of the school
56 | 38 | 6
Use of learning resources and accommodation
53 | 43 | 4
Financial planning
52 | 34 | 13
Value for money
42 | 50 | 8

0   20   40   60   80   100

■ good/very good   ■ satisfactory   ■ unsatisfactory/poor

These figures have been rounded and may not add up to 100 per cent

In the considerable majority of primary schools, the efficiency of the school is judged to be at least satisfactory. Indeed, arrangements for **financial control and administration** are good in around three-quarters of schools, with concerns raised in only one school in 30. Many schools are effectively employing a bursar, either as a member of the school staff or as part of a specialist service provided by the local education authority. Day-to-day administration is almost always efficient, with effective systems in place for budgetary control. Good use is made of external audits, and schools act quickly and successfully upon recommendations made.

---

[44] *The Annual Report of Her Majesty's Chief Inspector of Schools, 1995/96.* OFSTED, 1997.

Half the schools inspected in 1997/98 were good or very good at **financial planning**, with a further one-third satisfactory. Governing bodies are increasingly involved with their senior management teams in setting budgets and distributing funds; however, in about one in six schools, financial planning was insufficiently linked to development planning.

The following example, from **Merland Rise Primary School**, Epsom, Surrey, illustrates the complexity of issues faced by schools when setting financial priorities and targets. The essential involvement of governors is a feature of the good practice reported here:

> *The school's financial planning is very good. It is based on the school development plan which clearly identifies the priorities for change in the school. The governors have a very helpful and informative statement of the annual budget planning cycle which, month by month, indicates the tasks which must be carried out. The annual budget is very well managed and is considered with great care before being agreed. Governors and the headteacher are aware of long term financial implications of developments, but these have not as yet been written into a longer-term financial plan. There is currently a significant budget underspend, which has reduced steadily over a number of years as needed resources have been purchased. The underspend has existed since the formation of a single school from two separate schools. Money has been purposefully retained as the headteacher and governors are aware of the need for additional funds to cover the period when annual expenditure is likely to exceed annual income. This will occur when a larger number of pupils leave the school from Year 6 than enter into the reception class. Governors, the headteacher and administrative staff are fully aware of budget formulation and monitoring procedures, and where responsibilities lie. Following a governors' training session, an excellent document stating the school's standards of financial administration has been prepared. This clearly delineates tasks and responsibilities. The school's accounts have been recently audited and found to be in good order.*

The aspect of financial management which generally needs strengthening is that of monitoring the outcomes of expenditure; nearly half the schools fail to evaluate whether the money they have spent on a particular initiative has been money well spent. Not enough thought is given to establishing procedures for evaluating the cost-effectiveness or opportunity costs of spending decisions.

Budget surpluses vary considerably from school to school. At the end of the 1993/94 financial year, half of primary schools carried forward £18,000 or more, equivalent to about £100 per pupil. Budget surpluses have continued to vary, from about 2 per cent to 10 per cent of income. In most cases the larger surpluses are intentionally accumulated to pay for specific projects, such as refurbishing or improving a library. Most schools use the resources available to them well, and provide at least satisfactory **value for money**. Just under 10 per cent of schools, nevertheless, provide poor value for money. In those schools where poor value for money is provided, a combination of factors usually contributes to this: poor progress and attainment, unsatisfactory teaching, and weaknesses in the management, coupled sometimes with high unit costs.

Chart 39 gives an overall picture of the staffing, accommodation and learning resources in primary schools as at 1998. A more detailed analysis is given in the sections following.

Chart 39
Staffing, accommodation and learning resources in primary schools, 1997/98.
(percentage of schools)

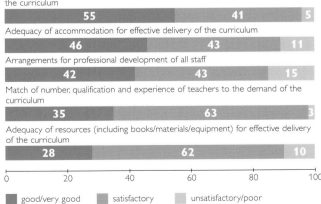

These figures have been rounded and may not add up to 100 per cent

5.7 Staffing

Average class sizes have risen throughout the period of the review. At Key Stage 1, by the end of the academic year 1997/98, 29 per cent of classes had more than 30 pupils, an increase of over one percentage point from the previous year.

Pupil–teacher ratios have also risen throughout the period, as indicated in Chart 40, and reached 24:1 by 1998; the ratio was 22.4:1 in 1993. To some extent this has been because schools have chosen to allocate a growing proportion of their budget to the employment of non-teaching staff such as classroom assistants and nursery nurses, recognising the cost-effective role that these adults can play in classrooms. Appropriately, many schools now choose to redeploy classroom support staff to the lessons in which a more focused approach to the teaching of literacy and numeracy is taking place.

Chart 40
Average pupil/teacher ratio 1994–98

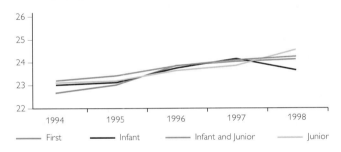

The match in terms of the **number, qualifications and experience of teachers** to the demands of the curriculum is good in over one-third of schools, adequate in about two-thirds of schools and inadequate in 3 per cent, as shown in Chart 39. The impact that teachers with a good subject knowledge can have on standards has, however, been a theme of this review, and clearly there are still a great many lessons where the unsatisfactory teaching is a direct consequence of teachers lacking the knowledge, skills or understanding to teach a subject well. It is a tall order to have this degree of specialist knowledge in all the subjects of the National Curriculum and religious education, and in some subjects – particularly design and technology and information technology – too many teachers either lack the essential, basic knowledge to teach the subjects properly or are getting left behind as the technology itself develops.

It is surprising that many headteachers report that when making appointments to class teaching posts, a candidate's subject specialism is a secondary consideration; they prefer to appoint a "good all-rounder" rather than a teacher with particular expertise in a subject, irrespective of the balance of subject knowledge already present among the staff. Part-time staff, on the other hand, are often appointed because of the subject expertise they bring – for example in music, physical education or technology.

Vacancy rates for full-time qualified teachers have almost doubled in the last five years, rising from 0.5 per cent of teachers in post in 1993 to 0.8 per cent in 1998.[45] The problem of unfilled vacancies is felt most strongly in London; in inner London over 2 per cent of all posts were unfilled at the start of the autumn term 1998, equivalent to about 700 posts (secondary and primary) in inner London alone. Many schools have no alternative but to employ a series of supply teachers, making it difficult to target effectively the necessary training for initiatives such as the National Literacy Strategy.

Nationally, 10 per cent of qualified teacher posts were advertised for a September 1998 appointment; the figure for inner London was 13 per cent. About half of the advertised posts received more than ten applications. In inner London, one in eight advertised posts remained unfilled, compared with only one or two in 100 in the north of England.

Vacancies for headships almost trebled in the period to 1998, rising from 0.5 per cent to 1.4 per cent. Recruitment of headteachers is becoming something of a problem in parts of London; there is a vacancy rate of 3.6 per cent in inner London. Recruitment of headteachers to schools seen as "difficult", often in areas of socio-economic disadvantage, is also a problem; the schools presenting the greatest challenges often find it the hardest to recruit headteachers of the necessary calibre to tackle these challenges.

Arrangements for the **professional development** of staff vary considerably in quality. They are good in two-fifths of schools but weak in one school in seven (see Chart 39). There continue to be

weaknesses in the arrangements for ensuring that staff who have attended courses can feed back effectively to the rest of staff. This "cascade" approach to in-service training has been at the centre of the implementation of the National Literacy and Numeracy Projects, and the success or failure of the national strategies will depend on the quality of the transfer of knowledge, skills and understanding from the local education authority consultants to the "key teachers" and from the key teachers to classroom teachers.

The literacy and numeracy projects provided useful case studies of the strengths and weaknesses of the cascade model. In both projects, a key role in their implementation was given to the key teachers or the mathematics and English co-ordinator. The choice of the key teacher was a crucial decision by the headteacher. Where the projects had little impact in a school and the training failed to bring about change, this was often due to a poor choice of key teacher. It was a worrying finding of the evaluation of the literacy project that half of the lessons in which unsatisfactory teaching was observed were taught by key teachers.

Nevertheless, in the numeracy project the co-ordinator role was carried out at least satisfactorily in well over half the schools, and very effectively in one in three schools. The provision of supply cover funded by the project to enable the co-ordinator to get into classrooms and work alongside other teachers, as well as giving them time to help with the planning of work and to review the school's progress, proved invaluable.

But not all key teachers had skills in training colleagues, and it is a demanding task to establish a programme of staff meetings, often to be conducted in "twilight" sessions at the end of a demanding day's teaching. It was not unusual to hear from key teachers that their best efforts were frustrated by a minority of teachers who were reluctant to change their practice to accommodate the structures of the projects.

Other factors also reduced the impact of the key teachers in some schools, often related to the particular features of the school: for example, a high level of staff turnover, especially at senior management level; insufficient support from the headteacher; and the allocation of too many responsibilities to the co-ordinator. In many

---

[45] The source of much of the data on staff vacancies is the School Teachers Review Body *Survey of Vacancies and Recruitment in Schools*, 1998.

schools the role of the key teacher was not fully developed. They were not always given clearly defined tasks and many were marginalised, often through the sheer accumulation of other work.

5.8 Accommodation

The accommodation in English primary schools, in terms of its quality and its adequacy for the effective teaching of the National Curriculum, is good in less than half of the schools. As shown in Chart 39, in 1998 inspectors judged it to be good in 46 per cent of the schools inspected, they judged a similar proportion to be satisfactory, and they judged 11 per cent – one school in nine – to have unsatisfactory accommodation. Even in schools looked upon as having generally good facilities, it was rare for an inspection report not to indicate some areas of concern. For example:

All classrooms and teaching areas are of adequate size, except the hall which is too small to accommodate the whole school for assemblies and is cramped at lunchtimes. Its small size also has a negative impact on the teaching of physical education, which is most noticeable with older pupils in gymnastic lessons.

Weaknesses in the quantity of accommodation have the most direct impact on the subjects of the National Curriculum when there is a lack of sufficient outdoor or indoor accommodation for the teaching of physical education, and a lack of access to running water, often in "temporary" classrooms, and particularly affecting the teaching of art. Needless to say, resourceful teachers get round these problems in a range of imaginative ways. The effects of poor-quality accommodation are more insidious: leaking roofs, crumbling plaster, flaking paintwork and bleak, unpleasant outdoor play areas. Where such poor-quality accommodation is found in conjunction with routine vandalism, such as graffiti, broken windows or damage to school grounds, the adverse effects on morale and the drive to raise standards can be considerable. It may be beyond the reach of a school to tackle some of these issues, particularly those requiring a change of direction in the local community or capital investment on a large scale. Where these features of poor accommodation are present, inspection reports make depressing reading. For example:

The standard of accommodation at Key Stage 2 is very poor. Although the classrooms at Key Stage 2 are of a good size, they are in an unacceptable state of repair, and are untidy and dirty. This affects standards because the pupils cannot, for example, sit together comfortably for a reading session because of the condition of the floor and the small, and rather dirty, carpeted areas.

The school's external environment is not attractive, and the Key Stage 2 building is bleak and uninviting. The extensive grassed area is poorly marked, the Key Stage 2 hard playing area is also unmarked and littered, and the Key Stage 1 hard playing area is too small.

Two aspects of progress with accommodation have recently been reported in a large number of schools. First – and often instigated by governing bodies in response to the tragedy at Dunblane – many schools, especially in urban areas, have greatly enhanced security arrangements, such as access codes for outside doors, security fences around play areas and car parks, and a greater degree of vigilance in ensuring that visitors to the school have bona fide reasons for their visit. Far from reacting negatively to the "fortress" appearance of some of these arrangements, staff, pupils and parents generally speak positively of the greater sense of security in their school.

The second aspect of improvement is that of enhancements being made to the school grounds. Many schools are making imaginative use of their grounds to support environmental education, and to make their buildings and grounds increasingly pleasant and civilised places in which to work and play. This aspect of the work of primary schools is often undervalued, but there are indications of some excellent practice and a widespread attention to the quality of the local environment, as well as a recognition of its value as a resource. The best examples are outstanding, with full use being made of school grounds: sculptures and murals created by pupils and professional artists; the development of "wild areas" in school grounds; environmental trails, including bird hides and "minibeast" sites; the adoption of local meadows and woodlands; and close links with local farms, parks and nature reserves. These resources, as well as motivating pupils and influencing behaviour and attitudes to conservation, can help to promote closer links between parents, the local community and the school.

5.9 Resources

The quality and quantity of learning resources are good overall in three in ten schools and are inadequate in one in ten, as indicated in Chart 39. One in eight schools has inadequate books for English, although there are signs that a significant reallocation of priorities towards literacy is helping to address this issue. Many schools have invested heavily in the purchase of enlarged texts ("big books") and sets of books to support the literacy hour, but many schools still have some way to go before they have sufficient books to meet all the requirements of the National Literacy Strategy.

Too many book corners still have worn and outdated books. Pupils rarely, if ever, look at such material. It reduces the impact of book corners and adds to the unnecessary sense of clutter in some classrooms. Many schools find it hard to supervise access to their libraries, with the result that valuable collections of books remain underused. Stocks of reference books, particularly for pupils towards the end of Key Stage 2, need to be increased; but, equally, schools need to do all they can to ensure that the stock they have is properly used.

Outdoor equipment is the weakest element of the resourcing for under-fives in primary schools, and there are shortcomings in the provision of books, language resources and construction materials in nearly one in five nursery schools.

Weaknesses have been reported over the four years in individual subjects. For example, in religious education, one-third of schools has insufficient resources to meet the requirements of the local Agreed Syllabus. Although there is a computer in most classrooms, many are old and unreliable and have an insufficient range of applications for pupils to develop fully their capability in information technology. Many schools have taken steps to improve the range and quality of musical instruments available for performing and composing during class lessons; however, there remain some schools where the instruments are in a poor state of repair, or little more than toys, or where younger pupils do not have access to chromatic instruments.

Clearly, schools have different priorities for spending; they also have different amounts of money available for the purchase of materials, books and equipment; and they have differential access to private fundraising. Schools allocate different proportions of their budgets to different aspects of resourcing, and they vary in the effectiveness with which they use these resources. HMI conducted a survey in 1996 of a sample of schools where resources were judged to be inadequate. In half the schools in the survey, the money spent on resources was ineffectively used. For example, several schools continued to spend heavily on improving their already adequate computing facilities even though there were severe shortages of books. Those subject co-ordinators who lacked expertise in their subject often made poor use of funds available to them, particularly in practical subjects such as art and design and technology.

A significant number of the primary schools admitted that they were unaware of the precise nature of the resource shortages in subjects other than English, mathematics and science until these were identified through inspection. Insufficient funding partly explained the unsatisfactory learning resources in one-third of the primary schools visited.

On the other hand, there are signs of a much closer link between available funding, development planning and the careful use of resources. For example, **Sir Harold Jackson Primary School**, Sheffield:

The school makes very efficient use of its resources, time, staff, materials and accommodation to provide a good quality of education. The governors and headteacher recognise the need to link the use of the school's resources to the achievement of its purposes. After staffing costs have been established, the school development plan is used effectively to decide upon the allocation of funds to appropriate targets. There is careful yearly monitoring of the cost-effectiveness of decisions taken in relation to the school development plan and priorities set, especially relating to curriculum, resources, energy saving and recreation service spending.

5.10 Management training

It has not been surprising, given the overwhelming evidence of the key role of leadership and management in determining the overall quality of a school, that in recent years several schemes aimed at improving the quality of leadership and management have been established. HMI were asked to contribute to the evaluation of two programmes, both administered by the Teacher Training Agency: first, the Headteachers' Leadership and Management Programme (HEADLAMP); and, second, the National Professional Qualification for Headteachers (NPQH).

The HEADLAMP scheme

The HEADLAMP scheme is a grant-supported training and development scheme for headteachers appointed to their first permanent headship from April 1995. The programme is open to headteachers of local education authority maintained and grant maintained schools in all phases and to headteachers of non-maintained special schools. A grant of up to £2,500 is offered, to be spent within two years of taking up the post. By the end of October 1997, 3,698 newly appointed headteachers had registered for HEADLAMP.

To underpin the HEADLAMP scheme, the Teacher Training Agency issued a procedural document setting out the details of the scheme and practical arrangements for participation. This document suggested that headteachers could benefit most from their participation in the scheme if they engaged in a thorough and accurate process of needs assessment before deciding upon a programme of training and development activities.

The document set out a list of HEADLAMP tasks and abilities.[46] For example, each programme needs to focus on one or more aspects of management, such as "selecting and managing staff, and appraising their performance and development needs". The programme also focuses on a range of leadership and management abilities, such the ability to "negotiate, delegate, consult and co-ordinate the efforts of others".

HMI made inspection visits to a sample both of providers and of headteachers (including 59 primary school headteachers), and the following findings emerged from these visits.

Most headteachers initially embarked on the scheme without a fully developed idea of what they expected to gain from HEADLAMP. Only a minority undertook a systematic process of needs assessment at the outset, and still fewer planned at all closely for their personal development. Headteachers who took the time to identify their needs and priorities and plan an appropriate programme to meet them gained most from their participation. The importance of needs assessment and proper planning became increasingly apparent to headteachers as their experience of the scheme grew. Some headteachers were attracted to the "package" courses because they took away the need for further thought and decision making. Overall, there were shortcomings in the quality of the needs assessment. Provision in many of the providers inspected was less than good, often being characterised by superficial analysis and insufficient focus on the HEADLAMP list of tasks and activities.

All participants appreciated the benefit of being given funding for their own training, which was on top of that allocated to the school generally. However, substantial numbers had not, at the time of the inspection, made full use of their HEADLAMP grants. For some, this was because they had decided to delay their start; for others, it was because of difficulty in identifying suitable providers of training. Some headteachers of small primary schools reported that they could not use the full allocation on their own training because of the need to purchase supply cover which exceeded the £500 allowable for this cover under the programme.

The training programmes offered by the registered providers were generally suitable, although they were not always designed with specific reference to the HEADLAMP tasks and abilities. Planning to meet the needs of the participants was not always effective, nor was the quality of delivery: shortcomings included an overemphasis on theoretical issues, slow pace and, in some cases, a lack of rigour and challenge. Few training and development activities made really effective use of the experience of high-quality serving headteachers.

---

[46] HEADLAMP tasks and abilities have now been superseded by the National Standards for Headteachers. Teacher Training Agency, October 1997.

The majority of headteachers reported positively on the training, particularly when it related closely to their own needs and those of their schools. However, others either were not fully satisfied with the quality of the provision or did not feel that it represented value for money. This was often because they did not feel it matched their needs, insofar as they had identified them, closely enough.

The HEADLAMP procedures suggested that headteachers, having identified their needs, should plan a programme to meet these needs. For example, a good personal development plan was prepared by the headteacher of a small primary school, after a process of needs assessment which was supported by a local education authority inspector. The plan identified ten training targets, all of which combined personal and school development needs. Each target was associated with a selection of the HEADLAMP tasks and abilities, and included a brief description of the training provision to be used, a section outlining the expected action which would follow and a set of criteria for the evaluation of outcomes. This was particularly beneficial both in helping the headteacher to develop and in improving the quality of education in the school.

Overall, there was evidence that some headteachers had developed new skills and gained in confidence in leadership and management as a direct result of their participation, but not all headteachers had changed or developed their styles of leadership and management as a result of their participation. There were general benefits, such as the closer attention given to issues such as: the effectiveness of communication; how to arrange and control meetings; how to set about the process of constructing and presenting development plans; and ways in which the work of the school might be evaluated.

The National Professional Qualification for Headteachers

At the time of writing, the Government has proposed in a Green Paper that it intends to make the NPQH a mandatory requirement for aspiring headteachers by 2002. HMI carried out a small-scale pilot study to consider the impact of the training on the development of an aspiring headteacher's leadership and management skills, and on school improvement – especially standards of achievement and the quality of education. The qualification is in a process of development, with issues being addressed in the light of evaluations. The following evidence is based on a small number of HMI inspection visits carried out during the summer term 1998.

While the training had helped the majority of the candidates visited to develop leadership and management skills, too many weaknesses in the process remain. For example, the headteachers in the candidates' own schools do not have enough information about the qualification or an understanding of what their role will be in the process. Headteachers rarely played a major part in the training and assessment processes, and often felt that their experience and skills were not used fully enough.

For many candidates, the generic nature of the NPQH programme was a positive aspect, but one-third of those seen felt greater differentiation was required to account for the needs of different school phases. The quality of the "action planning" varied considerably, and many candidates failed to recognise the importance and purpose of personal action planning. Only one-quarter of the action plans looked at by inspectors were good: typically these had been drafted in consultation with trainers or assessors and amended and refined through discussion with the candidate's headteacher. In the best cases the targets were clear and set against the national standards for headteachers, and they reflected appropriately the needs of candidates and tackled areas of value to the school. Of concern to a substantial minority of candidates was the need to find time to complete the course, particularly the assessment tasks, which were often described as burdensome.

The most significant positive impact of the training, reported by both the candidates and their headteachers, was the development of analytical skills. For many, confidence grew, and candidates generally had a clearer view of the roles and responsibilities of headship. Candidates also reported that they were better at chairing meetings and making presentations, and that they were clearer about strategic thinking and "vision".

The NPQH qualification is evolving in the light of evaluations. Many headteachers and aspiring headteachers welcome the idea of such a qualification in principle. Many, however, believe that it needs further work before it delivers benefits as it should. A new accelerated route to the qualification, for those candidates who are close to headship, is being trialled from September 1998.

6
ETHOS, BEHAVIOUR AND PUPIL SUPPORT

6.1 Behaviour and attendance

The good behaviour of pupils and the positive attitudes that they have to school are particular strengths of English primary schools. In 1997/98, behaviour of pupils was judged to be good in 80 per cent of primary schools and unsatisfactory in only 2 per cent. In a few schools, however, while there is generally good behaviour, the poor behaviour of a small group of pupils, often in one year group or class, has a depressing effect on learning, reduces the pace of lessons, and is extremely demanding for the teachers involved. Nevertheless, almost all schools are orderly communities. Pupils settle quickly to the routines of school life in their nursery and reception classes. At both key stages, primary pupils are usually enthusiastic about their work and co-operate well with one another.

In recent years there has been much public concern about bullying. Most schools, however, are responsive to these concerns and have clear policies and procedures, so that incidents of bullying are treated seriously and dealt with promptly and effectively. It is important for schools to establish a climate in which pupils and their parents feel able to raise issues such as bullying or harassment; they need to feel that their concerns will be taken seriously and acted upon. Although there has been a slight increase over the last four years in the number of pupils permanently excluded, the number remains very small – only 0.04 per cent of the school population. At least ten times as many boys as girls are excluded, the vast majority from Key Stage 2. A small number of schools serving severely disadvantaged areas accounts for a disproportionate number of exclusions.

There has been little change in attendance; it remains good in most schools. The national figure for attendance has remained at over 93 per cent and unauthorised absence is only about 0.5 per cent. In only about 4 per cent of schools does attendance fall below 90 per cent. Schools generally have systematic procedures for following up absence. Procedures for monitoring and promoting good attendance are effective in most schools, but are weak in one school in ten. However, despite this positive picture, a few schools do not monitor attendance sufficiently rigorously and do not contact parents quickly enough when pupils are absent. Given the vulnerability of primary age pupils, it is essential that all schools have proper procedures for dealing with unauthorised absence and implement them rigorously. The issue of pupils arriving late to school is most frequently raised in nursery classes, where although education is non-statutory, late arrivals can disrupt the programme of work of both the latecomers and the rest of the class.

6.2 Pupils' spiritual, moral, social and cultural development

It is the responsibility of schools to ensure that opportunities are provided which promote pupils' spiritual, moral, social and cultural development throughout the whole curriculum. This requirement is set out in Section 1 of the Education Reform Act 1988. Clearly the four elements overlap, but features of successful practice in each element emerge from inspection reports and are reported upon separately below.

Chart 41
The contribution of primary schools to pupils' spiritual, moral, social and cultural development 1997/98
(percentage of schools)

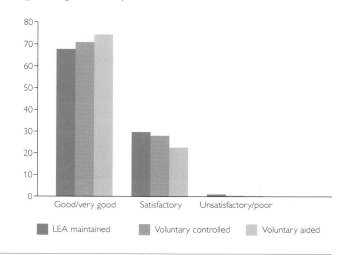

The overall quality of schools' contribution to pupils' spiritual, moral, social and cultural development changed little between 1994 and 1998. Not surprisingly, design and technology, science, mathematics and information technology have less impact on pupils' spiritual, moral, social and cultural development than do humanities and arts subjects. Chart 41 shows inspectors' judgements of the quality of the overall provision for spiritual, moral, social and cultural development in 1997/98, set out according to the form of governance in a school. There is slightly more good provision in voluntary-aided church schools than in other schools.

The features of schools where spiritual, moral, social and cultural development are strong include the clear presentation, often in the school

Chart 42
Provision for spiritual, moral, social and cultural development 1997/98
(percentage of schools)

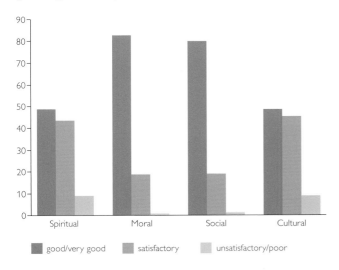

- good/very good
- satisfactory
- unsatisfactory/poor

Chart 43
Spiritual development by type of school 1997/98
(percentage of schools)

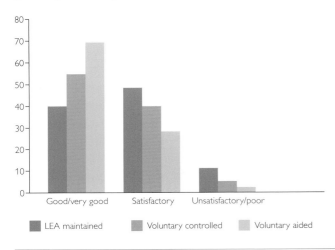

- LEA maintained
- Voluntary controlled
- Voluntary aided

prospectus, of the school's aims and, where appropriate, its religious principles; a detailed, well conceived policy, translated into practice by all staff; aims which emphasise valuing and respect for people and which permeate all areas of school life; good relationships and a supportive environment for adults and pupils; a strong sense of community, with all its members fully involved in the life of the school; and supportive governors and parents.

Primary schools are almost twice as successful in promoting moral and social development as spiritual and cultural development. The reasons for this are not always clear, but contributory factors include teachers' lack of understanding of the nature of spiritual and, to some extent, cultural development. Chart 42 illustrates differences in the quality of spiritual, moral, social and cultural development. Whereas provision for spiritual and cultural development is good in just under half of the schools, the provision for moral and social development is good in about four out of five schools. There are very few schools indeed where the provision for moral and social development is unsatisfactory.

6.3 Spiritual development

Nearly five in ten primary schools made good or better provision for pupils' spiritual development, but in just under one in ten schools, provision was unsatisfactory (Chart 42). There were significant differences in the provision for spiritual development between different types of school. Provision for spiritual development is strongest in voluntary-aided church schools, and weakest in LEA maintained schools. This situation is illustrated in Chart 43.

Religious education and acts of collective worship make the strongest contribution to spiritual development, a point frequently illustrated in inspection reports. For example, from **St Laurence CE Infant School**, Birmingham:

The school has a strong sense of Christian purpose, which is reflected in its caring ethos. A high priority is given to the acquisition of knowledge and insight into the values and beliefs of each other and everyone is treated with respect. This was noted in one class when the experience of a pupil from Hong Kong was valued and used to extend the knowledge of other pupils. The whole staff share a common purpose in providing positive role models and a sense of spirituality pervades the school. It is seen in music, the lighting of candles and prayer, time for reflection in lessons and the way everyone is treated in school. Pupils are sensitive to the needs of others to be respected and valued. The school's provision for spiritual development is very good. Spirituality is evident – and planned for – across the curriculum. Teachers promote spiritual development in their lessons. This was demonstrated when a pupil could not contain his excitement to become involved in music, or when gasps of wonder accompanied the uncovering of an ostrich's egg in science, or when calling up images from a CD ROM.

The following example is taken from **Heron Primary School**, Gloucester:

The school makes very good provision for pupils' spiritual, moral, social and cultural development. Some aspects are excellent. Pupils' creative writing shows that they are able not only to reflect on their own experiences, but to empathise with the experiences of others. Many teachers are skilled at grasping opportunities to further pupils' spiritual development. Pupils listened in rapt silence as one played the cello at the start of an assembly; encouraged by their teacher, they considered how the playing made them feel and were able to express their thoughts openly. Assemblies are carefully planned to make them an experience of quality. All reinforce the ethos of the school; most allow time for reflection and make a meaningful contribution to pupils' spiritual development.

Religious education often makes a particularly positive contribution to pupils' spiritual development. Through religious education, pupils have opportunities to enrich their spiritual development by, for example, visiting local places of worship to experience the atmosphere and meeting members of faith communities, talking to them about their beliefs; exploring ultimate questions, for example about why people suffer and die; learning about Christianity and other faiths, their forms of worship and contemplation; and understanding how for many people their beliefs affect their daily lives.

Most primary schools go beyond teaching about beliefs and values and promote desirable values in the school community. These values overlap with moral development but may have a specifically spiritual dimension. For example, pupils may be encouraged to consider the wonders of creation, and the importance of relationships and the worth of each individual. They may be given time for quiet reflection on significant experiences, and to develop a sense of "awe and wonder" – for example through listening to Psalm 8 while viewing slides of the stars and space.

Where provision for spiritual development is weak, there is rarely a shared understanding in the school of spiritual development and few planned opportunities to address it. While there may be opportunities for spiritual development taken from collective worship, no other aspect of school life is seen as contributing to it.

6.4 Moral development

Provision for pupils' moral development is good in over eight in ten schools (Chart 42). The aims and ethos of the school are often the starting points for promoting moral development, especially where these are shared with and agreed by parents. Where schools make good provision for pupils' moral development, there are usually clear statements of the moral values of the school, for example seeking to promote honesty, fairness, hard work, care, and a sense of right and wrong; and in physical education and games a sense of fair play will be promoted. Pupils are encouraged to think for themselves and to discuss a range of moral issues; and, most importantly, teachers and adults effectively promote moral principles through their interaction with pupils and each other. From **Newnham Junior School**, Ruislip, for example:

Moral development of the pupils is a strength of the school. The ethos of the school is firmly based on respect and care for others. There is an atmosphere of confidence and openness, and pupils show sensitivity and tolerance of the views of others. Teachers take care to show that all pupils are valued. Due attention is given to the reinforcement of the codes of behaviour and the sharing of positive values. Discipline is self-imposed and pupils are made aware of what facilitates an orderly school, through good examples given by the teachers, support staff, and the day-to-day interaction between the staff and pupils. The pupils enjoy their work and show care for the school, with a strong sense of belonging. Moral values are well taught through stories, songs and discussions.

Where the provision for moral development is good, schools put their moral values into practice. For example, schools free of litter and graffiti are likely to exemplify pupils' respect for each other and their environment; their good behaviour at lunchtime and breaktime illustrates their sense of self-discipline and responsibility; class rules demonstrate what constitutes acceptable and unacceptable behaviour; and there will be support for a range of charities.

Where provision for pupils' moral development is weak, typically school rules are not always understood by pupils and may be applied inconsistently by teachers; and opportunities for addressing moral issues are not taken up or planned for.

6.5 Social development

The provision of opportunities for social development is good or better in eight in ten of all primary schools, and unsatisfactory in only about one in 50 (Chart 42). In some schools, provision for social development is formalised through a personal and social education programme; in others, particularly those with younger children, "circle time" gives pupils opportunities to discuss problems which may arise within the lives of pupils at school. Where the provision of opportunities for social development is good, schools provide many opportunities for pupils to develop their interpersonal skills and a sense of responsibility.

In the best instances, social development is taught through the provision of opportunities to develop an understanding of society in all its aspects: its institutions, structures and characteristics, including economic and political organisation; and life as a citizen, parent or worker in a community. Pupils are helped in this through opportunities to exercise responsibility, and, in some schools, through democratically elected school councils. For example, **Rush Common County Primary School**, Abingdon:

Pupils are encouraged to be natural, open with

adults and to accept responsibility. The school is respected in the wider community, to which it makes a significant contribution through fundraising and entertainment, and there are many valuable community links. The School Council meets fortnightly and offers further opportunity for discussion about social responsibility. The pupils make very mature, responsible comments in the course of the meeting and report back to their classes, with the minimum of teacher intervention. Pupils from a local special school have a number of joint lessons weekly in a Year 1 class.

Where provision for social development is good, therefore, there will be opportunities for pupils to create a sense of community, through organising events such as the giving of Christmas gifts for the elderly. They may well become involved in local affairs such as development plans for the local area, and they may be given opportunities to debate environmental issues. They will have opportunities to hold positions of responsibility, such as classroom monitors, librarians or sports captains. They will also have opportunities to help younger children, for example helping Reception pupils to dress themselves; helping younger children with their learning, such as reading; and looking after younger children as they play at lunchtime. Many primary schools have a well developed environmental ethic, with pupils involved in the management of school grounds, in saving water and energy, and in recycling waste materials.

In those few schools which make poor provision for social development, weaknesses include insufficient provision of opportunities for pupils to take responsibility either for their own learning or for each other and younger children. The development of social skills is a prerequisite for progress and learning; where social skills are lacking, disruptive behaviour unsettles other pupils and hinders learning for everyone.

6.6 Cultural development

The National Curriculum requires schools to pay attention to a range of cultures, both Western and non-Western. Inspection shows that less than half of all primary schools make good or better provision for pupils' cultural development, as interpreted through the National Curriculum

(Chart 42). Most teachers stress the importance of all pupils understanding the cultural traditions of the United Kingdom. Where schools take this aspect of development seriously, a range of lessons includes the use of paintings, pottery, music, literature, poetry, architecture and costume in order to develop cultural awareness and appreciation. Pupils are given opportunities not just to study their own culture – although this is seen as the first priority – but to understand the beliefs, traditions and cultures of other countries. It is not unusual, however, to find teachers who are uncertain about the extent to which non-European cultures should be taught, particularly in classes in which there are pupils from a wide range of ethnic and cultural backgrounds.

In the best examples, provision for cultural development is not left to chance. For example, several subjects of the National Curriculum contribute strongly to pupils' cultural development at **Little Dewchurch CE Primary School**, Hereford. In history, pupils:

...have a good understanding of Victorian social history, the invaders and settlers, kings and queens, and the ways of life in town and country in past times.

In religious education:

The work reflects the main events of the Christian calendar, Bible study and the distinctive features of other world religions such as Hinduism. Work in religious education is complemented by well planned daily acts of collective worship, which are broadly Christian in character.

And as an element in the specific provision for pupils' spiritual, moral, social and cultural development:

The cultural development of pupils is excellent. Carefully planned schemes of work maximise every opportunity for extending pupils' awareness and understanding of life outside their own homes and for giving them greater appreciation of the richness and diversity of other cultures. Good use is made of all the local arts centres and theatres and the school enjoys visits from peripatetic music, dance and drama specialists. There are links with Tanzania and Bangladesh, and the school is very well provided with multicultural and multifaith resources.

6.7 Collective worship

Schools are required to hold a daily act of collective worship, which has to be "wholly or mainly of a broadly Christian character". Inspectors report on collective worship in the section on spiritual, moral, social and cultural development, to which collective worship should contribute. Importantly, worship may be planned to reinforce learning in National Curriculum subjects or religious education, but should not be used as a substitute for any subject, including religious education.

In 89 per cent of all primary schools inspected in 1997/98 there was no evidence of non-compliance with the requirement to provide a daily act of collective worship. This was an improvement on the previous year's figure of 75 per cent. Levels of non-compliance vary between types of school and are shown in Chart 44.

Chart 44
Collective worship in LEA and church schools: non-compliance 1997/98
(percentage of schools)

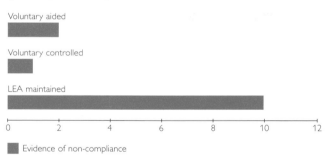

Voluntary aided

Voluntary controlled

LEA maintained

■ Evidence of non-compliance

Provision of daily collective worship does not necessarily ensure that spiritual development is promoted well. For example, from a sample of schools, provision for pupils' spiritual development was unsatisfactory in several schools which were complying fully with the legal requirements for collective worship.

In terms of quality, some of the best acts of collective worship are those where careful planning takes account of the school aims, the curriculum, major festivals and events, and yet is sufficiently flexible to enable the school to respond to important current issues. In the best examples, those leading worship take account of the beliefs or non-belief of pupils and teachers, thus minimising the occurrences of withdrawal. They encourage pupils to think about their lives and beliefs and the needs of others at home and abroad.

While most schools, therefore, comply with the requirement to provide a daily act of collective worship, the challenge facing many is to sustain the quality of this daily act of worship throughout the school year.

6.8 Support, guidance and pupils' welfare

Virtually every school gives a high priority to the care and welfare of its pupils. Most teachers tackle their pastoral role conscientiously and with commitment. Class teachers respond quickly and sensitively to the individual needs of pupils in their class. In 1997/98 the quality of the arrangements for the support, guidance and welfare of pupils was good in two-thirds of the schools inspected. Where weaknesses were identified, these were usually related to an overreliance on informal methods of monitoring progress and personal development; these can become unstuck if a member of staff leaves, when pupils move class or change school, or if problems faced by a family or a particular pupil suddenly require a greater reliance on monitoring and recording.

The positive picture of the level of support given to pupils and, often, their families is a theme running through many sections of inspection reports. For example, typically where the school's ethos is positive, a cluster of other positive indicators will be in place: spiritual, moral, social and cultural education; links with parents and the community; good behaviour and discipline; and support, guidance and welfare. An example of the overlap is illustrated from the recently opened **Jenny Hammond Primary School**, Leytonstone, in the London Borough of Waltham Forest:

The school has the advantage of having been established two years ago with a small reception class, and having then added a new intake each subsequent year. This has provided the ideal environment for pupils joining the school. Working in partnership, teachers, parents, governors, pupils and members of the local area have created a true community school. From the very beginning this has created an atmosphere and environment of caring support, where all are valued. Teachers know their pupils, and have built the school around the ethos of good behaviour, and value

and respect for others.

"Circle time" provides the opportunity for issues or personal concerns to be addressed in a safe atmosphere. Staff constantly monitor the progress of pupils, and parents are kept well informed of this progress through comprehensive reports which meet statutory requirements. There is a well established induction programme for new pupils entering school and a strong support system that enables them to make the transition into full-time education without difficulties. Parents are encouraged to spend time in the classroom before registration, listening to their children's reading and helping them to settle into the day. This support system is an integral part of school life which is recognised and valued by the parents.

Many similar examples can be found, and not just referring to the younger pupils. For example, **Carlton Netherfield Junior School**, Nottingham:

The staff work extremely hard to provide a caring and supportive environment and pupils respond positively to this. The pupils enjoy very good relationships with their teachers and are able to discuss with them any matters of concern. As a result, the support, advice and guidance have a positive impact on the pupils' progress, general confidence and ability to cope with everyday life at school... Pupils are confident to alert staff to any issues that concern them and know that their views will be taken seriously.

Almost every school has effective **child protection procedures** in place; these are known to all staff, and responsibilities and lines of communication are usually clear. All staff are generally aware of the procedures, for example for dealing with cases of suspected child abuse. Where issues are raised through inspection, they are most often related to the need for the training of personnel, particularly after staff changes, or the need for everyone, including ancillary staff, to be aware of procedures.

Health and safety procedures are also usually in place and effective; this is often an area in which governors take a keen interest and make a particularly influential contribution.

6.9 Partnership with parents and the community

Links between schools and parents are strong in about two-thirds of primary schools, and less than satisfactory in only about one school in 20. The quality of the information provided by schools for parents has improved over recent years; school brochures, for example, are increasingly seen as opportunities to attract parents and their children to a school, and are often professionally printed in a way which not only states but illustrates the range and quality of the work of the school. In several cases, responses to the pre-inspection questionnaire have encouraged schools to do more to inform parents about the work of the school and, in a growing number of cases, about ways in which parents can help their children with work at home. A typically positive picture is provided from **Gawsworth County Primary School**, Macclesfield:

The school communicates well with the community and with the parent body. A well-designed and particularly informative prospectus begins the process, followed by informal daily contact, twice yearly parents' meetings and a detailed report in the summer term. Termly newsletters and the close-knit nature of the parent body also help information to flow freely in both directions. Parents indicated in the pre-inspection survey and meeting that they feel well informed about their children's progress and the curriculum taught.

Many schools have homework policies which set out expectations of the school, the pupils and their parents, actively seeking the co-operation of parents with their children's homework. There is a particular emphasis on reading at home, with parents being encouraged to hear their children read aloud, and then completing a reading diary with scope for reporting on progress, problems and the interest shown in the book. Many schools ask parents to help their children learn their tables and number bonds; others send home "topic lists" on a regular basis, indicating what work is to be covered in the next half-term, seeking expertise and resources, and outlining how parents can reinforce the themes at home.

It is usual now for parents to be welcomed into the school; the days of the line of parents at the school gate are well and truly over. Particularly close informal links are made between most schools and the parents of the youngest children. Home visits are made by many teachers to the families of children about to enter a school; this provides a chance for parents to discuss concerns and any special needs, and helps teachers to gain an early view of a child's maturity and ability. Most schools establish close links with local playgroups. Frequently parents are encouraged to come into the nursery or early years classes at the beginning and end of the school session with their children, have a word with the teacher about pastoral or academic concerns or interests, talk to their children about the ongoing work, and assure themselves that their children are settled happily for the school work ahead of them. For example, **Shaw Cross Infant and Nursery School**, Kirklees:

In the nursery, information for parents is displayed in the entrance and parents and carers are a welcome part of life in the nursery. The ends of sessions are very positive times, when parents and carers may work alongside their children, talk with staff, look at displays and generally feel part of nursery life.

In the infant school, each classroom has its own noticeboard for parents as well as the general noticeboard in the main entrance. Parents receive regular information by letter and by phone call if necessary, and they know they are welcome in school at any time. The school's open and welcoming policy towards parents is appreciated and good use is made of this facility. Class teachers are generous with their time and are very approachable.

Many primary schools report relatively low attendance rates at parents' meetings by parents from some ethnic minorities. This appears to be a particular problem with isolated communities whose knowledge of English and the English education system is limited. Although some schools have seen a breakthrough in parental attendance (including women) at meetings and a greater willingness to be involved with the life of the school, others still find that, despite much effort, relatively few Bangladeshi or Pakistani parents come to school. The help of a local Traveller Education Service team can be a crucial factor in gaining the confidence of Gypsy Traveller families.

Governors are now required to present to parents

an annual report about the work of the school and the role of the governing body. There is a range of technical requirements about the content of the annual report which are not always followed fully; schools need to be more careful in checking the details of the requirements for these reports in order to ensure that they comply fully with the most recent circulars.

Most schools, whether through a formally constituted parent-teacher or "Friends of the School" association or not, benefit from fundraising and social activities, which bring tangible results in terms of enhanced resources and help establish good links between home and school.

Parents also contribute directly to the work of most schools by their involvement as volunteer helpers. Some of this help is "another pair of hands", helping with routine chores such as mounting work for display or photocopying. Increasingly, however, schools are recognising that, with some modest training and careful supervision, parents can make extremely useful contributions to the work in classes, such as supporting the literacy hour or hearing children read. They can also bring many areas of expertise, such as cooking, music, sport, art and craft, which enrich and augment the school's curriculum. Help is often provided by parents with safety at swimming lessons and extra adult presence on school trips.

Schools develop links with the local community in a variety of ways; much depends on where a school is and what sort of community it serves. Inspection reports illustrate an extraordinarily wide range of links: work with uniformed groups such as the cubs and brownies; links with a local church; charity links and help with old people's homes; penpal or email links with other schools and children in other countries; visits to the schools by local people such as the police, fire and ambulance services; and visits to people and places in the local area. Clearly many schools, especially in rural communities, are seen as the heart of the village or estate. Parent-governors can usefully support a school and the parents by asking pertinent questions which reflect local concerns.

There are some good examples of links with local businesses or industry, beyond fundraising and the collection of raffle prizes. **Lowfield Primary School**, Sheffield, for example:

Pupils visited the local wire-making factory and observed and described the work of the company: the standard operating procedures, the links between Pilkington Glass and Tinsley Wire, the processes involved in making wire and the many uses of different types of wire. They surveyed the perimeter of the factory site and reported back to the company with some recommendations about environmental improvement. They investigated the history of wire making in the area and the transport system that supported it. They looked at the recreational use and potential of the local canal by surveying the wildlife in the area and interviewing users of the canal such as fishermen.

Nevertheless, although there are some notable exceptions, links with local industry or businesses are the weakest aspect of primary school links with the local community.

7

THE CURRICULUM AND ASSESSMENT

7.1 Breadth and balance

The Education Reform Act 1988 required that the curriculum should be balanced and broadly based, that it should promote pupils' spiritual, moral, cultural, mental and physical development, and that it should prepare pupils for the opportunities, responsibilities and experiences of adult life. These requirements are generally met in most schools, although with slightly greater success at Key Stage 1 than Key Stage 2. Chart 45 illustrates the overview of the balance, breadth and relevance of the curriculum at both key stages in 1997/98.

Chart 45
Breadth, balance and relevance of the whole curriculum in primary schools 1997/98
(percentage of schools)

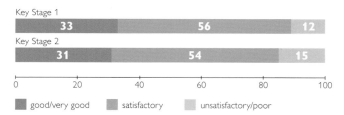

Key Stage 1

| 33 | 56 | 12 |

Key Stage 2

| 31 | 54 | 15 |

0   20   40   60   80   100

■ good/very good   ■ satisfactory   ■ unsatisfactory/poor

These figures have been rounded and may not add up to 100 per cent

There are tensions embedded in the curriculum requirements which every school has to address. Given the limits to the time available, one tension is that between breadth and depth; another lies in the requirement to give sufficient time and attention to literacy and numeracy, while still providing sufficient time for worthwhile study of all the National Curriculum subjects and religious education. From September 1998 schools have been given some guidance about the selection of priorities: statutory requirements have been relaxed for subjects other than English, mathematics, science, information technology and religious education. Nevertheless, schools are still required to teach a curriculum which is broad and balanced. Some schools, while teaching the National Curriculum and religious education in line

with statutory requirements, also choose to include their own emphasis: a strong creative arts curriculum, environmental education or a modern foreign language, for example.

Resolution of these tensions is shown in some inspection reports. For example, **Charlestown County Primary School**, Cornwall:

In Key Stages 1 and 2, the curriculum is broad; it covers all the National Curriculum subjects and religious education and meets all statutory requirements. With few exceptions, it provides the right experiences for pupils to attain the appropriate level and to make sound progress in their subjects. It also fosters very good personal development. Whilst the school places an appropriately strong emphasis on English and mathematics, the curriculum provides balance in the range of subject it offers. It is enriched by the effective integration of subjects, and teachers generally plan carefully to ensure depth for each subject. Some of the best curriculum provision occurs when pupils work on problems from everyday life. For example, when older Key Stage 1 pupils designed and made sandwiches for their class café, this involved in-depth coverage of science, design and technology, and data handling in mathematics. Pupils applied their scientific and mathematical knowledge to design and technology very well.

The tensions are also revealed by the overall judgement in 1997/98 that the balance, breadth and relevance of the curriculum were good in less than one-third of schools at both key stages. In the previous year, at Key Stage 2 the balance and breadth of the curriculum were good in only one in five schools. Where an imbalance is reported, it is often through insufficient emphasis on the two elements of technology, but significant issues were also raised in one in five schools about art and music, and in one in six schools about geography and religious education. Indeed, almost one in ten primary schools did not meet fully the requirement to teach religious education in accordance with the appropriate Agreed Syllabus. On the other hand, especially in schools serving more advantaged areas and with easy access to continental Europe, the inclusion of a modern foreign language – usually French – in the curriculum is increasing. About one in five primary schools now teach a modern foreign language.

Even in those schools where the curriculum breadth and balance are good, concerns are reported. For example, differences in the length of the school day and the amount of teaching time available:

The total time allocated to teaching the curriculum at both key stages is about an hour a week below the recommended minimum time. As a result, work sometimes becomes rushed towards the end of units of work, and extension work has to be curtailed.

The variation in the amount of time given to subjects by different teachers is also reported. For example:

The time allocations for subjects are generally satisfactory, although they do vary significantly between classes. Pupils spend insufficient time on information technology.

7.2 Equality of access

Throughout the four-year period, equality of access to the curriculum has been at least satisfactory in most schools, although some concerns are raised in about one in 12 schools at Key Stage 2 and one in 20 at Key Stage 1. Concerns may be about curricular entitlement, for example, and, typically, boys having access to a richer and more challenging range of opportunities in physical education and extracurricular activities with a higher profile in the school. They may also be related to unchallenged attitudinal issues; one inspection report, for example, states that, "in some classes, particularly at the end of Key Stage 2, some girls are being disadvantaged by the domineering and unsatisfactory behaviour of a minority of boys".

An example of good practice is **All Saints' CE Primary School**, Whetstone, Barnet:

The aims of the school's policy on equal opportunities are effectively implemented in all areas of the curriculum. Pupils mix together confidently and well in class and in extra-curricular activities. Older pupils have opportunities to help and support younger pupils; boys and girls are actively encouraged to take part in all activities. They have positive attitudes towards themselves and each other and have equal access to all subject areas.

The resources provided throughout the school, such as books, pictures and home play areas, show a sense of value and respect towards all pupils and families that make up the school community.

The progress of equal opportunity aims and practice is monitored effectively by the deputy headteacher. All new and revised policies include equal opportunities statements and strategies for their integration.

7.3 Curriculum planning

Schools have committed a great deal of time and effort to curriculum planning and organisation in recent years, and the quality of planning continues to improve. In 1993/94 inspectors judged curriculum planning unfavourably in about half the schools at Key Stage 1 and rather more than half the schools at Key Stage 2. Many schools had policy statements for most or all subjects, but these policies had not always been translated into schemes of work specifying the detailed coverage required to ensure progression and continuity from year group to year group. By 1997/98, although things had improved, many schools were found still to have a long way to go.

Written policies are insufficient in themselves to ensure that pupils receive increasingly demanding work in a subject as they move through school. These general policies need to be backed up by schemes of work which provide detailed statements of what is to be taught to particular year groups or groups of pupils. A growing number of schools are preparing such schemes of work, giving clarity to teachers about what needs to be taught, and setting expectations appropriate for the pupils. For example, **William Ford CE Junior School**, Essex:

The curriculum is very well planned and makes a significant contribution to the school's high standards. The general requirements of the National Curriculum are mapped out clearly across the four year groups, ensuring full and systematic coverage.

For each subject there is a more detailed plan, showing the work to be covered in each half term. This is then broken down into very clear and practical descriptions of what is to be taught and the standards for which the school aims. The standards set are ambitious and are often higher than the levels expected nationally by the age of eleven. The plans are supported by a good range of well thought-out teaching resources. These arrangements make it clear to teachers what they need to cover and the standards to be achieved. The teaching is very systematic. It develops pupils' skills, knowledge and understanding gradually and progressively. As a result the vast majority of pupils make very good progress.

Despite the efforts that have gone into curriculum development and planning over recent years, and the structure provided for all subjects by the National Curriculum and Agreed Syllabuses, about one-third of schools lack effective schemes of work (Chart 46). Further, in most schools there are few opportunities for subject co-ordinators to monitor what goes on in classrooms in their subject and evaluate the success of their curriculum planning. The schools in the National Literacy and Numeracy Projects, however, reported how helpful the detailed frameworks of these projects were in establishing progression within English and mathematics.

Chart 46
Planning for progression and continuity in primary schools 1997/98
(percentage of schools)

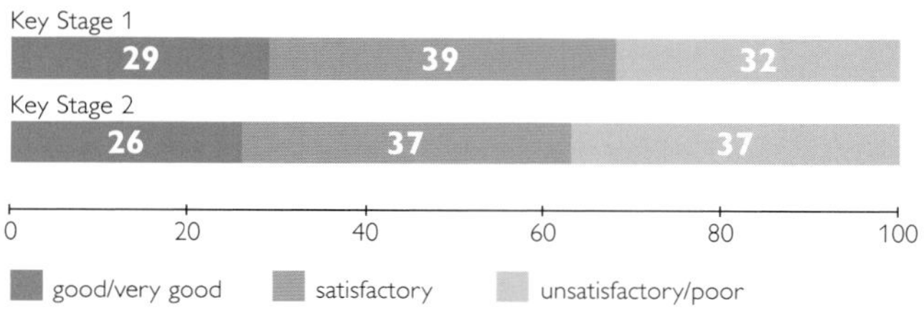

Key Stage 1

29	39	32

Key Stage 2

26	37	37

0   20   40   60   80   100

■ good/very good   ■ satisfactory   ■ unsatisfactory/poor

These figures have been rounded and may not add up to 100 per cent

Wide-ranging topic work dipping into several subjects has continued to give way to work which is focused on a single subject, although, of course, within a subject such as history or geography pupils apply, consolidate and improve their skills in aspects of other subjects, such as literacy or data handling. In many schools there is a continuum from Reception and Year 1, in which much of the work is integrated in broad topics covering several subjects, to the end of Key Stage 2, by which time most if not all of the work is taught in separate subjects. Even for the youngest pupils, the notion of a fully integrated curriculum is more myth than

reality: they are usually taught numeracy and literacy as clearly discrete parts of the school day, and other subjects – especially music, physical education and art – are often taught separately. It is rare to find a school maintaining the view that all the curriculum should be taught through broad-ranging topics; but it probably always was less common than was generally supposed.

7.4 Extracurricular provision

The range and quality of extracurricular provision is a strength in over one-half of schools at Key Stage 2, and the variety of activities undertaken is wide. Many inspection reports include reference to this aspect of school life – an example of the commitment, enthusiasm and range of skills which many teachers bring to their work. Pupils' attitudes to these opportunities are invariably good, they are appreciated by parents and, as many reports indicate, they can make a positive contribution to the quality of work in the National Curriculum. For example, **Wimbledon Chase Middle School**, Merton:

The school offers an impressively large number of extracurricular activities such as choir, recorders, orchestra, chess, gardening, art, computer, French, mathematics and science clubs and various aspects of sport including football, netball, hockey, badminton, dance and basketball. The curriculum is also enriched by a programme of trips, fieldwork and residential visits to France and south Wales, which not only provide opportunities for increasing children's personal and social development but enable them to learn through first-hand experience.

7.5 The assessment of pupils' attainment

The use of day-to-day assessment as an aspect of teaching is reported on in some detail in Chapter 4 herein on teaching. The assessment of pupils' performance and the use of the outcomes of that assessment to inform the planning of work remains problematical in many schools. While there are signs of improvement, procedures for assessing pupils' attainment in 1997/98 were unsatisfactory in about one-quarter of schools, and the use made of assessment to inform curriculum planning was weak in almost one-half of schools. Having moved away from the ticksheet approach which characterised much of the assessment in the early days of the National Curriculum, many schools have yet to find an approach to assessment

Chart 47

Procedures for assessing pupils' attainment in primary schools 1997/98

(percentage of schools)

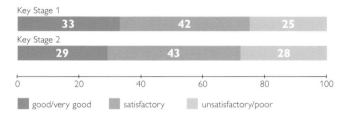

These figures have been rounded and may not add up to 100 per cent

Chart 48

Use of assessment to inform curriculum planning in primary schools 1997/98

(percentage of schools)

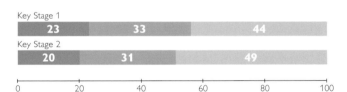

These figures have been rounded and may not add up to 100 per cent

which is manageable and works effectively.

Examples of good practice reveal several important features: for example, a close link between a planned curriculum and the setting of learning objectives which can be assessed; effective monitoring and improvement of the curriculum; the involvement of the governing body; thorough and well documented assessment procedures; the tracking of pupils' progress through the school; and consistent marking and appropriate target setting. An example from an infant and nursery school illustrates good practice:

Because the curriculum is well documented, teachers are able to use the identified skill sequences when planning their work and to set realistic learning objectives in their termly, weekly and daily plans. They consistently

address the differing needs of the children and cater for all levels of ability to ensure that pupils progress. Effective monitoring of the curriculum is carefully documented and findings acted upon to ensure continuous improvement. The governing body plays a full role in the production and implementation of policies through minuted sub-committee meetings and direct observation of teaching and learning.

Assessment procedures are well documented and thorough. Entry assessment in the nursery is used to plan what the child needs to do next. Nursery staff are currently involved in entry assessment initiatives, with a view to improving present good practice. Baseline assessment tests are also administered in the reception classes. School analyses of national test results are acted upon to ensure continued high attainment. The school and local education authority have recently assessed and tracked pupils' progress from nursery to the end of Key Stage 1 from 1993 to 1996. Results show that pupils make at least sound, and often good or very good, progress.

The school keeps detailed records of pupils' achievements in all academic subjects and records on personal development are also kept. Whole-school portfolios have been compiled on the core subjects of English, mathematics and science which are carefully annotated, and individual portfolios contain photographs and a varied range of examples of pupils' work. Good-quality advice and guidance from the local education authority has been acted upon and the co-ordinator has worked very effectively with staff to provide a consistent assessment process, which is used to plan the next stage of learning.

Marking of pupils' work follows a consistent pattern, and both teachers and pupils are involved in setting targets for future improvement. Weekly assessments of a particular aspect are used effectively and work is evaluated at the end of each topic.

Greater use is being made of end-of-key-stage National Curriculum test data, optional National Curriculum tests in Years 3, 4 and 5, and standardised tests. Increasingly, schools are able to record the attainment and track the progress of individual pupils and to use this process as the basis for the setting of targets. However, in many schools assessment data is not used to full effect in planning teaching and bringing about improvement. For example, insufficient monitoring, using this information, is undertaken to analyse the attainment or progress of different groups of pupils, such as boys and girls or pupils from different ethnic backgrounds.

7.6 Issues for the future

From September 1998, primary schools have been expected to move towards implementing the National Literacy Strategy: the teaching methods, the structure of lessons and the termly objectives in the Framework. From September 1999 they will be expected to follow a similar approach in the teaching of numeracy by implementing the National Numeracy Strategy. At the same time, the statutory requirement for the full coverage of the programmes of study for non-core subjects of art, design and technology, geography, history, music and physical education has been relaxed. Three principal issues emerge for schools from these factors. First, schools will need to ensure that they continue to provide a broad and balanced curriculum which includes all the subjects of the National Curriculum and religious education. Second, a relaxation in the statutory requirements for the non-core subjects does not imply a relaxation in the drive to achieve the highest possible standards. Third, religious education and information technology, neither of which are subject to a relaxation in the statutory requirements, are both subjects in which many teachers require further training in order to improve their subject knowledge and confidence.

8
THE EDUCATION OF UNDER-FIVES

8.1 Standards of achievement and the quality of teaching

The Framework for Inspection requires inspectors to evaluate aspects of the education of pupils under five as follows:

For pupils under five, the report must contain an evaluation of the strengths and weaknesses in attainment, pupils' attitudes, teaching and other provision across the areas of learning.

The inspection of under-fives work covers a wide range of types of national provision and also takes account of the variable time that pupils may spend in designated "reception" classes. Inspection takes account of the work of mixed-age classes where under-fives and over-fives are in the same class, and the fact that some pupils who are still not five years old may well have moved from the Desirable Outcomes for Children's Learning[47] into the programmes of study of the National Curriculum.

Pupils made good or very good progress in about half the nursery sessions inspected. In less than one school in 20 is the progress of under-fives in nursery classes judged to be poor. Chart 49 illustrates that in the large majority of schools pupils make at least satisfactory progress towards achieving the Desirable Outcomes for Children's Learning, and that over the past two years the rate of progress made by pupils in reception classes has improved. Many pupils, particularly those entering school with low levels of attainment, make

---

[47] *Desirable Outcomes for Children's Learning.* SCAA, 1996. The Desirable Outcomes are goals for learning for children by the time they enter compulsory education, which begins in the term after a child's fifth birthday. The Desirable Outcomes cover children's development in six areas of learning: personal and social development; language and literacy; mathematics; knowledge and understanding of the world; physical development; and creative development.

particularly good progress in their first year or so at school. However, in some schools there is a continued focus on the Desirable Outcomes, when pupils – particularly the more able – have already achieved them. For these pupils, more advanced knowledge and skills should be developed.

The quality of teaching in both nursery and reception classes was good in over 45 per cent of the lessons observed throughout the period, and considerable improvement is reported. Chart 50 illustrates this. Indeed, the greatest proportion of lessons in primary schools in which the teaching is good or very good has consistently been in nursery classes, closely followed by teaching in reception classes. Improvement has been particularly noted

Chart 49

Progress by pupils under five, 1996/97 and 1997/98

(percentage of lessons)

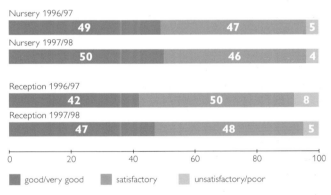

These figures have been rounded and may not add up to 100 per cent

Chart 50

The quality of teaching in reception and nursery classes

(percentage of lessons)

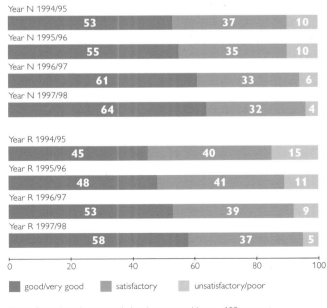

These figures have been rounded and may not add up to 100 per cent

in the development of more detailed curriculum planning and greater co-operation between classes with the same year groups. This helps address the issue of inconsistency of practice and provision within a school, one of the concerns raised in one in eight schools with under-fives provision in 1994/95. The establishment of the Desirable Outcomes has helped clarify the nature of the early years curriculum for many teachers, and this has led to a greater consistency in planning.

However, the quality of the teaching of under-fives has been a cause for concern in a significant number of small schools (with less than 100 pupils). Many teachers find it hard to set work of appropriate challenge and range for a class in which there are under-fives working towards the Desirable Learning Outcomes and older pupils who are being taught the programmes of study of the National Curriculum. The provision is more likely to be weak in those classes where there are only a few pupils under five. There is a danger that these pupils are either moved on too quickly towards National Curriculum work or given an insufficiently structured early-years experience. Inspection reports on small schools frequently include reference to the variation in the quality of the provision for the youngest pupils in such schools, but there are signs that the issue is being addressed by an increased provision of teaching assistants for these pupils, which is particularly effective when the assistant has NNEB training.

Good use of teaching assistants is a consistent feature of effective under-fives provision, especially since 1995. There has been an increased emphasis on the provision of training for teaching assistants in nurseries and on the careful deployment of all available adults. For example, at the **Margaret McMillan Nursery** in Islington:

All staff including teachers, nursery nurses and assistants build on their existing skills, knowledge and understanding to enable them successfully to further the children's learning in the areas of the curriculum and promote the values of the school. There is a very strong sense of community, and all the staff work well together and share responsibilities. Their consistency of approach makes a significant contribution to the good standards of attainment and of behaviour.

To provide the well planned and structured

staff training and in-service training programme, use is made of the good expertise available at the school. The commitment to staff development is a significant strength, and this is evident in the very good quality of the provision and teaching.

A significant development has been the improvement in the balance between under-fives work directed by the teacher and that undertaken within free or guided choice by the pupils. This is an interesting development in the light of the current debate about the nature of early years education. Again, the improvement in planning and the use of the Desirable Outcomes may be supporting the trend towards a more appropriate balance between direct teaching and free play.

Planning has improved in its thoroughness and consistency over the four years of the review period. Daily planning is generally better than longer-term planning, but in more than one in ten of nursery classes insufficient attention is given to the setting of objectives in the plans. On the other hand, there has been a significant reduction in practical activities which lack a clearly specified purpose. Where the purpose of activities is clearly established and children's work given more structure, teachers achieve a closer match between the work and pupils' abilities.

The quality and use of assessment has also improved over time. The range of assessment procedures has grown and teachers are increasingly skilled in techniques of observation. But a feature of the reports on the most sophisticated and successful assessment methodologies is usually a comment about the demands they place on busy teachers. For example, **Merrivale Nursery School**, Nottingham:

The assessment, recording and reporting arrangements are excellent. The school uses an effective range of techniques and recording systems in order to assess accurately the progress of individual children. Assessment is firmly rooted in sound observation techniques, whereby three children each session are closely observed by staff. In this way all children are assessed over a period of two weeks. These observations cover academic success, social interaction and behaviour.

The staff come together eight times a week to discuss and record these observations, which

are transferred to the children's records and are central to the assessment, recording and reporting system. Two members of staff also focus on a particular activity each day in order to make detailed observations of both children and tasks. Information about the children's involvement in specific tasks is marked on checklists so that staff can be sure that all children have been actively involved in all aspects of the curriculum. In addition to this, the school uses other appropriate assessment procedures. These include a baseline assessment and a special folder in which work worthy of note is selected by both staff and children. These are collected and compiled into a book which the children take with them when they leave.

The school also uses procedures, for example the "pride vine", which is a large display of records of achievement. The school records and displays the academic, physical or social activities a child is working towards... The assessment, recording and reporting systems used by the school are valuable but demand a great deal of time from the staff.

Baseline assessment has developed throughout the four years of the review period. About one in eight reports referred to its use in 1994/95, compared with half of the reports in 1997/98. The introduction of baseline assessment is helping schools to focus more sharply on starting points, against which progress can be measured and planned. For example, in 1997/98, the limited language skills of pupils on entry were reported in two in five schools as a cause for concern.

The overall picture of the quality of teaching, planning and assessment is one of developing detail and rigour, with an increased focus on identifying the strengths and weaknesses in individual pupils' performance.

8.2 The curriculum

Reporting on trends across the four years of the inspection cycle has to take account of the introduction of the Desirable Learning Outcomes in 1996. The curriculum for the under-fives has been carefully developed by many schools during the four years. The use of the Desirable Outcomes has provided a clearer focus for work, which, together with improved planning and assessment, has produced a more rigorous view of what knowledge and skills children should develop and how this is to be done. Remaining weaknesses include the slow pace of work in a small minority of classes, a feature much more frequently mentioned than work being too demanding of the under-fives. Where excessively demanding work for the youngest pupils is noted, it is almost always in those classes which include older pupils as well as reception-age pupils. Inspectors very rarely report that pupils are being pushed too early into the National Curriculum or that they are being given unduly "formal" work.

Provision for pupils' **personal and social development** is a major priority and a considerable strength of the work of most schools. Schools place a high priority on the promotion of a positive attitude to learning, good behaviour and a lengthening concentration span. Schools are particularly successful at helping young children settle to the routines of school life. This is a wide-reaching aspect of the inspection of nursery classes and schools, and is often reported on most clearly in the section on attitudes, behaviour and personal development. For example, at the **Dorothy Gardner Centre**, Westminster:

The nursery is a hive of activity. Children often initiate their own activities and are able to sustain concentration for long periods. During role play in the construction area and in the home corner, they initiate lengthy sequences of events, including rescues from top-storey fires and cures for hospital-bed ailments. Children are responsible for the tasks they set themselves, but readily request help when needed. They respect property and tidy up after themselves. They appear happy, and on the few occasions a child is in distress, staff quickly resolve the problem.

Children celebrate a range of religious and cultural festivals. Visiting the Hindu temple during the celebration of Divali, they experience feelings of wonder at the majesty of the building and a sense of awe by being present during a ceremony.

Standards in **language and literacy** (formerly reported under English) have risen throughout the period of the first inspection cycle, and they were at least satisfactory in 85 per cent of schools by

1997/98. The proportion of schools with good achievement in language and literacy rose from 16 per cent to 28 per cent during the four years of the review period. Nevertheless, there are overall weaknesses in language and literacy in one in eight schools.

The quality and range of provision for language work in a school with good practice in this area is illustrated in the report on **Strong Close Nursery School**, Keighley:

A high priority is given to the language and literacy area of learning. Pupils, including those with special educational needs, are achieving levels at least appropriate to their abilities, with many achieving levels which are high. Teaching takes account of those pupils for whom English is a second language; dual language texts and materials are provided, and this enables pupils to make good progress.

In both small and large groups, pupils listen attentively, talk about their experiences and confidently share ideas. They listen well to stories, songs, nursery rhymes and poems and respond enthusiastically when questioned about them. Most have learned some songs and rhymes by heart and many are confident in reciting these to others in the group. Pupils demonstrate an increasing awareness of a wider range of vocabulary in many areas of learning. They follow instructions and verbal directions effectively and show by their responses that they have understood key words and ideas.

Pupils enjoy books and handle them appropriately, particularly some of the tiny "pop-up" books which require great care. They generally realise how books are organised and most systematically turn pages correctly from the beginning of the story, making relevant comments as they move through the text. Most know that pictures carry meaning and many demonstrate an understanding that print also carries meaning. Many recognise their own names and sometimes they recognise their friends' names. Pupils are beginning to recognise letters of the alphabet by both the shape and sound and a few are beginning to apply this knowledge when reading.

Pupils' understanding of the writing process is developing well. They show awareness of the different purposes of writing and often communicate their learning using pictures, symbols and some familiar words and letters. Most are developing appropriate control of pencils and pens. A significant number of pupils can write their own names with a reasonable level of accuracy.

The development of speaking and listening skills has been given high attention, although many schools need to promote more intensively a broadening of children's vocabulary. The vast majority of pupils engage in early reading and writing activities, which include some elements of phonic work, letter recognition, reading familiar words and name writing. On the whole, however, this aspect of the programme is less systematic than it needs to be.

The range of **mathematics** seen in schools with good practice is summarised, for example, in the report on **Clervaux Terrace Nursery School**, Jarrow:

Pupils achieve high standards in the wide range of mathematical experiences which are provided in the nursery. They make good use of the many opportunities to investigate and learn about number in activities such as number songs, in the sorting and matching of objects, and in a wide range of counting and ordering tasks which are an integral feature of the school day. Even at snack time, pupils are keen to count out fruits or crisps and to compare their sizes. Pupils have a very good knowledge of space and shape. They learn to make patterns and can use correct mathematical language to describe them.

The great majority of schools teach children to recognise and write numbers and to count, recognise mathematical shapes and use simple mathematical terms to describe shape, position, size and quantities. Shopping activities usually form part of an early mathematics programme, but pupils are not always taught the necessary skills to enable them to succeed.

Knowledge and understanding of the world is the broadest of the six areas of learning, and involves early historical, geographical, environmental, scientific and technological learning. Many schools find it hard to cover the full range satisfactorily and it is the area in which the fewest schools secure good provision and response. Most schools tackle this area by integrating the various strands into a topic such as "homes", and often use visits to local places of interest to back up work undertaken in class.

Creative development receives a high priority in most under-fives classes and is at least satisfactory in over nine in ten schools. Art and music are generally well developed. **Physical development** is generally well promoted in terms of developing children's co-ordination and movement skills through using tools and a range of materials requiring increasingly complex manipulative skills. Weaknesses are usually a result of restrictions on space and equipment, either indoors with climbing apparatus, or outdoors where space may be limited or non-existent. Schools with cramped or unsatisfactory accommodation often take imaginative steps to overcome these difficulties and cope despite the problems. Nevertheless, the gap between the good and poor provision for physical development is very wide.

The absence of policies for some curriculum areas (or subjects) was a feature of about two in five schools for the first three years of the present period. This is a particular cause for concern when core areas such as mathematics and language and literacy are involved. Although the proportion fell to one in five in 1997/98, it is still too high.

The provision of a "broad and balanced" curriculum for under-fives has been increasingly observed over the four years. In the best examples, schools are clearly making decisions about the balance of the curriculum in the light of their assessment of the needs of their pupils. For example, at **Powers Hall County Infant School**, Witham:

> *Pupils' attainment on entry to the nursery and early years classes is often below expectations for the age group... The early years curriculum places an appropriate and necessary emphasis on developing the children's skills in language and literacy, and mathematics, and on their personal and social development.*

8.3 Partnership with parents

The partnership between schools and the parents of the youngest children is strong in the great majority of schools. Parents are generally welcomed into nursery and reception classes at the start of a session, and are encouraged to take an interest in their children's progress, the work being undertaken, and to discuss any problems with the teacher. This is usually backed up by newsletters and noticeboards, and many schools provide written or photographic explanations of the purposes of the various activities provided, indicating to parents how they can help their children at home.

Inspectors have increasingly raised concerns about the number of children arriving late for the start of sessions in early years classes. While attendance is not compulsory before statutory school age, the disruptive impact of late arrivals is significant. Late arrivals in the year when many schools first admitted younger four-year-olds, or "rising fours", when the nursery voucher scheme was introduced nationally, has presented many schools with an issue that they are addressing but which is still not resolved.

8.4 Issues

In the last year of this four-year period, changes in government policy had the potential to affect previous practices significantly. The introduction of early years development plans and the associated partnerships to match provision with need across the range of pre-school services, came too late to have an impact on inspection reports. Similarly, it is too early to report on the impact of the support given to integrated child-care and education services, notably through the Early Excellence Centre programme.

However, by the end of the inspection year 1997/98, some references were beginning to be made to the implementation of a "literacy hour", and to a lesser extent a mathematics lesson, for pupils towards the end of their reception year. The few comments made were positive and referred to the appropriately and sensitively staged introduction of such work with young children. Other early signs are of materials such as "big books" being used for story sessions in younger reception and some nursery classes as a means of very gradually introducing the literacy resources and practices used elsewhere in the school. From the evaluation of the National Literacy and Numeracy Projects, there was no evidence of the literacy hour or numeracy lesson being introduced too rapidly in reception classes during the pilot stage of these schemes.

Particular challenges exist when reception-age pupils are taught in mixed-age classes with older pupils, especially in small schools or schools where teaching support is limited. The issue has been resolved to some extent by the introduction of the Desirable Learning Outcomes, which have helped teachers of such classes by distinguishing between the curriculum appropriate to children under five and those over five who are engaged on the programmes of study of the National Curriculum. It is proving to be less of a problem in language and mathematical work than in knowledge and understanding of the world, where scientific work across mixed age groups is most commonly noted as a problem.

Improvements in planning, especially since the advent of the Desirable Learning Outcomes, are significant. Yet there remains a number of schools where policies, schemes of work and overall planning have significant gaps – for example, where subjects or areas lack relevant schemes of work. In 1997/98, one in five schools with early years provision had insufficient or inadequate documentation to support the curriculum for under-fives.

8.5 Section 5 inspections

During the 1994-98 period, Section 5 nursery voucher (later nursery grant) inspections were established. These nursery inspections covered non-local education authority provision operated by providers in the private, independent, voluntary and social services sectors. After a pilot phase in four local education authorities (Norfolk, Westminster, Wandsworth, and Kensington and Chelsea) in 1996/97, the scheme was launched nationally in 1997. The Section 5 inspections use a different inspection framework and process from that of Section 10 inspections of local education authority provision, and the findings of the two approaches cannot be compared statistically. Section 5 inspections assess how far the nursery's programme promotes the Desirable Outcomes, has weaknesses or is poor. It is a judgement on whether pupils are likely to have achieved the Desirable Outcomes by the age of five. By contrast, Section 10 inspectors judge the current

achievements of the pupils in relation to the Desirable Outcomes or to the National Curriculum if this is considered appropriate.

Over the period of this review there has been a determined effort by the Government to provide non-statutory nursery places for all children from the age of four. More recently, the Government has announced a programme of expansion of non-statutory nursery education to include places for three-year-olds. In step with these developments, and at the request of the Secretary of State for Education and Employment, OFSTED has inspected the quality of provision in all publicly funded pre-school settings for four-year-olds in primary school reception classes.[48] Inspection has taken full account of a key condition of funding, notably that all these settings should promote the Desirable Outcomes for Children's Learning.

An emerging issue in several schools and other institutions is the growth in services for parents and pre-school children which are not subject to OFSTED inspection and yet which significantly extend the provision – for example, adult education (often informally organised), parent and toddler groups, "drop-in" services, before- and after-school clubs, and other services. These can have a major impact both on the education provision for the children and on links with the wider community.

Given the diversity of settings receiving funding, it is not surprising that some have found it easier to meet the requirements of the funding than others. Table 1 shows how well the various types of setting promote the Desirable Outcomes for Learning.

Across all types of setting, moreover, some of the areas of learning have proved more difficult to promote than others. Table 2 shows in rank order the areas of learning where the promotion of the Desirable Outcomes was secure, across all institutions.

Despite a great deal of debate about what should constitute an appropriate curriculum for early years education and how it should be taught, the introduction of the Desirable Outcomes for

---

48 Inspections of private, voluntary and independent sector nursery settings were carried out under Section 5 of the Nursery Education and Grant Maintained Schools Act 1996. Inspections of local education authority and grant maintained schools with four-year-olds were carried out under Section 10 of the School Inspections Act 1996.

Table 1 The percentage of nursery settings, by type, likely to promote the Desirable Outcomes for Learning 1997/98

Areas of learning	Playgroup	Private nursery school	Independent school	Local authority day nursery	Private day nursery	Other
Personal and social development	83.5	87.5	89.7	94.1	86.9	91.3
Language and literacy	54.3	80.8	94.3	65.0	73.9	69.8
Mathematics	59.4	82.6	91.8	66.9	74.7	76.1
Knowledge and understanding of the world	52.7	68.3	81.0	69.2	64.6	68.0
Physical development	77.0	72.5	80.4	82.3	78.0	80.2
Creative development	72.9	75.3	80.0	82.3	77.0	80.2

Table 2
The average percentage of nursery settings likely to promote the Desirable Outcomes 1997/98

Personal and social development	86%
Physical development	77%
Creative development	75%
Mathematics	69%
Language and literacy	65%
Knowledge and understanding of the world	60%

Learning has undoubtedly helped providers in at least two ways. It has helped them to plan and prepare a more coherent, broad and balanced curriculum which takes account of young children's physical, intellectual, emotional and social development. It also dovetails sensibly into the start of the National Curriculum. Furthermore, inspection itself has helped to focus the attention of providers on advancing the strengths and addressing the weaknesses of their programmes. For the most part, they have responded quickly and positively to the key issues for action identified in the published report of their inspection.

As the provision of early years places expands, the Government's intention to match the increase in the capacity of the system to improvements in the quality of education, irrespective of the type of setting, will depend principally upon the availability of well trained teachers and other staff responsible for the day-to-day planning and implementation of the programme. The range of qualifications held by early years staff is wide, and the Government's intention for registered providers to involve a qualified teacher in their plans from September 1999 should help to improve the consistency of provision across the sector.

Clearly, the dependency of young children on

adults for care and welfare is greater in these settings than at any other time in the education service. It follows that early years settings must do more than provide education even in its broadest sense. They must demonstrate and reassure parents and others that young children are safe and well cared-for. The Government is conducting a wide-ranging consultation on these matters and at the same time encouraging, through targeted funding, innovative, integrated early years services such as Early Excellence Centres. These approaches should do much to overcome the historical problems of piecemeal provision which have dogged this sector of education for so long.

The value of good early years provision is beyond dispute. Among other things, it promotes children's personal and social development, inspires confident learning, and boosts self-respect and respect for others. It is key to the formation of positive attitudes which ensure that children are well disposed to statutory schooling and which are of fundamental importance to children's educational success as a whole. It also provides crucial opportunities to promote close ties with parents and thus set the direction for continued support from home, which is vital for children's progress at school.

9
SMALL SCHOOLS

9.1 Small schools: a distinctive element of the primary education system

There has been a debate about the most effective size of school since at least the 1960s, when the Plowden Report[49] suggested that small schools lacked the resources to provide an effective education, limited pupils to a narrow range of opportunities and were unable to provide the necessary range of specialist teacher knowledge for the primary curriculum. The arguments and discussions continued; ten years later it was suggested that a school needed at least eight teachers to provide an adequate range of subjects and that every school should be large enough to provide all pupils with a "broad, balanced and differentiated curriculum".[50] The arguments against small schools were summed up as "The three Cs: curriculum, culture and cost".[51]

Some parents, of course – particularly those living in rural areas and without access to convenient transport – had no choice in the matter and the local village school was automatically the one to which they sent their children. Other parents, against the trend of the education reports of the day, specifically chose to send their children to small schools. They appreciated the special qualities, such as the "family atmosphere", that many small schools provided.

Researchers, therefore, began to look more closely at the small schools that had survived the rounds of closures and amalgamations. They found that small schools could provide a caring, stable environment where pupils' progress could be tracked more closely and problems identified earlier than in larger schools.[52] The professional isolation of teachers was perceived rather than real, with teachers in small schools just as likely to have attended courses, observed colleagues at work, had visits from advisers and worked with peripatetic staff as teachers in larger schools.[53] Small schools benefited from their place in the local community, and teachers had more frequent informal discussions with parents; closer links were established between home and school; and pupils did not have to adjust to a series of teachers.[54]

Undoubtedly the dual role of headteachers of small schools, combining a considerable class teaching commitment with management responsibility, makes great demands on those headteachers, especially at times of major policy shifts. Nevertheless, the substantial teaching role enables headteachers to have a more direct influence on curriculum development and a closer working understanding of the processes of change; pupils of different ages can work together when appropriate; and clustering arrangements between groups of small schools widen the opportunities for interaction and the sharing of ideas and experiences of staff and pupils.[55]

With the introduction of local management of schools, small schools initially had to manage with a budget based largely on the number of pupils on roll. Many small schools had to campaign to stay open as local education authorities began to rationalise their provision, targeting small schools with high unit-pupil costs. A report by the Audit Commission in 1990 estimated that within the primary sector there were 900,000 surplus places, with a considerable proportion of them in small schools.[56]

[49] *Children and their Primary Schools* (The Plowden Report). HMSO, 1967.

[50] *Primary Education in England. A Report by HMI.* DES, 1978.

[51] Harrison, Diane A (1995). "Small Schools, Big Ideas: Primary Education in Rural Areas", *British Journal of Educational Studies,* Vol 43, No 4.

[52] Arnold, R and Roberts B (1990). "Small Primary Schools: A report for education officers and advisers", *International Journal of Education Management,* Vol 4, No 5.

[53] Patrick, H (1991). "Teachers in Small Primary Schools", *Aspects of Education,* (Journal of the Institute of Education), University of Hull, No 44.

[54] Hopkins, D and Ellis, P D (1991). "The Effective Small Primary School: Some Significant Factors", *School Organisation,* Vol 11, No 1.

[55] Waugh, D (1991). "Implementing Educational Change in the Small Primary School", *Aspects of Education* (Journal of the Institute of Education), University of Hull, No 44.

[56] Audit Commission (1990). *Rationalising Primary School Provision.* London: HMSO.

This chapter draws together principally evidence from inspection reports, but refers also to inspection evidence from HMI and analysis of National Curriculum test data. For the purposes of this chapter, a "small school" is defined as one with up to 100 pupils; where the distinction is possible, these schools are split into "very small schools" with fewer than 50 pupils and "small schools" with between 51 and 100 pupils. Only pupils of statutory school age are included in these figures. There are about 2,700 small schools, of which about 700 are very small.

About two-thirds of small schools are church schools, generally affiliated to the Church of England; there are few small Roman Catholic schools. The percentage of ethnic minority pupils in small schools is relatively low, with few having more than 5 per cent. The exceptions are usually schools with considerable numbers of Gypsy and Traveller pupils.

9.2 Standards of achievement

Pupils in small schools are not disadvantaged in comparison with those in larger schools simply because of the size of the school. Small schools are capable of providing an effective education, and many are among the most successful schools in the country. At the same time a disproportionate number of the smallest schools have serious weaknesses or require special measures.

In the end-of-key-stage National Curriculum tests, small schools achieve on average higher scores than larger schools. The very small schools, while also achieving test results well above the average overall, are more variable in their performance. The schools in the 51–100 band are the most successful. For example, in the 1998 National Curriculum English tests at both Key Stage 1 and Key Stage 2, pupils in schools with between 51 and 100 pupils achieved results around six percentage points higher than those in larger schools. Several factors contribute to this positive picture: the quality of the school and its teaching, of course, but also the fact that the majority of small schools are in relatively affluent areas with above-average indicators of socio-economic advantage. Among the schools of between 51 and 100 pupils, the most effective are the small, rural, church primary

schools in advantaged areas, typically within commuting distance of towns and cities. The range of achievement of small schools is, however, very wide; some small schools achieve an average level of almost Level 5, while there are others averaging just over Level 3.

When National Curriculum test data is used to compare small schools with others in similar socio-economic circumstances, there is little difference in performance; if anything, the balance of judgement moves in favour of larger schools. In other words, factors other than size probably have a greater overall influence on standards in small schools. On the other hand, many parents choose to send their pupils to small schools for a wide range of reasons, such as the ethos of the school, the attention that parents consider can be given to the particular needs of their children, and the links that the school maintains with its local community.

Small schools – and, in particular, very small schools – have small cohorts of pupils in each year group. The results of the end-of-key-stage National Curriculum tests can inevitably fluctuate widely from one year to the next, because the scores of one or two pupils can have a significant influence on a school's results. For this reason the Key Stage 2 results for cohorts with less than eleven pupils are not published separately.

From an analysis by school size of the results of the Key Stage 2 National Curriculum test results, several features emerge:

- In the performance tables of the 1996–98 Key Stage 2 results for English, mathematics and science, there were between 20 and 30 small schools each year in the highest-achieving 100. This is at least twice the number that might have been expected on purely statistical grounds; and it does not include those successful very small schools with cohorts of less than eleven pupils and whose results were not published.

- At the other end of the scale, there were between three and ten schools in the table of the lowest-scoring schools. Again, these numbers do not include the very small schools, but the presence of some of these in the "serious weakness" and "special measures" categories would increase the number of small schools in the bottom 100.

- The number of small schools in the list of successful schools published in HMCI's Annual Report has included a larger number of small schools than would have been expected.

- The number of small schools (51–100 pupils) which have been judged to require special measures or to have serious weaknesses is a little below the average for all schools, but the number of very small schools requiring special measures is much greater than the average. The number of very small schools with serious weaknesses is higher than the average.

9.3 The quality of teaching

The quality of the teaching in small schools is slightly better than in larger schools; the influence of the teaching of the headteacher, which may account for as much as one-third of the teaching seen during an inspection, has a very strong, and usually positive, impact on the overall judgement about the quality of the teaching in a small school. Overall, the teaching in schools with between 51 and 100 pupils is marginally stronger than in schools of other sizes. By contrast, the quality of the teaching of the under-fives in small schools often compares unfavourably with the rest of the

Chart 51
The quality of teaching according to the size of the school 1997/98

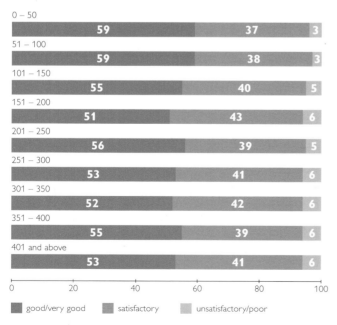

0 – 50: 59 | 37 | 3
51 – 100: 59 | 38 | 3
101 – 150: 55 | 40 | 5
151 – 200: 51 | 43 | 6
201 – 250: 56 | 39 | 5
251 – 300: 53 | 41 | 6
301 – 350: 52 | 42 | 6
351 – 400: 55 | 39 | 6
401 and above: 53 | 41 | 6

■ good/very good   ▩ satisfactory   ▢ unsatisfactory/poor

These figures have been rounded and may not add up to 100 per cent

teaching in the school and with the national picture. The teaching of the under-fives is more frequently unsatisfactory than in larger schools. Chart 51 illustrates the quality of the teaching according to the size of the school.

There is no evidence to suggest that pupils in small schools are disadvantaged because their teachers lack sufficient subject knowledge, understanding and skills to teach the required broad curriculum with appropriate academic challenge. This reflects very well on the arrangements for the in-service training of teachers and headteachers in small schools. For example, **Delamere CE Primary School**, Cheshire:

Despite the small number of staff there is an adequate spread of subject specialisms. The school has concentrated its in-service training effort mostly on developing expertise in curriculum areas because of the multiple subject responsibilities of individual members of staff. Teachers are committed to improving their performance and have given a great deal of time to extra training in subjects and other cross-curricular areas such as special educational needs. The school has benefited substantially from this.

In tackling the challenge of providing sufficient expertise in all subjects, small schools make good use of their strengths, both within their own teaching staff and the local community. There are many examples of the effective use of part-time specialists and volunteers from the community, well planned use of non-teaching staff and good management strategies to enable the teachers to be as effective as possible; for example, teachers exchange classes to enable them to teach their strong subjects to as many pupils as possible. Indeed, in a recent survey by HMI,[57] some of the best examples of the successful use of subject specialists were found in small schools, reinforcing the view that small schools work hard to ensure that their pupils have access to adequate expertise to teach the full range of skills, knowledge and understanding required by each subject.

West Meon CE Primary School, Hampshire, recognised the challenges facing three full-time teachers in teaching eleven subjects to classes containing pupils from as many as three year

[57] *The Use of Subject Specialists in Primary Schools. A Survey by HMI.* OFSTED, 1997.

groups. Where necessary and possible, the school brought in outside help, often from the local community, to extend the curriculum or to plug gaps. The small size of the school was exploited as a strength rather than a constraint: all the teachers knew what each other was doing, and all the pupils (about 60) knew all the teachers; they also knew the additional adults, most of whom were living in the village. With so few staff involved, changes could be made relatively easily. The arrangements change from year to year, and a change of staff can make a big difference, but the school was very much alert to subject needs when new appointments were made. In 1997, for example:

- the mathematics co-ordinator took her own class (Years 5 and 6) for mathematics and extended the work of Years 3 and 4 by taking their class once or twice a week;

- this allowed a straightforward exchange with the art specialist, who therefore taught art to all Key Stage 2 pupils;

- a part-time physical education teacher was employed to teach gymnastics to the Key Stage 1 pupils and the Year 3 and 4 class, so that a relatively modest expenditure extended the quality and range of the teaching;

- the Key Stage 1 teacher (the English specialist) took the Year 5 and 6 class for writing once a week and also taught reading skills once a week;

- the part-time special needs teacher took the top class for personal and social education once a week; and once a week the rector (this is a church school) discussed a moral or ethical issue with the Year 6 pupils;

- other volunteers made valuable contributions: a rota of parents and friends heard readers; a play-reading session was taken by a volunteer from the village; and the choir was taught by a local musician.

Small schools usually have classes containing pupils of more than one age group, and sometimes from more than one key stage. The wide range of age and ability in a class places great demands on the teacher, but effective teaching of these mixed-age classes is consistent with the planning and classroom organisation frequently seen in these classes. The behaviour of the pupils is almost always good, and class sizes are usually smaller; teachers know their pupils particularly well, often teaching them for more than one year. Group sizes are smaller, and the teacher can increase the amount of direct teaching provided for a pupil or a group of pupils. Where teaching is weak, ineffective planning fails to take account of the range of age and ability in a class and proper academic challenge is lacking. The potential impact of a weak teacher on the school career of an individual pupil and on the overall quality of a school can be considerable, and much greater than in a larger school where others can compensate to some extent for a particular weak link.

Provision for pupils under five is a cause for concern. Overall judgements made by inspectors relating to all aspects of the quality of teaching are considerably more critical than those given in larger schools, where the quality of the teaching of the youngest children is often the strongest element of the teaching. Teachers clearly find it hard to pitch work of appropriate challenge and range for a class which contains under-fives working towards the Desirable Learning Outcomes and those older pupils embarking on the National Curriculum programmes of study. On the one hand, there are pupils who have already achieved the Desirable Outcomes and should be moving on to more challenging work; on the other hand, there are pupils who are not given an appropriate early years curriculum and are moved on too quickly. In general, the provision is least effective when there are only a few pupils under five and where these pupils, of necessity, form a minority group within a class of largely older pupils. There are signs of improvement, however, and many schools are supporting the youngest pupils with teaching assistants – all the more effective when the assistant has NNEB training.

9.4 The curriculum

It is well within the capacity of small schools to teach the full range of the National Curriculum. Many do it well, making good use of their environment and the community. They often supplement the strengths of staff with outside help, which provides not only better provision for the National Curriculum subjects but also extends the range of curricular and extracurricular activities on offer; a remarkable number of the most successful small schools offer a modern foreign language, for example. At the other end of the spectrum, however, there is a significant minority of small schools which do not provide a broad curriculum and offer little by way of enrichment or special interest.

The curriculum of small schools at both key stages is generally as broad and as balanced as that of larger schools, but, as has already been reported above, can be weaker for the under-fives. As with the majority of schools, small schools have moved towards a more subject-based curriculum over the four years of the inspection cycle; specialist teachers and members of the local community are frequently involved in the teaching of some subjects, particularly music, design and technology, and physical education. The challenge of teaching numeracy and literacy to mixed-age classes from Frameworks which spell out what is to be taught to specific age groups but which also emphasise the value of whole-class teaching is one with which small schools are beginning to grapple. But, this challenge is nothing new; small schools have always had to choose appropriate content and pedagogy for their mixed-age classes, and inspection evidence shows that they have generally been successful in this.

Most small schools provide a range of extra-curricular activities, and take their pupils on visits, both local and residential. They often go to considerable lengths to involve the pupils in local sports and musical activities, including the opportunities to enable children to play and work with children of their own age from other schools. The quality of such provision depends very largely on the enthusiasm and ingenuity of individual teachers, but it is also related to access to local facilities such as sports halls or leisure centres. Provision is often weakest where local facilities are poor or non-existent, or where a catchment area is very widespread and the pupils have long distances to travel. Curricular provision both in and out of school hours is strongly supported and much appreciated by parents; their involvement in their children's learning is a strength of the large majority of small schools.

9.5 The ethos of small schools

One of the great strengths of small schools is their ethos. Very good provision for the spiritual, moral, social and cultural development of pupils, considerable parental involvement in their children's learning, and strong links with the community all contribute significantly to the establishment of caring, welcoming schools often seen as playing an essential role at the heart of a local community. The best small schools recognise the dangers of isolation and tackle the issue head-on. For example, **Grade-Ruan VC Primary School**, near Helston, Cornwall:

Cultural education is a strength of the school. Pupils are taught about the historical and living culture of the Duchy and this is well-integrated into all areas of the curriculum. Pupils take part in musical events, in local pageants and festivals and visit local art galleries and museums. They are also taught to understand and respect other cultures. There are good links with other countries: the oldest children go each year on a residential trip to Brittany and attend a partner school. Pupils keep in touch by letters and by fascimile, exchanging data as well as news of more personal interest. There are also links with a school in Kenya. Visitors to the school, such as a Japanese teacher, enhance cross-curricular links. These are well followed-up and enrich the curriculum in many subjects. Although the school is geographically isolated, this has not prevented the staff from ensuring that pupils are well aware of the world outside the peninsula.

Links with industry have been established through liaison with the Confederation of British Industries and the Cornwall Education Business Partnership. Particularly noteworthy initiatives have been visits to the Architects' Department and Buildings Office at County Hall, the monitoring of the Global Challenge Yacht Race with the help of British Telecom and work with RNAS Culdrose for a project on the weather.

The provision for spiritual development in small schools with close church links is stronger than that for larger schools. Schools in less advantaged areas which achieve well are reported to have a particularly strong ethos, often enabling them to handle difficult pupils well.

Even small schools with weaknesses in the teaching or with unsatisfactory standards tend to have a positive ethos, although when things get sufficiently bad for a school to have serious weaknesses or to require special measures then, not surprisingly, weaknesses in the provision for spiritual, moral, social and cultural development are reported.

9.6 Leadership and management

The majority of headteachers of small schools provide clear educational direction for their school, although as with schools in general there are weaknesses in the leadership in around one school in seven. The role of the headteacher in a small school is, however, different from that of a headteacher in a larger school. Workloads are balanced in a different way for the teaching headteacher; smaller numbers of pupils make some tasks lighter, but others prove more demanding and time-consuming because teaching and management work overlap during the school day. There are also, of course, fewer adults. It is unlikely that a small school will have a deputy headteacher, and the concept of a senior management team is unlikely to be appropriate; the school secretary is likely to have less hours each week than in a larger school. All adults, especially the headteacher, are likely to carry multiple responsibilities, not just in terms of management but for the co-ordination of subjects.

Combining leadership with a substantial teaching role can, however, be a powerful way to influence the process of change. The teaching commitment enables a headteacher to "lead from the front" and to understand the processes involved in curriculum development. It also ensures that the headteacher knows at first hand what pupils know and can do; and it should reveal priorities for spending or training very clearly. On the other hand, weakness or enforced absence through, for example, illness or even secondment to alternative work can have an immediate and depressing effect on a small school.

Good teaching and good management are, not surprisingly, the two most significant

characteristics of effective small schools. In practice, this means that the influence of the headteacher is a more than usually important factor in determining the quality of a small school. When the teaching or the management, or both, are weak, there are few ways to cushion the adverse effects. By the same token, however, the strength of the headteacher's influence in a small school also means that change and development can be brought about more quickly than in a larger organisation.

Governors are increasingly aware of the supportive role they can play. In many small schools they, too, have multiple roles, and inspection reports show how strong this partnership can be. At times, however, the governors leave too much to the headteacher and the resulting overload can lessen the effectiveness of the leadership.

9.7 Finance and efficiency

Small schools have higher unit costs than larger schools; they cost more per pupil than larger schools, and the cost per pupil rises as the school gets smaller. Judging value for money in a small school is a complex exercise; even successful small schools cost more to run per pupil than larger schools. What is clear, however, is that in most small schools day-to-day administration is efficient and there is usually careful financial planning and budgetary control. In addition, many small schools are particularly good at raising funds in the local community. By and large, small schools spend what money they have wisely and effectively.

Most small schools have sufficient resources to teach the National Curriculum. However, there is a wide spread of provision and the smallest schools often have the weakest resourcing. Local fundraising can play a particularly important role in enhancing the resources of a small school.

The quality of the accommodation in small schools is adequate in three-quarters of the schools. In one-third of the schools the accommodation is good. In an effort to modernise and to provide for the National Curriculum, many small schools have been given new or refurbished premises and now have good facilities. The demise of the outside toilet has been a long time coming, but much appreciated by caretakers, staff and pupils alike – especially in winter!

Nevertheless, overall, small schools have poorer accommodation than larger schools, and the smallest schools have the least satisfactory buildings: one-quarter of the smallest schools and one in five of the small schools have inadequate accommodation. Problems include cramped classrooms; insufficient facilities for the youngest children; a lack of space for outdoor play; and complicated arrangements for physical education, dinners and wet weather playtime. Many of these schools, however, have ingenious ways of circumventing their difficulties, often making good use of alternative local facilities such as church halls.

9.8 In conclusion

The features which make a small school successful are often those which combine to make a larger school successful, and inevitably include good teaching and good management. More specific to the small size of a school, and often directly related to the typical rural location and favourable economic circumstances of many small schools, are the close involvement of the local community in supporting the day-to-day work and extra-curricular activities of the school; the strong personal links between parents and the teachers; smaller class size and continuity of staffing; the ingenuity of the staff in overcoming problems with the accommodation, resources or expertise available; the establishment of networks of support from clusters of small schools; and a commitment by parents and the school to achieve the highest possible standards. The strength of "save our school" campaigns in rural areas is testimony to the warmth often felt by a local community for its school.

There remains a sense of vulnerability in small schools, however. If things go wrong and a school's reputation declines, parents are quick to register their protest by moving their children to another school. A weakness in the teaching or leadership can have a devastating impact on the school career of a pupil. It only takes the loss of a few families to have a significant impact on the organisation and morale of a small school. Fortunately, though, such schools form a small minority and, as this chapter indicates, most small schools are achieving standards and providing a quality of education at least as good as those achieved in larger establishments.

10 SPECIAL EDUCATIONAL NEEDS

10.1 Provision

OFSTED is publishing separately a four-year review based on the inspection of every special school in England. This chapter reports on the provision in mainstream primary schools for pupils identified as having special educational needs. It also reports on the implementation of the Code of Practice and includes evidence about the provision of "units" for pupils with special educational needs in primary schools. Provision for pupils with special educational needs is good in the majority of primary schools (six in ten in 1996/97, for example), and is rarely inadequate.

Provision for pupils with special educational needs was the focus of considerable change between 1994 and 1998. This was mainly as a result of the 1993 Education Act and the subsequent guidance in the Code of Practice[58] on the identification and assessment of special educational needs and in Circular 6/94 on the organisation of special educational provision. A significant and positive change in primary schools has been, over the past four years, the establishment of the role of the special educational needs co-ordinator (SENCO). The expectations on this role have been substantial, but considerable expertise has been acquired by many SENCOs and their work has been influential and effective. It has generally been the SENCO, with support from the headteacher, who has driven forward the changes required by the 1993 Act and the Code of Practice. SENCOs have established appropriate procedures for keeping a register of pupils' special educational needs and for preparing and revising individual education plans. However, these are time-consuming tasks, and many co-ordinators have

been concerned about the time taken by their role; indeed, some have been unable to complete the recommended termly reviews.

The estimations made in 1978 (the Warnock Report[59]), that 20 per cent of pupils would have special educational needs at some time in their school careers and that 2 per cent would have long-term needs which would require a Statement of Special Educational Need, have continued to be reflected in recent legislation. A Statement of Special Educational Need follows a detailed multi-disciplinary assessment of a pupil's needs and sets out the special educational provision required to meet those needs. The statement is a legal document and is kept under statutory annual review. It is expected that pupils with special educational needs, including those with statements, will be educated in mainstream schools if:

- their needs can be met;
- the education of the other pupils is not hindered;
- the placement meets with the wishes of the parents; and
- the placement represents an efficient use of resources.

In January 1998 just under 3 per cent of school-age pupils had a Statement of Special Educational Need and 20 per cent of all primary-aged pupils were identified as having special educational needs, including those with statements. Both the percentage of pupils with a statement and the proportion of these pupils placed in mainstream schools increased steadily throughout the 1990s. Fifty-eight per cent of pupils with statements were placed in mainstream schools in 1998 compared with 48 per cent in 1993. Of the children for whom a statement was first written in 1997, 71 per cent were placed in mainstream schools, compared with 66 per cent in 1994 and 59 per cent in 1992. Roughly twice as many pupils in Key Stage 2 have Statements of Special Educational Need than in Key Stage 1. The majority of schools identify between 10 per cent and 24 per cent of pupils as having special needs; over a quarter of schools identify more than 25 per cent of pupils as having special needs.

There are considerable variations amongst local education authorities in relation to the numbers of

---

[58] *Code of Practice on the Identification and Assessment of Special Educational Needs.* DfEE, 1994.

[59] *Special Educational Needs – Report of the Committee of Enquiry into the Education of Handicapped Children and Young People.* HMSO, 1978.

pupils with statements. These often reflect a local education authority's policy in respect of the way funding is allocated for the provision of pupils with special educational needs. Some have relatively high percentages of pupils with statements, while others have relatively few such pupils. The proportions vary from over 5 per cent to just over 1 per cent. In addition, the proportion of pupils with Statements of Special Educational Need taught in mainstream schools as opposed to special schools differs widely between local education authorities. For example, a few local education authorities have over 90 per cent of their pupils with statements in mainstream schools. At the other extreme, a few have less than 35 per cent of their statemented pupils in mainstream schools. This is clearly related to the number of special schools that a local education authority has decided to maintain.

10.2 Promoting high achievement for pupils with special educational needs

In 1996, OFSTED published the results of a survey[60] conducted by HMI of how schools identified pupils with special educational needs, the provision made for these pupils and their achievements in mainstream schools. In general, HMI found that the quality of teaching and learning of pupils with special educational needs had major shortcomings in too many lessons. In particular, the survey found that:

- throughout the primary phase, the quality of teaching and learning and the standards achieved by pupils with special educational needs were frequently too variable, both within and between schools;

- where support was not available, or where it was insufficiently well informed, both the standards of achievement and the quality of education suffered;

- where no extra support was present, pupils with special educational needs benefited no less than others from good teaching, which took full

account of the needs of all pupils;

- the most influential factor on the effectiveness of in-class support was the quality of joint planning of the work between the class teacher and the support teacher or learning support assistant;

- all pupils gained from extra in-class support, but pupils with special educational needs gained the most;

- learning support assistants were effective in helping to raise the standards achieved by pupils with special educational needs;

- the quality of educational provision in withdrawal sessions, outside the classroom, was generally sound but focused almost exclusively on literacy skills.

The key features of lessons in which effective learning took place, including withdrawal groups and individual support lessons, were:

- activities which were clearly targeted, focused and challenging for the pupils;

- careful planning, which responded to the specific nature of a pupil's individual learning needs;

- the tracking of individual progress against carefully constructed programmes of work;

- sessions linked to the work being undertaken by the rest of the class, with the class teacher being aware of what was taking place and sharing records;

- teaching which fitted into whole-school approaches, such as concentrating on a school approach to teaching phonic skills;

- time used flexibly so that pupils did not lose their curricular entitlement, for example not always being withdrawn from music.

The following example illustrates good practice where pupils are withdrawn from mainstream classes for individual or group work:

Ten pupils are withdrawn from two classes in Year 3 and Year 4 as they have similar literacy difficulties. They are achieving around Level 2 for reading and writing, below age-related expectations. The focus is on reading for meaning, writing and spelling, with the specific aim of developing levels of concentration. The

[60] *Promoting High Achievement for Pupils with Special Educational Needs in Mainstream Schools.* OFSTED, 1996.

work is linked to a whole-school anti-bullying programme. The planning and organisation of the session by the class and support teachers show a thorough understanding of pupils' individual needs. A range of appropriate worksheets, carefully selected, supports reading and writing activities, and computer software with a voice synthesiser encourages independent learning. Pupils enjoy these thrice-weekly sessions, can articulate why they need extra help, but display good levels of self-esteem. They apply previously learned skills to the new words and sentences. Progress is clear, carefully monitored and conveyed to their class teachers.

At the time of the 1994 survey, the majority of schools were in the process of reviewing their policies for special educational needs in the light of the Code of Practice. While considerable progress was being made, initially the main thrust in most schools gave priority to procedural and administrative detail. Less than half the schools in the survey provided appropriate guidance for class or subject teachers on strategies for teaching the range of pupils with special educational needs.

10.3 The Code of Practice

In 1997 HMI published a survey[61] into the implementation of the Code of Practice on the identification and assessment of special educational needs and found that steady progress was being made in almost all primary schools. In particular:

- most schools were aware of the major implications of the Code of Practice for all teachers;

- increased attention was being given to special needs issues in primary schools, especially to the need to provide pupils with special educational needs with a broad and balanced curriculum, including the National Curriculum;

- there was a better match between the educational provision made and pupils' special educational needs;

- schools were more successful at identifying pupils' learning and behavioural problems;

- almost all primary schools had a designated SENCO and best practice occurred when the SENCO had sufficient time to liaise, co-ordinate and support staff throughout the school;

- most schools were establishing procedures for keeping a register of special educational needs, for preparing and reviewing individual education plans, and for liaising with parents, colleagues and external support services;

- local education authorities had produced good-quality guidance for schools on the implementation of the Code of Practice, although there was little assistance on how to apply the guidance effectively.

Some areas of difficulty remained, however, in particular:

- while better identification procedures were in place, teachers were less successful in monitoring the progress of pupils or the effectiveness of the teaching and additional support that pupils receive;

- many schools could not provide detailed information about their funding arrangements for special educational needs, often due to unclear information from local education authorities but more frequently because the school itself did not have a clear rationale for the proportion of its funds which should reasonably be spent to support pupils with special educational needs;

- the majority of special educational needs policies did not comply totally with the statutory requirements. Teachers, and particularly governors, were often unclear about their statutory duties, most often in relation to the statutory requirement on governors to report to parents annually on the success of the school's special educational needs policy and practice;

- changes to the organisation and funding of health authorities had left schools very confused about who is responsible for making provision, and in particular with whom to liaise, for the support of pupils requiring physiotherapy and speech therapy;

- the lack of adequate support from some local education authority support services for pupils with more serious difficulties, although without a statement, which as a consequence often led to a statement being necessary.

---

[61] *The SEN Code of Practice: Two Years On.* OFSTED, 1997.

Of all the recommendations made by the Code of Practice, the writing and reviewing of individual education plans continued to give the greatest cause of concern to SENCOs, with many reporting that they did not have the time to complete the recommended termly review of individual education plans, especially without access to clerical assistance.

The DfEE, in its most recent publication,[62] recognises the need for further development in special educational needs policy and practice as part of the Government's school improvement strategy. The recommended programme of action sets out an expectation that the proportion of pupils with statements being educated in mainstream schools should be increased over the next four years. In addition, it sets out plans to produce a revised Code of Practice to take effect during the academic year 2000/01.

10.4 Additional special educational needs provision or "units" for pupils with special educational needs in primary schools

While a high proportion of pupils with statements are educated in mainstream primary schools, this is often in additional-provision or specially resourced designated "units", usually additionally funded by the local education authority. Much of this provision has been well established over many years. Many local education authorities are increasing this type of provision, sometimes to replace special schools, most often those for pupils with visual or hearing impairment, or physical disabilities.

Additional special educational needs provision is usually for a specific group of pupils, almost always with a Statement of Special Educational Need – for example, pupils with hearing impairment, including those who use signing either as their primary means of communication or as a supplement to hearing and lip-reading; visual impairment, including pupils who use braille; speech and language difficulties; and physical difficulties, including those using wheelchairs and with severely reduced mobility.

Admission policies for additional provision are usually negotiated between the school and its governors and the local education authority. In some provision, the placement of pupils has gradually changed – for example, increasing numbers of pupils with emotional and behavioural difficulties in a moderate learning difficulties provision. In the best practice, admission policies are kept under careful review and, where changes occur, staff have opportunities to undertake additional training. Some admission policies emphasise the intention to reintegrate pupils into their own mainstream schools or to retain pupils for a specified length of time, as is often the case for many pupils with speech and language difficulties. In some local education authorities a mismatch of provision between primary and secondary schools leads to considerable difficulties for the placement of pupils in Key Stages 3 and 4.

Additional special educational needs provision is inspected as part of the inspection of the host school. Inspection reports and HMI surveys[63] have indicated much good practice, which has improved over the four-year period, often in line with the positive developments which have taken place as a result of the Code of Practice.

The attainment of pupils in additional provision is usually below – and often well below – national expectations, but there are exceptions. For example, in a survey of the teaching of reading to pupils with hearing impairment, HMI found[64] that one-third of the pupils attained standards in line with those expected for their ages. In several schools with provision for pupils with visual impairment, it was found that at the end of Key Stage 2 more-able pupils who were competent braillers were able to read and write as well as their sighted peers. The emphasis in inspection reports, however, for most pupils with special educational needs is usually on the progress that they as individuals make over time rather than comparisons with national expectations.

Progress made by pupils with a range of special educational needs was judged to be satisfactory

---

[62] *Meeting Special Educational Needs: a Programme of Action.* DfEE, 1998.

[63] *Promoting High Achievement for Pupils with Special Educational Needs in Mainstream Schools.* OFSTED, 1996.

[64] *The Teaching of Reading to Pupils with Hearing Impairment in Mainstream Schools.* OFSTED, 1998.

and often good. For example, in a survey of provision for pupils with specific learning difficulties HMI found that the pupils made good progress in reading, and satisfactory progress with spelling and writing. The greatest variation in progress reported by inspectors was for pupils with moderate learning difficulties, and emotional and behavioural difficulties. In some schools there was insufficient planning for these pupils and insufficient challenge in order to raise standards.

In most cases teachers working in specialised provision had additional qualifications in an aspect of special educational needs and they were skilled and experienced mainstream teachers or occasionally had a special school background. In most cases the quality of teaching was sound or better, but there were exceptions. In the best lessons which covered all types of special educational needs:

- individual education plans had targets which were clear and precise, they had a specified timescale – for example six to eight weeks – and they could be monitored simply, for example by ticking whether the skill had been achieved;

- support staff and learning support assistants were well briefed;

- planning took good account of the individual needs of the pupils;

- activities were well matched to the pupils' needs, ensuring a level of success;

- positive feedback was given to the pupils, spelling out exactly what was good about their work;

- good relationships enabled pupils to feel valued and supported;

- pupils, often as young as seven, knew their targets and strived to reach them;

- day-to-day assessment of pupils' progress facilitated good planning for the next lesson.

Some excellent lessons were seen with pupils with emotional and behavioural difficulties, in which each had a set of targets in literacy which were assessed at the end of every lesson by recording the skills acquired. The pupils developed a tremendous sense of achievement, which they were proud to share with others.

The majority of pupils placed in additional special educational needs provision had access to a broad and balanced curriculum, and there was no disapplication from the National Curriculum. However, the provision often catered for a wide age and ability range, at worst two key stages and at best two year groups in a single key stage. Balancing integration opportunities in mainstream classes with specialist teaching and the deployment of staff to support pupils was a difficult process which needed continuous monitoring. In many cases it worked well, especially when the support in mainstream classes was well deployed, as in the case of many pupils with hearing, visual and physical difficulties; but integration in mainstream classes was most difficult for pupils with moderate learning difficulties or emotional and behavioural difficulties. At times there was too much emphasis on core skills at the expense of other areas of the curriculum, while at the same time there were instances of a lack of support for pupils in foundation subjects.

In most cases, pupils were on the register of the appropriate mainstream class. They had opportunities to work in this class and to develop friendships, and they had additional support in withdrawal groups. Much depended, however, on the quality of communication between the specialist teacher and the mainstream teacher so that literacy and numeracy skills, for example, could be reinforced in other curricular areas. In the best practice the specialist teacher joined in the shared curriculum-planning process with other teachers, and there was added strength where this also included the school SENCO. In these situations, staff could share in contributing to the overall provision of the school and, from this, specific projects such as family literacy initiatives sometimes emerged.

In much of the provision for pupils with speech and language difficulties, the joint work between speech therapists, teachers and learning support assistants was excellent in the quality of support it gave pupils. Likewise in the provision for pupils with physical difficulties, the joint work with physiotherapists was equally valuable for pupils' progress. Services from outside the school were well used to develop the curriculum for pupils with special educational needs. Educational psychology services frequently provided good advice on developing individual education plans for pupils with emotional and behavioural difficulties. Appropriate attention was usually, but not always, given to developing mobility skills for pupils with visual impairment and the development of their social skills in some schools, but this was not consistent for these pupils.

Assessment practices were usually at least satisfactory, with effective baseline assessment and good-quality individual education plans. While in the survey of the teaching of reading to pupils with hearing impairment in mainstream schools no pupils had been disapplied from the statutory tests completely, in some cases pupils had been disapplied from the written tests but not from teacher assessment. Annual reviews were usually well managed and transition to secondary schools well thought-out.

Partnership with parents was an important goal and in some cases this was very well achieved. In the best practice, teachers made good links with parents, some of whom lived a distance from the school. They provided home–school books and termly meetings focusing on the progress made by the pupil and social events. In one school with provision for pupils with speech and language difficulties, parents, alongside mainstream pupils and staff, attended classes to learn signing so that they could use it with their children.

The management of additional special educational needs provision was usually good. In the best provision, the specialist staff were committed to, and clear about, their goals. The headteacher had a good knowledge of special educational needs issues and undertook a role in monitoring the quality of the specialists' work. This commitment was also reflected by the governors, who understood the role of the provision and actively supported it in the school. School development planning included development targets for the provision. There was, however, almost no evaluation of the effectiveness of the provision in order to plan its further development.

In most cases the provision was adequately staffed, with teachers and learning support assistants suitably qualified and experienced. In a number of schools the specialist teacher was also the SENCO for the whole school; where time had been made available this was a valuable role in giving the specialist teacher an overview. It also enabled mainstream staff to see the teacher as a full member of the school's staff. In some schools, however, the specialist teacher promoted a separateness which was not in the best interests of the pupils.

Specialist teachers had sufficient access to in-service training but their choice of professional course was more often focused on special educational needs issues than on subject development issues. There were good examples of in-service training to the whole of a school's staffing, before additional provision was established and periodically as needs or staff changed.

Resources for learning were sufficient overall, except for the use made of information and communication technology for pupils with all types of need. For example, pupils with moderate learning difficulties, who would have benefited from using computers, and in particular concept keyboards, to develop their writing skills, sometimes had no access to this equipment. The underuse of computers for developing reading skills with pupils with hearing impairment delayed progress. However, there was good use of supportive technology such as closed-circuit television to support pupils with visual impairments.

Accommodation for additional special educational needs provision was usually appropriate to the needs of the pupils and in many cases has become available because of falling rolls in the host school. Appropriate modifications have often been made, such as soundproofing to assist pupils who are deaf and improved floor surfaces for pupils with physical difficulties. Inspectors often commented positively on the location of a base room when it was in the heart of the school rather than in a separate building or located at the end of a corridor; location was important to the achievement of a sense of inclusion for pupils with special educational needs.

Funding for the additional special educational needs provision for pupils with hearing and visual impairments was usually centrally managed by the local education authority, which enabled the provision to be managed flexibly as the incidence, age and location of pupils with these disabilities changed. Funding for all other types of provision was often delegated, and in the best practice it was supported by a service-level agreement. In most cases funding was sufficient to meet the needs of the pupils, but it was not always based upon clear criteria for allocation.

11 LITERACY AND NUMERACY

11.1 Inspection evidence

In 1994/95 inspectors reported that pupils achieved well in about half of primary schools in English, and in a little over two in five primary schools in mathematics. The Annual Report for 1994/95 concluded that: "In Key Stage 2 standards (in English) require considerable improvement in about one-tenth of schools. In mathematics standards require considerable improvement in about one-sixth of schools." This view from inspection supported claims from researchers involved in international comparisons that English pupils achieved relatively poorly in mathematics in comparison to Pacific Rim societies such as China, Korea and Taiwan.[65]

There is ample evidence to show that the performance of pupils in England lags behind that of many of our international counterparts in important aspects of mathematics. The Third International Mathematics and Science Study (TIMSS)[66] of pupil performance pointed to long-standing weaknesses in the performance of English nine-year-olds, particularly in number. In the TIMSS, the same teachers and pupils took part in both the mathematics and the science assessments of the nine-year-old pupils. These same pupils performed well in science and considerably less well in important aspects of mathematics. The findings, therefore, reinforced the view that it is what schools and teachers do which makes a substantial difference to pupils' performance rather than other factors such as home background or the ability of pupils, which are "outside their control".

---

65 See, for example, *Worlds Apart? A Review of International Surveys of Educational Achievement involving England,* David Reynolds and Shaun Farrell, OFSTED, 1996.

66 *Third International Mathematics and Science Study.* NFER, 1996 and 1997.

67 *Access and Achievement in Urban Education: A report from the Office of Her Majesty's Chief Inspector of Schools.* HMSO, 1993.

In 1993, OFSTED published its report on *Access and Achievement in Urban Education,*[67] which drew attention to the underachievement by significant numbers of pupils and students in urban schools and colleges. One of its themes was that pupils in schools in disadvantaged areas require particularly skilled teaching in oral and written communication, including reading.

Chart 52
Speaking and listening
(percentage of schools)

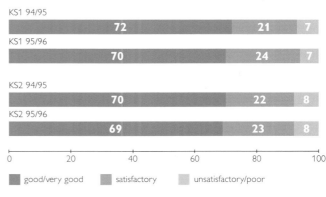

These figures have been rounded and may not add up to 100 per cent

Chart 53
Reading
(percentage of schools)

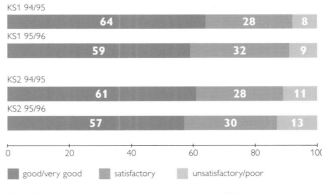

These figures have been rounded and may not add up to 100 per cent

Chart 54
Writing
(percentage of schools)

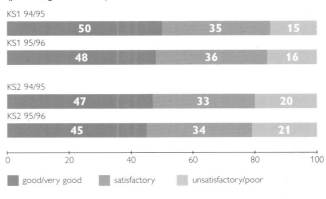

These figures have been rounded and may not add up to 100 per cent

Chart 55
Numeracy
(percentage of schools)

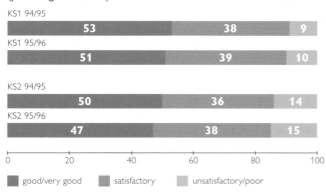

These figures have been rounded and may not add up to 100 per cent

OFSTED responded to the growing debate about the teaching of numeracy and literacy by requiring inspectors to report more directly on literacy and numeracy skills in 1994/95 and 1995/96. Charts 52–55 summarise inspectors' judgements on literacy and numeracy skills for the two years (1994/95 and 1995/96) at Key Stage 1 and Key Stage 2.

On the basis of the inspection evidence, the conclusions from the 1995/96 Annual Report were:

Pupils' skills in **speaking and listening** *are generally good. Pupils listen attentively, talk confidently about their work and express their ideas clearly. In over half of schools, pupils'* **reading** *skills are good in both key stages, but in just under one in ten in Key Stage 1 and one in eight in Key Stage 2 they are poor. Many pupils are not able to read accurately. Phonic work in particular still needs to be strengthened in many schools.* **Writing** *skills remain weaker than those in speaking and listening, and are poor in Key Stage 2 in one-fifth of schools: weak spelling and sentence construction, limited vocabulary and lack of attention to improving work by redrafting are the main problems. Too many children continue to leave their primary schools poorly equipped with the essential skills of reading and writing.*

In mathematics, standards in **number** *are good in about half of primary schools, but are poor in one in seven in Key Stage 2. Standards in* **shape and space** *and* **data handling** *are generally higher than those in number. In Key Stage 2, pupils spend too much time unproductively repeating work that they have already mastered. This slows progress in Years 3 and 4, but there is an improvement in Year 6.*

In schools where a substantial amount of mathematics is taught directly to the whole teaching group or class, and pupils regularly undertake oral and mental work, standards are generally higher than where the approach is overwhelmingly that of individual work.

Inspection evidence, therefore, was beginning to demonstrate a strong relationship between standards of reading, writing and numeracy and the method of teaching. In 1995, Her Majesty's Chief Inspector announced that he would follow up the inspection evidence and the findings of the Access and Achievement in Urban Education report. HMI, working closely with three local education authorities in London (Islington, Southwark and Tower Hamlets), inspected the teaching of reading in 45 primary schools, 15 from each authority. The inspections concentrated on the teaching of reading in Year 2 and Year 6 in each school, and were backed up by a common test of reading administered by the National Foundation for Educational Research to the Year 2 and Year 6 pupils in the survey schools.

The following year HMI conducted a similar survey into the teaching of number in Year 2 and Year 6 in 45 schools in three other local education authorities (Greenwich, Newham and Knowsley). In both surveys the local education authorities were selected because their publicly available indicators – National Curriculum test scores, and General Certificate of Secondary Education grades for English and mathematics – were comparatively low. All six authorities face some of the most severe socio-economic conditions in the country, including high proportions of low-income families, areas with high and long-term unemployment, and (in most cases) high proportions of families for whom English is an additional language.

One outcome of the considerable interest in, and concern about, the teaching of literacy and numeracy was the establishment in September 1996 by the DfEE of the National Literacy Project and the National Numeracy Project. The approaches taken by these projects were extended nationally into the National Literacy Strategy in September 1998 and the National Numeracy Strategy from September 1999. Finally, in the summer of 1997 a small number of "Summer Literacy Schools" was established, followed the next year by a larger number of literacy and numeracy summer schools.

This chapter draws principally on five sources of evidence in its review of literacy and numeracy: the two surveys of the teaching of literacy and numeracy in three urban local education authorities; the evaluations, conducted by HMI, of the National Literacy Project and the National Numeracy Project; and initial reports on the 1998 summer literacy schools.

11.2 *The Teaching of Reading in 45 Inner-London Primary Schools*

In the survey referred to above,[68] intakes of the majority of the schools represent some of the highest levels of disadvantage in the country. They generally had higher proportions of pupils eligible for free school meals, higher numbers of pupils with English as an additional language, and both higher pupil turnover and higher staff turnover than the national averages. These are challenging circumstances in which to teach reading and the central problem, reflected in the under-achievement of many pupils in reading, was the wide variation in the quality of the teaching.

Reading scores in the standardised tests were significantly below national norms, and a large group of white pupils from disadvantaged backgrounds performed poorly. In Year 2, only about one in five pupils achieved a reading age at or above their chronological age. Almost one in five achieved no score at all. Of those achieving no score at all, about half were from non-English-speaking home backgrounds. In Year 6, two pupils in five achieved a reading age at or above their chronological age; about one-quarter of the pupils in Year 6 were one year or more ahead of their age norms.

However, four out of ten of the pupils in Year 6 achieved reading ages which were two years or more below their chronological age. Black African pupils performed better than other ethnic groups at both Year 2 and Year 6. Bangladeshi pupils achieved low scores in Year 2 but performed better in Year 6. White pupils from disadvantaged backgrounds performed least well and constituted the largest group of underachievers at Year 6.

The commentary on these test results is unequivocal, and the spotlight falls fairly and squarely on the quality of the teaching in the classroom, namely how reading is taught:

> *The wide gulf in pupils' reading performance is serious and unacceptable. Some schools and pupils are doing well against the odds while others in similar circumstances are not. It is clear that it is what individual schools do that makes the difference to their pupils' reading performance. It follows that the underperforming schools must do things differently if the large numbers of low-achieving pupils are to receive the quality of teaching they need and deserve to make the progress of which they are capable.*

The survey challenged directly several well established aspects of the teaching of reading, including:

- free reading with little or no intervention by the teacher;

- too much time spent hearing individual pupils read;

- the overuse of undemanding and time-consuming worksheets.

The survey identified the weaknesses of the teaching, including:

- insufficient attention to the systematic teaching of an effective programme of phonic knowledge and skills;

- insufficient attention to the development of reading beyond the basic stages, such as the development of pupils' abilities to question, evaluate and respond in depth to what they read;

- the use of too narrow a range of texts (largely narrative fiction), giving pupils insufficient opportunity to encounter progressively more demanding texts, including reference materials;

- insufficient direct and explicit teaching of specific aspects of reading;

- a lack of any detailed analysis of pupils' errors in reading.

At the time of publication these criticisms of the teaching of reading were seen as a broadside assault on the methods used in many English

---

[68] *The Teaching of Reading in 45 Inner London Primary Schools.* OFSTED, 1996.

primary schools. Nevertheless, they have been addressed through the establishment of National Curriculum assessment arrangements such as the use of "running records", and within the Framework and teaching approaches of the National Literacy Strategy.

11.3 *The Teaching of Number in Three Inner-urban Local Education Authorities*

As with the survey of the teaching of reading, the schools participating in the number survey[69] were mainly in areas of severe socio-economic deprivation, with high proportions of low-income families and high levels of long-term unemployment.

Scores in the National Curriculum tests for mathematics at both key stages in 1995 were below the national averages in two-thirds of the schools. In 1996, however, many of the schools showed significant improvements in their test results. The pupils in Year 2 and Year 6 also took standardised mental and written number tests. Overall, the mental and written test scores of Year 2 pupils were comparable with the national norms, but the Year 6 pupils performed less well and their scores were below those of the national sample.

In a similar picture to that seen in the reading survey, the test scores indicated substantial variation in attainment between schools. This variation indicated that some aspects of number work received too little attention or that they were badly taught. Too many pupils were ill-equipped to work out basic calculations in their heads, and they were slow and often inaccurate when using pencil-and-paper methods.

The performance of pupils from different ethnic groups showed considerable variation. Black African, Bangladeshi and Pakistani pupils achieved low scores in both Year 2 and Year 6. The small group of Chinese pupils performed well.

The report comments on the cultural acceptance in England of not having a "head for figures", unlike illiteracy, to which a critical social stigma is

attached. Nevertheless, despite the fact that, overall, the schools in the survey scored close to the average in the standardised tests, the variations in standards and in the quality of teaching were, as the report states, "too wide and call for urgent attention".

The variation in the quality of the teaching was striking. At best some excellent teaching was seen in all three of the authorities. In contrast, there was some confused and confusing teaching, leading to poor attitudes, and anxieties about number, in many pupils.

Weaknesses in the teaching of number were highlighted in the report, and included:

- in half the lessons at Key Stage 1 and one-third at Key Stage 2, insufficient attention was given to securing the confident recall of number facts;

- in several schools there was no clear expectation that multiplication tables were to be learned by heart;

- "a debilitating overuse of individual work", often linked with an overreliance on worksheets and published schemes, where reliance on individual work isolated pupils in ways which made it difficult for them to receive any sustained, direct teaching;

- inappropriate expectations in terms of the "pitch" of the work and the pace of the lessons, often linked to weaknesses in teachers' curricular knowledge about how to progress number work. Examples of pupils receiving work that was too easy for them far exceeded those where the work was too hard.

There was another side to the coin, however. Good lessons were seen, with positive features including:

- a higher proportion of time spent teaching the class together, often at the start and sometimes at the end of the lesson;

- a well-judged mix of whole-class, group and individual work, developing a common gain in core knowledge and skills and enabling re-inforcement or extension through individual work;

- clear explanations and instructions;

- the teacher's ability to ask relevant questions and engage pupils in exchanges which promoted confidence and familiarity in using mathematical language;

---

[69] *The Teaching of Number in Three Inner-urban Local Education Authorities.* OFSTED, 1997.

- good modelling of mathematical ideas and knowledge of using simple resources such as a number line;

- an insistence that pupils should learn number facts and tables by heart.

A recognition of the weaknesses to overcome and the strengths on which to build has been a feature of the National Numeracy Project and its wider dissemination as the National Numeracy Strategy. The importance of tracking progress throughout the primary years, rather than just at the end of the key stages, has been acknowledged by the QCA; schools are now offered up-to-date standardised tests to help monitor pupils' progress more systematically and to help teachers plan their work more effectively.

It was encouraging to find that some schools in the survey were at or close to the national targets set by the Government for primary pupils in mathematics for the year 2002. That is to say, 75 per cent of their eleven-year-olds were achieving Level 4 or above in mathematics. While schools serving the areas of social disadvantage generally did less well than those in schools serving more favourable circumstances, this was not the whole story: some schools serving the poorest areas managed to achieve the national target and have done so since national testing began.

11.4 The National Literacy Project

The National Literacy Project was set up by the DfEE in September 1996 and was funded through Grants for Education Support and Training at a cost of £12.5 million over five years. Eighteen local education authorities were involved in the Project, involving initially 266 primary schools. HMI evaluated the Project by visiting a 20 per cent sample of schools.[70] Three visits were made to each school in the sample and over 300 "literacy hours" were observed.

Most of the schools had entered the Project because they had weaknesses in reading and writing, particularly at Key Stage 2. OFSTED inspection reports had also, in many cases, indicated unsatisfactory performance in other key

areas, including leadership and management and the monitoring and evaluation of standards of work by both headteachers and subject co-ordinators.

The Project's aims were to raise standards of literacy in primary schools in line with national expectations. It targeted two key areas for improvement:

- the quality of literacy teaching in the classroom;

- the management of literacy throughout the school.

The Project established a detailed Framework of teaching objectives for reading and writing structured as a termly programme based on three levels of work:

- word level: phonics, spelling and vocabulary;

- sentence level: grammar and punctuation;

- text level: comprehension and composition.

The Project also provided guidance on how to teach these three levels of work through a daily literacy hour. Pupils were taught during this time through a mix of whole-class teaching, group teaching and individual work. As part of their work in promoting, managing and monitoring the Project, local education authorities appointed literacy consultants who trained and supported the "key teachers" designated by schools to take the lead in implementing the Project in their schools.

The progress of the pupils in the Project schools was also monitored by the use of nationally standardised tests, taken at the start of the Project in October 1996 and again in March 1998. Pupils also completed a questionnaire to assess their attitudes to reading and to see whether these had changed.

The Project was able to claim some important successes. Teaching improved, and many pupils made good progress. The Project was an important catalyst in the majority of schools in tackling deep-seated problems in literacy. While the picture was mostly positive, some schools remained in a trough of low standards, with only marginal improvement over the first five terms.

The Teaching Framework and the Literacy Hour required focused, direct teaching; both were well received by teachers, who appreciated the clear structure of the Literacy Hour and the detailed

---

70 *The National Literacy Project. An HMI Evaluation.* OFSTED, 1998.

teaching objectives of the Framework. The Framework helped to establish demanding and clear expectations for reading and writing in primary schools, an essential precondition to the raising of standards. The Project had a positive impact on pupils' attitudes and interest in reading and writing; they recognised the importance of what they were doing and afforded the Literacy Hour a high status.

HMI found that the Project had a clear, positive influence on the teaching of literacy and the test results for pupils in the first cohort of schools indicated that the majority of pupils had improved their reading scores. Nevertheless, HMI also reported that there remained a number of weaknesses in the teaching of literacy, disturbing variations in the standards being achieved in the first cohort of project schools, and insufficient progress being made by a significant minority of schools. These weaknesses were not considered to be intractable, but HMI concluded that if they were to be remedied, they would require:

- stronger leadership in schools where standards had not, thus far, begun to improve. Support from the headteacher was weak in just over one in five schools;

- a faster pace of change in classrooms where the teaching was unsatisfactory;

- a much greater degree of support and a more carefully targeted programme of intervention in the schools with weaknesses in leadership, management and teaching;

- improvements in teachers' knowledge about the teaching of phonics in order to improve the teaching of "word level" work.

Notwithstanding these weaknesses, the overall quality of the teaching was at least satisfactory in seven out of eight lessons, and in half of the lessons the teaching was good. The features of the good teaching can be illustrated by reference to the teaching at **Mary Trevelyan Primary School**, Newcastle upon Tyne, a school achieving test results above the national averages from a pupil population with 83 per cent eligibility for free school meals:

All teachers are thoroughly well informed teachers of English, confident in their strategies for teaching phonics and spelling and including all aspects of English in demanding

lessons. They are very familiar with the Project Framework.

All the teachers seen managed the literacy hour extremely skilfully. The class teaching was direct, demanding, involved accurate instruction and engaged all the pupils. Direct teaching was precisely linked to clear objectives. Groups were organised quickly with clear instructions. Pupils were very good at working independently, within a very well organised set of sensible classroom routines.

Expectations were universally high, and the Project Framework was helpfully guiding teachers as to where to pitch things. This meant, for example, that much greater emphasis on the vocabulary of English (verb, sentence, adverb, for example) was placed with younger pupils; and the blends of letters ("oo" and "at" in a Year 1 lesson, for example) were used earlier than before. Lessons progressed at a good pace, although the Year 5 teacher was frustrated that the pace was not even faster.

A small number of schools in the Project were high-achieving primary schools. Schools with outstanding English test results are understandably reluctant to abandon tried-and-tested good practice. Reference to **St Oswald's RC Primary School**, Newcastle upon Tyne, illustrates the tensions as well as the approach taken. HMI noted:

Appropriate but unusual adaptation of the Project approach to match the particular demands of this high-achieving school. The school is not prepared to discard its previous successful practice which seemed to emphasise depth and quality, features which the school believes could get lost, especially by Year 6 in a 60-minute session.

The school has decided to teach "formally" the literacy hour for two lessons a week at Key Stage 2 and for three lessons a week at Key Stage 1. Other sessions are used for extended writing and other literacy activities, including handwriting and spelling. All the objectives of the Framework are covered; this has proved a very useful checklist for the teachers to ensure that their English scheme of work covers everything.

The school teaches well beyond the Framework,

both in level and depth. Its scheme of work has been mapped against the Framework and at least covers it all. The Year 6 teacher plans her English against National Curriculum Level 5, for example.

Given the national concerns about the underachievement of boys, the school has emphasised the need for all pupils to write complex and accurate sentences. An example from a Year 6 boy illustrates their success, included verbatim:

The Telegraph April 30th 1912

UNSINKABLE?

The Telegraph Asked Mr. C. H. Stengel a survivor from the great Titanic accident to write an account on what he felt on the night everything went wrong and here was what he came up with.

It was a cold night on the 14th April 1912 and I, Mr C. H. Stengel, was enjoying a party with my fellow friends from Belfast as an almighty crash interrupted the party. My friends, Maids and I all made our way out of the room we were occupying passing a clock showing us the time... 11:40pm it was almost midnight. I made my way onto the deck and looked around. I heard an announcement saying the ship had struck an iceberg but I thought nothing of this as the ship was unsinkable... wasn't it?! I went back to my room to inform my friends as to what I saw on deck.

There were big blocks of ice falling from the iceberg and I was beginning to get worried... I rounded my friends up and told them to follow me onto the deck, they obeyed me and followed. We passed the stage and I noticed the band were still playing.

I ran towards the lifeboats and attempted to climb in through the crowds of other people but stopped as a badly aimed shot from a pistol just missed me, only to carry on and hit a bystander. I ran back through the crowds of hysterical women screaming and running wildly. I forgot about my friends for the time being so I ran to the stern, kicked off my shoes and dived into the deep blue sea.

The shock of the coldness of the water was amazing and I'm surprised I didn't die on impact, but still I was alive and that's all that mattered for the time being. Bits of ice were falling all about me but, with a bit of luck and great difficulty I avoided them just... I swam round to the front of the boat passing the hysterical crowds and men jumping overboard as I did In a last hope to stay alive.

Waves were lashing against the side of the boat and the stern rose higher and higher into the air. The crashing of the furniture and belongings smashing and tearing could be heard along with the exploding engines.

I was about to give into the mean and unkind Atlantic ocean when I spotted a wooden lifeboat nor far off. I got

an adrenalin rush and seemed to find superhuman strength to swim or rather grind out the last few metres toward the small craft but then, I collapsed...

Lucky for me a friend of mine on board the small boat spotted me and reached out to me. She just caught me by the collar as I was sinking along with the ship and she hauled me on board... I was told later I stopped breathing for a while but thanks to a brave sailor who gave me C.P.R. I survived. I regained consciousness and watched in silent awe and hope the Titanic against a clear black sky with a full moon settled right in the middle of it.

I said a silent prayer for my friends as I watched the Titanic a 66000 ton monstrosity tilt back even further until it was at a right angle with the water.

A strange force made me turn away and I wept hoping at some moment I would be pinched by someone and wake up but this was no dream or even nightmare. It was really happening and there was nothing I could do to change the events of the last few hours of hell.

I turned around to face the ship one more time, just as it sank below the water and there was an eerie moment of silence apart from the sucking of the water as it was sucked down along with the Titanic and many people to nothingness.

I would never forget that night as long as I live and every night since I have prayed to God to thank him for sparing my life from the cruelness of the sea.

Mr. C. H. Stengel was one of about 850 people who survived the terrible tragedy of the Titanic from the 2228 who sailed in her. At about 6:00am the same day the Titanic sunk the Carpathia a lifeboat arrived but it was to late.

The gains made by some groups of pupils in schools across the Project, as measured in reading scores, were greater than others; for example, girls recorded greater gains than boys, pupils eligible for free school meals made smaller gains than those who were not eligible; and pupils at advanced stages of the special educational needs Code of Practice made smaller gains than pupils with no defined special need. This finding indicates that the Project did not offer a completely watertight solution to the real challenge of the English system, namely the underachievement of boys in socio-economically disadvantaged areas.

Even after five terms, the rates of progress made by some schools were still not good enough. In the sample of schools visited by HMI, nearly one-third of the Year 6 age groups made less progress than the national average.

The dissemination and implementation of the Project, as with the National Literacy Strategy, relied on the "cascade" model of training. This placed a heavy responsibility on the key teachers, most of whom performed well. But the cascade model only works if the key teachers have the necessary skills and resources, and the support of the headteacher.

The contribution of the consultants was generally good and sometimes outstanding. Most developed an impressive range of skills, essential to sustaining the impetus of the work. Their role has been very demanding indeed, particularly when facing headteachers who were reluctant or unable to implement the Project in their school.

In most local education authorities the support for the consultants was at least satisfactory, and several effective literacy centres and literacy steering groups were set up. In three of the 18 authorities, however, the promotion and management of the Project never fully recovered from an unsatisfactory start because of poor internal communication and a lack of coherent strategies for linking the Project to other priorities. It was at the level of the individual school that the local education authority support was weakest, particularly in those schools which required the most help because they were not making enough progress.

Teachers found it difficult to organise the group-work element of the literacy hour in such a way that they were free to teach one or two of the groups, while the other groups undertook worthwhile tasks rather than low-level "holding" activities: at worst, wordsearches and colouring exercises.

Most schools worked hard to ensure there were adequate resources for the teaching of the literacy hour. Often, this meant diverting money from one priority to literacy in order to increase the stocks of books, particularly "big books" and sets of books used in "guided reading" sessions.

11.5 The National Numeracy Project

Two hundred and thirty-three primary schools set about implementing the National Numeracy Project.[71] Over one-fifth of these were located in

---

71 *The National Numeracy Project. An HMI Evaluation.*
OFSTED, 1998.

inner London and a further 46 per cent in metropolitan areas. They were generally in areas of socio-economic disadvantage and the performance of the "numeracy schools" was generally lower compared to schools nationally.

The Project was well received in the vast majority of the schools. In many schools the introduction of the Project's Framework for Teaching Mathematics, with its detailed planning requirements and well-defined learning objectives, required a major change. The quality of planning for mathematics quickly improved and teachers found the Framework structure very helpful, especially in mixed-age classes. The level of detail offered by the Framework was welcomed by teachers working with pupils with special educational needs.

The initial requirement to devote at least four 50-minute lessons a week to numeracy was implemented speedily. For some schools, this involved allocating more time to mathematics than before, and in a few this was reportedly at the expense of other subjects.

The audit process, which included the identification of targets and how to address them, helped many schools to raise their expectations of what pupils could achieve in mathematics. Many headteachers found target setting difficult, and in about one-third of schools the targets had an insufficiently strong emphasis on standards. In a significant minority of schools, expectations were too low and were unduly influenced by teachers' perceptions of the effects of pupils' backgrounds.

Most schools had sufficient resources to support the Project and were able to fund non-contact time for the co-ordinator and key teachers. As with the literacy project, problems emerged for schools with a high turnover of staff, particularly where new co-ordinators needed to be trained or supply teachers needed to be informed about the Project.

The quality of the teaching improved during the life of the Project and by the end was satisfactory or better in four-fifths of the lessons observed, although the figure of one in five lessons in which the teaching was unsatisfactory is high.

The amount of detailed and systematic planning required by the Project was considerable, and teachers found this to be very time-consuming.

The Project had a positive impact on the teaching

of mathematics. Effective direct teaching was evident in most lessons, although not always sufficiently sustained. In particular, many teachers lacked confidence in using questions with the whole class. Teachers began to use the oral work and mental calculation activities as opportunities to develop a much more informed view of pupils' strengths and weaknesses.

Most pupils showed a positive attitude to the mathematics lessons, although their response to the introductory oral work and mental calculations was generally better than the demands of staying on task in the middle part of the lesson. Pupils often lost concentration when they were not working directly with the teacher.

The quality of the training for the teachers has been one of the crucial determinants of success. Again, as with the National Literacy Project, the quality of the headteacher's leadership and management and the status given to the Project have also been strongly associated with its success or failure at school level. Some schools clearly needed greater support than others from consultants and the local education authority in order to improve the quality of teaching and manage change.

11.6 Summer Literacy Schools

In 1997, 1,600 pupils took part in Summer Literacy Schools in 50 schools. In 1998, the scheme was extended considerably, involving over 16,000 pupils in approximately 500 schools. The aim was to improve the reading and writing skills of pupils on entry to Year 7 and help prepare them for the challenge of the secondary school curriculum. Summer schools formed part of the National Literacy Strategy and were expected to use the good practice described in the strategy. The pupils targeted were mostly those working at Level 3; in other words, not those one in ten pupils, largely boys, who fail to reach Level 3 in English.

Typically, the schemes involved 30 pupils from the feeder primary schools of a secondary school. The teachers involved were usually secondary school staff, often from the English or special needs departments. Most schools ran for five hours a day, with structured literacy activities during the

morning and a range of sporting, technology or drama activities in the afternoon.

The strengths of the scheme included:

- a sense of shared purpose, with highly motivated pupils and good relationships between teachers and pupils;

- generally good co-ordination of the scheme, and careful monitoring by the local education authority;

- good teaching in half of the lessons observed by HMI, and satisfactory teaching in a further 35 per cent of lessons;

- good planning of literacy-related work, generally linked to the Framework for teaching.

Weaknesses included:

- inadequate assessment information from the feeder primary schools;

- some lack of knowledge of the National Literacy Strategy approach on behalf of the secondary school staff involved;

- a minority of reluctant staff, or a lack of continuity because of the use of a great many part-time staff;

- occasional overuse of worksheets or computer programs, reducing the amount of teaching of key literacy skills.

In summary, the vast majority of the Summer Literacy Schools were successful in meeting their objectives and provided good value for money. The quality of literacy teaching, the range of activities and the response of the pupils were all good features in these schools. In a few schools there were weak elements in the provision, mostly associated with too little training and preparation and a limited understanding of the principles and practice of the National Literacy Strategy. These lessons have been taken to heart and incorporated into the guidance for summer school providers in 1999, linking summer schools much more closely to the National Literacy Strategy.

12
WORK IN
SUBJECTS

12.1 English

Standards of achievement

At Key Stage 1, National Curriculum test results show some recent improvements in reading and spelling but little change in the quality of pupils' writing, which remains the weakest aspect of English. For example, in 1998, while 61 per cent of pupils achieved a Level 2B or above in reading, only 48 per cent did so in writing. Many pupils reaching 2C failed to make the necessary progress to reach Level 4 by the end of Key Stage 2. The gap between boys' and girls' performance by the end of Year 2 was ten percentage points in 1998, reflecting an increasingly well-documented problem during this period.

At Key Stage 2, there has been a steady improvement over the four years. While 48 per cent of pupils reached Level 4 or above in 1995, 65 per cent did so in 1998 and 79 per cent of girls were at or beyond this level in reading – close to the Government's overall target for English in 2002. The gap between boys and girls has remained high: 16 percentage points at Level 4 in 1998, and the number of boys achieving Level 5 being half that of girls. It is particularly worrying that one in ten pupils still leaves primary school without achieving Level 3 in English.

Inspection evidence reflects these figures, including the improvements in attainment at Key Stage 2. However, in both key stages, in about one in ten lessons, pupils have consistently failed to make sufficient progress.

In 1994, pupils achieved well in English in about half of primary schools; speaking and listening were generally strong features. Standards in writing were, and remain, poorer than in reading, or in speaking and listening. This picture has not changed significantly. Although children enter school with a wide range of communication skills, most make good progress as speakers and listeners. They readily take part in conversations

with teachers and peers and learn how to adapt their speech for different purposes, using standard English when appropriate. In Key Stage 1 they begin to discuss the books they are reading and by the end of Key Stage 2 they can explain their preferences. Most pupils develop the ability to read aloud with confidence, accuracy and expression; and can make brief presentations to the class or in assembly. Children enjoy making up and performing stories, taking on roles and exploring topics, relationships and emotions in drama. By the end of Key Stage 2, many pupils can take on different roles in discussion, for example acting as chair, mediator or spokesperson. This requires good listening skills: paying attention to instructions and to the contributions of others.

A significant minority of pupils fail to make this degree of progress. They have limited powers of concentration and are poor at developing their ideas in discussion. Often, they find it difficult to distinguish between formal and informal language, failing to grasp and use the grammatical constructions and vocabulary of standard English.

Despite the worries of some teachers that the National Literacy Project would sideline the spoken word, the introduction of the literacy hour can enhance both speaking and listening. For example, it has shown the need for pupils to listen carefully during shared reading and word-level work. The recent emphasis on improving pupils' phonic knowledge and phonemic awareness has pointed up the need for young children to be trained to listen carefully to sounds in words. Further, the structure of the literacy hour provides opportunities within question-and-answer elements and in discussion to use language. Unfortunately, in many classrooms, drama has consistently been undervalued as a way of strengthening pupils' skills in speaking and listening, as well as exploring topics, relationships and emotions.

The introduction of the revised National Curriculum in 1995 clarified for teachers the range of knowledge, understanding and skills needed in a balanced approach to the teaching of reading. Although this led to some improvements in the teaching and learning of reading, it has taken the National Literacy Project to emphasise the importance of phonic knowledge in such a programme. Most pupils swiftly learn the conventions of print and come to enjoy stories and books at an early age. Good readers learn to use a wide range of strategies to decode unfamiliar words, and they rapidly acquire a good sight vocabulary. They use these skills to read widely for information and enjoyment. By the end of Key Stage 2 they can empathise with characters and show a critical appreciation of stories, poems and plays. None of this is accidental: phonemic awareness is achieved through well sequenced and carefully structured teaching. For the vast majority of teachers this new approach and rigorous knowledge of phonic work has been hard-won. Moreover, many teachers are still in need of training to boost their understanding of phonics.

During the four years of the review period, inspection evidence and National Curriculum test results have highlighted two problems. Firstly, about 10 per cent of pupils fail to reach Level 3 in the Key Stage 2 English tests, and clearly have not acquired the skills and understanding necessary for them to make satisfactory progress as readers. They find it difficult to identify the sounds in words and to blend them together into words: grammatical and contextual clues in a text provide little further help. They read aloud in a stilted manner and lack the skills which would allow them to correct their errors. A second, larger group of pupils fails to build on their basic reading skills, and this means that they read a narrow range of unchallenging literature; rarely move beyond literal understanding to the ability to infer meaning or predict what might happen next in a story; and, in following up an interest or seeking help with a topic, they select information from a narrow range of sources. Towards the end of the four-year period, the National Literacy Project was beginning to show how both groups of pupils could be helped to become better readers.

Standards of writing have shown little change. In fact, in 1998 in Key Stage 1 fewer pupils achieved Level 3 or above than did so in 1995. Nevertheless, inspection evidence and National Curriculum test results help build up profiles of successful and weak writers and suggest ways of improving pupils' writing. Good writers soon learn pencil control and form letters well. They learn how to spell simple words through using their phonic knowledge and through familiarity with words from a wide experience of books. They enjoy communicating their ideas, feelings and reactions and do so in an increasing range of styles; and

they learn how to draft and edit their writing, sometimes using computers to do so. By the end of Key Stage 2, they have developed good cursive handwriting skills and can also print clearly to label diagrams and charts. They use dictionaries, thesauruses and spellcheckers as a matter of course and have learned effective note-making techniques.

However, OFSTED has consistently reported that too many pupils leave their primary school unable to produce sustained, accurate writing in a variety of forms. The definition of a literate primary pupil in the National Literacy Strategy Framework for Teaching provides a good checklist for teachers seeking to improve their pupils' standards of writing. Weak writers in Key Stage 1 often fail to grasp basic spelling patterns and fail to hear the individual sounds in words. They do not move beyond simple sentence structures and rarely write at length. As they move through Key Stage 2 they seldom attempt anything but straightforward narrative. Early errors tend to remain, for example: inconsistent use of tenses; using commas instead of full stops to demarcate sentences; and insecure use of the apostrophe.

The quality of teaching

The quality of teaching has improved over four years: in 1995 it was unsatisfactory in one lesson in five, but this figure had dropped to fewer than one in ten by 1998, and in more than half of the lessons the teaching was good or very good. Teachers' knowledge and understanding of the subject, their planning and management of pupils, and their methods of teaching and organising work have all improved in the last four years. Teachers have become more confident in their understanding of the National Curriculum, and the National Literacy Project has sharpened their focus on the need for better subject knowledge, in particular the aspects of children's language acquisition and development and the demands of word-level work. The Project has led to an increase in the amount of direct teaching of whole classes and groups and better knowledge of books to be shared with pupils. Above all, it has begun to raise teachers' expectations of what pupils can achieve. Over the four years inspectors have noted, as features of the best work in English, teachers' ability to ask searching questions; provide good models of speech and writing; demonstrate their own enjoyment of books; link work in the three attainment targets (speaking and listening, reading and writing); and concentrate on basic literacy skills.

For many teachers, the National Literacy Project made demands which they have found difficult to meet: moving away from regularly hearing each pupil read; confident and coherent teaching of phonic skills; and using the last ten minutes of a lesson (or "plenary") to review, reflect on and consolidate learning. Other weaknesses have emerged during the four years. For example, although school libraries have improved, teachers have not always used them well to improve pupils' reading and research skills. Moreover, while National Curriculum and standardised test data have become more readily available, the use of all forms of assessment was still poor in two out of five schools in 1998. Despite the overall improvement, the quality of teaching has remained best in Year 6 and weakest in Year 3, reflecting a similar pattern in the progress made by pupils.

The demands on the role of the subject co-ordinator have increased over the four years of the review period. In 1995 the co-ordination of English was weak in one-fifth of schools in Key Stage 1 and a quarter in Key Stage 2; the influence of the co-ordinator was seen as crucial in ensuring well planned and coherent provision; and co-ordinators lacked adequate time to carry out their responsibilities. The most recent findings show that leadership and management of the subject have improved, but remain poor in one school in ten; and that lack of time is still a problem. Yet the management of literacy is a major strand in the National Literacy Project and the co-ordinator is now expected to have a firm grasp of the Framework for teachers; to train colleagues to introduce the literacy hour; to influence practice to promote high standards; to monitor and evaluate work; and to help to set targets for individuals, classes and the whole school.

The curriculum

The revised National Curriculum for English was regarded by many teachers as an uneasy compromise. It gave due attention to the main language modes: speaking and listening, reading and writing. It specified the range of reading and writing and it listed five essential approaches to the teaching of reading. There was a suitable emphasis on technical accuracy and an

acknowledgement of the importance of drama, media education and information technology. In practice, some sections of the programmes of study, including those on standard English and language study, proved difficult to translate into classroom practice and many teachers found it difficult to use the document as the basis of their own schemes of work. By the end of the four-year period, the National Literacy Project was beginning to help teachers solve these problems, and in particular the Framework for Teachers set out what should be taught and when in an integrated approach to reading and writing.

The National Curriculum, in its two versions, has set out a demanding range of books and other materials for pupils to read and use. By the end of Key Stage 2 they are expected to be "enthusiastic, independent and reflective readers". Although pupils read more widely than they did four years ago, inspectors continue to note many gaps. For example, few pupils experience a good range of poetry, non-fiction or texts from a variety of cultures and traditions. Just as worrying has been the number of schools lacking sufficient resources for English. Despite a small improvement over the four years, in 1998 one in ten schools did not have an adequate range of books and other materials – and this coincided with the introduction of the National Literacy Strategy and the National Year of Reading.

The revised National Curriculum established the importance of drama, aspects of media education and information technology in the English programmes of study. All three enhance work in the three attainment targets for English, as well as offering worthwhile areas of study in their own right. Where they are taught regularly, pupils' response is usually good and standards often high. However, inspectors have frequently noted their absence over the four years. In 1995, the use of information technology was underdeveloped; in some schools it was absent. There was little evidence that drama had the place prescribed for it. The situation had not changed significantly by 1998.

Improving standards of English: the way forward

The Government has set a national target of 80 per cent of eleven-year-old pupils reaching Level 4 or above in National Curriculum English tests by

2002. Despite the improvements over the last four years, much remains to be done if the target is to be met, as follows:

- The National Literacy Strategy and its Framework for Teaching need to be accepted by all schools as a way of planning, structuring, teaching and evaluating their work in reading and writing. Teachers in National Literacy Project schools saw the benefit of more direct teaching, pupils' growing familiarity with the literacy hour, and the increased expectations of pupils resulting from the word, sentence and text-level work.

- The teaching of word-level work, ie phonic work, within the literacy hour remains the weakest and yet most crucial element in the teaching of reading. Schools need to address this with a greater sense of urgency, and those responsible for training teachers in the requirements of the literacy hour must make sure that the quality of the training for teaching phonic work is of the highest order.

- Teachers need to plan carefully their coverage of the whole of the English curriculum, including speaking and listening, extended writing and drama; the literacy hour is a basic minimum, and is likely to need reinforcing at other times in the school day and by giving more attention to those aspects of literacy which feature in other subjects.

- Schools will have to continue to give attention to the needs of all their pupils, including the most able. However, three groups in particular require immediate consideration: boys; the pupils who leave primary schools lacking the literacy skills to cope with the demands of the secondary curriculum; and those pupils who fail to develop their sound basic skills.

- There is now sufficient inspection and research evidence to suggest that boys can be helped from an early age. The clearly defined tasks and outcomes, structure and pace of the literacy hour have begun to make a positive contribution to boys' attitudes and performance. Teachers should ensure that they include a good balance of fiction and non-fiction in their reading programmes and they need to value the voluntary reading of boys. A full English curriculum will include drama and work which involves the use of information

technology, both fields in which boys often excel. In their oral work, boys in particular need to be encouraged to talk about their feelings and emotions.

- If improvements are to be made, many teachers need to upgrade their knowledge and expertise beyond the initial Literacy Strategy training. In particular, they need to consolidate their knowledge of word-level work, especially the teaching of phonics; to make clear to pupils the specific language objectives of a lesson; to monitor pupils' work in class, making appropriate and helpful interventions; to develop their own knowledge of children's literature, guiding pupils' private reading and conveying an enthusiasm for books; to make effective use of support staff and teaching assistants, especially during the literacy hour; and to provide a good blend of teaching and learning styles, including the direct teaching of whole classes, managing group work and setting tasks for individual pupils.

12.2 Mathematics

Standards of achievement

The National Curriculum test results indicate gradual improvements over the four years 1994–98. There was, however, a worrying dip in performance at Key Stage 2 in the 1998 tests. At Key Stage 1 performance has been maintained, with 84 per cent of pupils achieving Level 2 or better. Girls' performance continues to be marginally better than that of boys at Level 2 but below that of boys at Level 3. In 1998 the proportion of pupils achieving Level 2C increased by five percentage points to 23 per cent. There is, however, growing concern as to whether these pupils will make the progress necessary to reach Level 4 by the end of Key Stage 2.

At Key Stage 2, the steady improvements made from 1995 to 1997 were not sustained in 1998, in part attributable to the introduction of a statutory mental arithmetic test. In 1998, 59 per cent of pupils achieved Level 4 or above, well below the Government's target of 75 per cent for 2002. The proportion of pupils who achieved Level 2B or better at the end of Key Stage 1 in each of the four years indicates the extent of the improvements that need to be made if the target is to be met. For example, 55 per cent of the 1995 Year 2 cohort achieved Level 2B or better; this cohort takes the Year 6 tests in 1999. The rate of pupils' progress early in Key Stage 2 will have to increase considerably and match that achieved in Years 5 and 6.

Inspection evidence has consistently highlighted the dip in pupils' progress in mathematics as they move from Key Stage 1 into Key Stage 2. In 1998, in three in ten Year 3 lessons pupils made good progress; in over one-third of lessons in Years 1 and 2, and in nearly one-half of lessons in Year 6, progress was good. The expectations that teachers have of pupils of different ages and the teaching methods employed have a significant impact on pupils' progress. In too many Year 3 and 4 classes, pupils repeat earlier work and consolidate skills they have already grasped. In National Numeracy Project schools, Year 3 and Year 4 pupils made the greatest progress. Inspection evidence showed that teachers had raised their expectations of pupils' achievement and pupils responded well to these higher demands. There have been improvements in attainment in some aspects of mathematics, reflecting corresponding improvements in teaching. Teachers who are confident and competent to discuss mathematics with pupils help raise attainment by developing pupils' breadth of understanding. Teaching correct mathematical vocabulary and notation, and efficient mental strategies, gives pupils confidence. They do not have to fall back on inefficient methods such as counting on fingers.

Underachievement is greater at Key Stage 2 and there are too many pupils who leave primary schools with only a very basic knowledge of mathematics. Unless identified and supported, they quickly fall behind their peers who are better equipped to cope with the demands of secondary education, some of whom make very rapid progress. Schools have not given sufficient attention to reducing the attainment gap in mathematics. The overreliance on individualised schemes and worksheets has had the effect of widening the gap between high and low attainment. The National Numeracy Project's emphasis on direct whole-class teaching has succeeded in closing the attainment gap, with more rapid progress being made by lower-attaining pupils. Emphasis on the acquisition of knowledge and skills at the expense of securing an

understanding of the underlying concepts is a notable feature in schools where there is a greater range of attainment. Pupils are not necessarily able to connect the different skills they acquire and too readily forget what they have been taught. They find it more difficult to solve problems that are set in less familiar contexts.

Over the four years of the review period, inspection evidence has painted a consistent picture of achievement. While standards are usually satisfactory or better in Shape, Space and Measures, there are weaknesses in all the other aspects of mathematics. The good attainment in Handling Data at Key Stage 1 is not maintained; there is too little progress at Key Stage 2. There are improvements in pupils' recall skills, although their mental calculation strategies remain weak. Pupils' ability to use written methods of calculation for addition and subtraction is more secure than for multiplication and division. Of the four operations, division skills are the weakest. Pupils have difficulty with work that involves fractions and the idea of proportion. Algebraic knowledge and skills are generally poorly developed, and there are few schools where algebra is a strength. Pupils' ability to use and apply their mathematics is very variable, reflecting opportunity, experience and teaching styles.

Towards the end of Key Stage 2, the late acceleration in progress made by many, but not all, pupils enables them to meet the standards expected for their age. They understand the number system and can calculate accurately on paper and mentally. Their mathematical vocabulary is sufficiently developed to enable them to explain their methods and describe properties of common two- and three-dimensional shapes. Some pupils have developed the problem-solving skills needed in mathematics and other subjects to explore relationships and patterns. They can present reasoned arguments and justifications, occasionally using algebra to generalise patterns and to describe graphs.

The quality of teaching

The quality of teaching of mathematics has improved steadily over the last four years. Now one-half of the lessons are taught well, compared with 1995 when teaching was good in just over one-third of lessons. There is proportionally less unsatisfactory teaching, down from one-fifth to one-twelfth of lessons. A major reason for the improvement is quite simply that there is more direct teaching taking place. Four years ago, for many pupils, mathematics meant working from a published scheme at their own pace. The teacher rarely intervened to teach the class. Support was provided only when a pupil was stuck; pupils had little opportunity to discuss their mathematics. Administration of materials had replaced mathematics teaching.

The poor performance of pupils in England, a fact brought to light in a major international survey, triggered concerns at all levels. Attention was drawn to the way in which pupils in England were being taught mathematics, and number skills in particular. In 1996 the National Numeracy Project was introduced into selected schools to improve the quality of teaching. Other initiatives took root, and increasingly schools began to review their teaching methods. Over time, the greatest improvements have been made to the way that teachers plan and organise their lessons and manage time, resources and pupils. Lessons are now better directed and pupils are more productive. These improvements have led to teachers gaining in confidence with the subject. They rely less on published materials to determine the mathematical experience for pupils, and are becoming more discerning about how to use them.

Improvements have, however, been uneven. Year 1 and Year 6 are still the best-taught year groups; in Years 3 and 4, where the quality of teaching has continued to be the weakest, improvements have been slower. Pupils' progress also slows in Year 3, at a time when many key mathematical ideas need to be established to maintain and build on the progress made in Key Stage 1. The National Numeracy Project has helped teachers to identify mathematical progression across the year groups, which has in turn raised teachers' expectations of what pupils are capable of achieving. However, in too many classrooms mathematical expectations are low and the pace of learning follows the slower pupils. While repetitive and undemanding tasks may keep pupils busy, they do not extend or consolidate their understanding. The rate of improvement in organisation and management has yet to be matched by improvements in expectations and the pace of learning.

Teachers have made too little use of assessment information to guide planning and teaching; it

remains a weakness in over one-quarter of schools. Teaching a class without good assessment information makes it difficult to group pupils by attainment and to set work at the appropriate level of difficulty. Consequently, there is a tendency to pitch work at the middle ability range in the class. Inspectors frequently state that high-attaining pupils are insufficiently challenged and mark time.

Over the four years of the review period, there has been a shift away from mixed-ability teaching. Grouping pupils on the basis of their prior attainment within classes or in sets across classes accounts for one-quarter of lessons at Key Stage 1 and one-third of lessons at Key Stage 2. Inspectors judge teaching in classes where there is such grouping to be better; it helps teachers to manage and limit differentiation, to teach the whole class and groups of pupils, and to set levels of expectation more accurately. In small schools setting may be impractical, but grouping in the class is often an essential organisational strategy. Setting does not in itself improve teaching, but schools that choose to set tend to use the organisation well, occasionally adapting it, for example to run intensive workshops or to engage outside help.

There has been an increasing willingness by most teachers to examine and to change their teaching methods. The Numeracy Task Force restated the importance of direct teaching with frequent, well-directed oral and mental work. More lessons now start with some mental activity. Teachers are providing more instruction to pupils and more proactive, rather than reactive, support to pupils as they work; and lessons have an identified ending. In more classrooms the elements for good mathematics teaching are in place; it is the quality of implementation that still varies. For example: the oral work may help pupils to get a right answer but does not challenge and enhance understanding; the mental work may test but not strengthen pupils' recall skills and calculation strategies; instructions are clear, but there is no dialogue during which pupils can sort out their ideas with the teacher's help and get used to using the correct mathematical terminology; there is direct support to individuals, but it is uneven and not planned or monitored. Practices are gradually improving within each element, but teachers find it hard to sustain higher-quality practice across the lessons.

When commenting on good teaching, inspectors note how the teacher orchestrates the whole class for the whole lesson; uses mathematical terminology accurately; illustrates number structures and other properties with well-chosen resources; and shares and promotes a spirit of enquiry into mathematics with the pupils. Typically, good teachers provide: a prompt start to the lesson with some intensive mental work, which is then discussed to elicit understanding and to promote recall or calculation strategies; clear explanations and demonstrations along with skilled questioning of pupils, whose responses inform the teaching; carefully planned tasks, with the teacher continuing to teach a targeted group of pupils; and a conclusion when the teacher identifies progress and rectifies remaining misconceptions.

Inspection evidence has shown that teachers cannot easily change their own practices without guidance and support. Over the four years under review, the management of in-service provision has shifted from local education authorities and more responsibility for identifying need and organising provision has been devolved to schools. However, development planning for mathematics is weak in nearly one-quarter of schools, and the monitoring of mathematics teaching is unsatisfactory in nearly in one-quarter of schools. In 1995, in one-fifth of schools, the poor management of mathematics was a significant factor in producing low standards. Management is better, though still of concern in one-eighth of schools. Finding time to carry out their management responsibilities, particularly making visits to other classrooms to monitor mathematics teaching, has been a long-standing problem for co-ordinators. Inspection of the National Numeracy Project highlighted the key role of the mathematics co-ordinator in keeping teachers informed, directing their teaching practices and raising pupils' attainment. Crucially, inspection evidence also shows that this is not possible without good support from the headteacher. Such combined and effective leadership and management provided by headteacher and co-ordinator together are essential factors in improving teaching and standards in mathematics.

The curriculum

Schools are expected to devise their own scheme of work which identifies how they intend to provide pupils with a broad and balanced mathematics curriculum meeting the National Curriculum requirements. Inspectors judge that one-third of schools do this well, but in one-tenth of schools there are significant weaknesses in provision. Revisions to the National Curriculum sought to reduce teachers' assessment burden. Replacing statements of attainment with Level descriptions helped. However, schools found the reduction in detail contained in the programmes of study more difficult to translate into a scheme of work. For example, teaching pupils to "develop a variety of mental methods of computation" and "develop a range of non-calculator methods of computation" were open to many interpretations by teachers. Establishing smooth progression and continuity across year groups while meeting all National Curriculum requirements was a daunting task for schools; many consequently resorted to published schemes. It has taken time to rectify the consequent overemphasis on written work, but slowly, and sustained by the national drive to improve pupils' mental calculation strategies, the mathematics curriculum is being regenerated in schools.

Over the four years of the review period, number has always received a high priority in both key stages; Using and Applying Mathematics has been underrepresented in many schools. Such imbalances in curriculum provision are long-standing. For example, the development of pupils' mathematical language and communication has continued to be identified as a particular aspect of curriculum weakness. This reflects the paucity of opportunity that pupils have been given to talk about mathematics and to present a reason for their own methods and solutions. The expectation that pupils' application skills should be "set in the context of the other areas of mathematics" has not been met. Guidance on how schools should build this into their planning of provision has not given sufficient help. Pupils' curriculum experience has become dislocated, topics change quickly, and pupils are not helped to establish essential connections – for example, knowing that "4+4=8" means "double 4 is 8", or that division is the inverse of multiplication.

Schools in the National Numeracy Project have used the Framework for Teaching Mathematics to guide their curriculum planning. The year-by-year learning objectives have helped teachers to identify progression within and across year groups. Greater attention is given to developing pupils' mental calculation strategies and their ability to communicate their mathematical ideas and methods. However, in many schools there remain imbalances in their curriculum provision. There is still an overemphasis on written work early in the curriculum before pupils have a secure understanding of number. Few schools include the use of information and communication technology in mathematics teaching. Particular topics such as division, negative numbers and fractions get insufficient attention, while other topics are regularly revisited – sometimes unnecessarily so as pupils have already acquired the necessary knowledge, skills and understanding.

Improving standards of mathematics: the way forward

The preparations for the National Numeracy Strategy give schools an opportunity to review their mathematics teaching and to evaluate the standards attained by pupils. Using this information together with the training and support provided, schools should:

- identify strengths and weaknesses in teaching and determine what good practices can be built on and what areas need to be improved, and take action to improve them;

- review their mathematics curriculum plans, ensuring there is a good breadth and balance for all pupils and that all pupils receive sufficient attention;

- use the Framework for Teaching Mathematics to direct medium- and long-term planning strategies, identifying clear progression within and across year groups and from Key Stage 1 to Key Stage 2;

- ensure that expectations of what pupils can achieve are high enough to challenge all pupils and to raise standards to the level that pupils are capable of achieving;

- establish procedures to identify pupils who are underachieving and provide them with the support they require to progress at the rate expected of them;

- use assessment information to organise pupils in ways appropriate to the school's circumstances, which help with the teaching of mathematics;

- establish a daily mathematics lesson for all pupils with a clear beginning, middle and end, adopting the flexible structure identified in the Framework for Teaching Mathematics;

- monitor and review the balance in the time pupils spend on oral and mental work in mathematics lessons, in particular to ensure:

  - written methods are not introduced before pupils acquire appropriate understanding of the mental strategies that support them;

  - pupils are taught to use precise mathematical language and recognise words and symbols in regular use;

  - pupils have the opportunity to develop their communication skills and learn how to explain their methods and present a reasoned argument;

- audit the availability and use of teaching materials in the classroom, including information and communication technology resources, and provide teachers with guidance on their use, particularly those that can model mathematical structures and operations;

- ensure that mathematics co-ordinators receive the support of the headteacher in order to be able to undertake the role expected of them, including the monitoring and influencing of practice and the raising of attainment.

12.3 Science

Standards of achievement

Standards of achievement in science have risen over the four years under review as the National Curriculum has become more firmly established in primary schools. In 1994 the main obstacle to higher standards in science was teachers' lack of expertise in what was, for many, still a relatively new curriculum area. Confidence and expertise have grown considerably since then, and as a result standards are now higher and far less uneven than they were at the start of the review period.

The proportion of pupils achieving national expectations at the end of Key Stage 1 has remained nearly constant at 85 per cent, but there has been a slow increase in the incidence of higher levels. At Key Stage 2, the proportion of pupils reaching Level 4 or above has risen slowly, although in 1995 an unexpectedly high number attained Level 5; this was attributed to the changes in the National Curriculum Order and the decision to base national tests on the reduced curriculum.

Standards in Life Processes and Living Things remain slightly higher than other sections of the programme of study, partly because this area is the most familiar to many teachers. Although Experimental and Investigative Science incorporates elements of pre-National Curriculum primary practice, standards in this section are the most variable. In some schools excellent investigative work is carried out and pupils achieve high standards; able pupils at Key Stage 2 are, however, not always given the opportunities to achieve the higher levels of which they are capable.

The progress made by pupils in science at Key Stage 1 has improved steadily and now compares favourably with that in other subjects. For example, by the end of that key stage most pupils are able to name the external parts of their bodies and can recognise how the five senses help them to find out about the world around them. They know what is needed to sustain life and that differences in local environments affect which plants and animals are likely to be found. Techniques for simple classification are well understood, although pupils often have more experience of grouping materials than living things.

Through practical activities such as cooking, pupils learn that materials can change. Work on electricity, light and sound is well established and the majority of pupils have a good understanding of Level 2 expectations in these areas. In all these contexts, pupils are able to engage in simple practical work and to make and record appropriate observations, and most are able to describe what happened and compare this with what they expected. Pupils' use of simple scientific terminology has improved but excessive use of worksheets for recording is still too common. Pupils recognise the need for scientific tests to be "fair" but only a minority understand the significance of this in a range of contexts.

Progress during Key Stage 2 is far less steady, although overall it is now better than in other subjects. There is an established "dip" in progress at the start of the key stage. This has become less marked recently but Year 3 remains weak, with many pupils marking time following good progress in Key Stage 1. By contrast, most pupils make very good progress in science during Years 5 and 6.

By the end of Key Stage 2 most pupils know the scientific names for major organs of human body systems, can identify where these are and have some knowledge of their function. They recognise that feeding relationships exist between plants and animals in a habitat but many have difficulty in representing these by food chains in less familiar contexts. Pupils are able to explain how materials can be classified by their properties and the simple techniques used to separate mixtures, although dissolving, evaporation and condensation are often not well understood. Knowledge of electrical circuits is extended to switches and their function, with a minority of pupils gaining an understanding of electric current as a flow which can be changed. Ideas about gravitational attraction, balanced forces and shadow formation are, however, not well understood.

The quality of teaching

Teachers' knowledge of science and confidence in teaching it have grown considerably during the period 1994–98. As a result, the quality of teaching has improved and now compares favourably with that in most other subjects. Science co-ordinators have had a major influence on the quality of teaching and it remains the case that teaching is often strongest where the co-ordinator is most influential and well informed.

For some years after the introduction of the National Curriculum, science teaching was weaker at Key Stage 2 than Key Stage 1. Many teachers who lacked qualifications in science struggled with the concepts and methodology involved. Difficulties were greatest at Key Stage 2 where there were most demands on teachers' subject knowledge and in physical science, which for many was the least familiar area. A combination of training, self-help and the clarification provided by feedback from tests has greatly improved the knowledge base of teachers and has enabled almost all to reach an acceptable level of competence. There are still a few residual difficulties; teachers' knowledge of physical science remains weaker than other areas and so standards are lower, and their uncertainty about higher-level scientific ideas holds some abler Key Stage 2 pupils back.

The most effective teaching makes use of discussion and probing questions to encourage pupils to talk through their ideas and so develop understanding. More teachers now feel sufficiently confident in their own knowledge to embark on discussion and allow pupils time to attempt their own explanations, as in the following lesson:

Before starting an investigation [into] dissolving jelly in water, the children discussed with the teacher what questions they would try to answer, how they would go about doing so and what they expected to happen. One pupil suggested that separating the jelly cubes would "make it easier for the water to get to the bits", another suggested that hot water would make the jelly "melt more easily", another that stirring would "help keep the water and jelly mixed up". The teacher responded positively to all these suggestions but reminded the children about earlier work they had done on melting and made a note to check again later that they understood the distinction between this and dissolving.

Where teachers stay well within their sphere of confidence, this can result in narrow lesson objectives, a restricted range of teaching approaches and an undue emphasis on the transmission of factual information.

As teachers' own confidence has grown, their expectations of what pupils can achieve have been raised; they are now high (good or very good) in almost half of schools. In the small proportion of lessons where expectations are low, this is often because the focus is upon the activity rather than the science to be learnt. Planning has improved considerably, particularly at Key Stage 2, where the increase in single-subject teaching has led to improved development of pupils' ideas. Exemplar schemes of work produced by local authorities and, more recently, the QCA have greatly helped and have enabled teachers to concentrate on preparing lessons for their own classes. However, some of this short-term planning fails to identify in enough detail the science which pupils at different levels of attainment should learn from activities, an essential prerequisite of effective day-to-day assessment.

Curriculum and assessment

When first introduced, National Curriculum science occupied a large proportion of taught time

(up to 20 per cent) and many topics had a scientific theme, often at the expense of non-core subjects. Since 1994, moves towards the discrete teaching of subjects, particularly at Key Stage 2, have accelerated, and science now typically occupies 10 per cent of taught time at Key Stage 1 and a little more at Key Stage 2; this is sufficient to cover the programme of study. Most schools have a "rolling programme" which ensures that sections of the programme of study are revisited every two years; this is particularly important at Key Stage 2, where mid-key-stage expectations have been too low. National tests have had an impact on the curriculum. They have given teachers a clearer idea of what pupils are expected to know and do and have sharpened teaching. Many schools spend a substantial amount of time on revision for tests in Year 6; at best this consolidates pupils' knowledge and broadens their understanding but can, when too closely focused on test items, be unproductive.

Whole-school and class planning have also improved considerably during the four-year review period, but in about a quarter of schools insufficient attention is given to structuring the work so that it builds on previous learning and becomes progressively more demanding. Where the purpose of classroom activities is not sufficiently well defined, this can lead to the same ground being inadvertently covered at a later stage. For example:

Initial planning identifies a two-year cycle but the broad brushstrokes of this, which are directly related to the National Curriculum, are not precisely elaborated in the medium term to ensure progression through the elements of the programmes of study. Short-term planning does not identify possible opportunities for progression within lessons to ensure that the more able pupils are challenged and that the lessons move forward at the appropriate pace. The activities suggested in the scheme of work are not in sufficient detail – this has led to misinterpretation, leading to repetition in Years 4 and 5.

Procedures for assessing pupils' attainment in science have improved slowly at Key Stage 2. The data obtained is usually used to monitor progress towards test targets and inform reports to parents. The use of assessment information to inform discussion about teaching approaches and the curriculum is far less common, although there is more good practice; for example, some schools make good use of the end-of-Key-Stage 2 tests to diagnose strengths and weaknesses in their science curriculum.

Leadership and management

One of the strongest influences on the development of science in primary schools has been the subject co-ordinator. This has been a particularly crucial role in science, because for many it has been a relatively new subject and one in which relatively few primary teachers have an initial qualification. The co-ordinators' role has broadened considerably. Initially they saw their principal tasks as the organisation of equipment for practical work and the provision of day-to-day support for colleagues; now most become involved in planning for science across the school and, as time permits, visiting lessons and working with colleagues in order to monitor and improve the quality of classroom practice. Much of the progress made in implementing National Curriculum science can be attributed to good leadership by co-ordinators as in the following examples:

The curriculum leader has no formal science qualifications but has attended many courses and is interested and enthusiastic. She supports teachers in planning, knows where weaknesses lie and has taken steps to address them, eg tracking strands of Attainment Target 1. Planning is monitored and teachers supported with practical help and advice.

The efforts of the knowledgeable and effective co-ordinator have been influential in raising standards in science over the three years she has been at the school. She has worked closely with staff, carried out informal visits to lessons and provided ongoing support. Staff have worked with the co-ordinator to produce a clear policy and a very good scheme of work which incorporates a well-defined assessment procedure.

Improving standards of science: the way forward

In order to raise standards further, schools should:

- take steps to ensure that all sections of the programme of study receive sufficient attention, including the important guidance given in the introduction to each attainment target;

- use the Year 4 assessment tasks or other means to check that pupils are making sufficient progress in the first half of Key Stage 2;

- continue to support those teachers who are less confident in teaching science by the use of training and detailed planning;

- review planning to check that the scientific outcomes of lessons are clear and that these take account of pupils' prior experiences and learning. The QCA exemplar scheme of work provides a helpful model and suggests, for each unit of work, what pupils should be able to know and do by the end;

- develop their own manageable ways of recording pupils' progress so that this can be used when teachers prepare lessons and evaluate the success of complete topics at a later date;

- continue to seek ways of enabling co-ordinators to maintain a whole-school perspective of the science curriculum and teaching.

12.4 Art

Standards of achievement

Standards of achievement rose steadily in art in primary schools between 1994 and 1998. The proportion of good or very good work rose from about one-quarter in 1994 to one-third in 1998. In the same period, the proportion of unsatisfactory work fell overall, at Key Stage 1 from about one-fifth to well below one-tenth, and at Key Stage 2 from one-fifth to just above one-tenth.

The level of skills in handling familiar two- and three-dimensional materials was progressively raised, and pupils had better knowledge of and opinions on art by 1998. Nevertheless, standards of art still varied considerably between and within schools. In too many schools and classrooms, art remains an undemanding subject in which teachers have low expectations and pupils lack sufficient understanding of the subject. In these schools, insufficient attention has been given to the development of skills and techniques, or to encouraging pupils to talk about art.

Pupils enjoy art. They respond with good levels of concentration to opportunities to work with two- and three-dimensional materials. Less able pupils frequently respond particularly well to art and make good progress. Where the teaching is good and standards high, pupils can talk about their work and say something about how their ideas originated and how their techniques developed. Increasingly, pupils are able to talk about the work of other artists; in the best cases, pupils in Years 5 and 6 have a lively awareness of the work of some important artists. For example, in one school a group of Year 6 pupils had studied the paintings of Leger, had made drawings from his work in their sketchbooks, and had produced very large group paintings which showed how volume could be represented through tone and colour. They were able to talk about Leger's work and describe its characteristics.

The quality of teaching

The quality of teaching in art has improved throughout the period from 1994 to 1998. For example, the proportion of good lessons has risen from one-third to one-half. In the best lessons, teachers plan well, organise materials and equipment carefully, make their classrooms attractive with displays of pupils' work and artefacts, and capitalise on children's curiosity and readiness to experiment. These teachers have a clear idea of what constitutes good standards in art, and have high expectations of their pupils. They share these expectations through direct instruction in the classroom, through discussion and through the display of art in school. A proper emphasis is given to the teaching of skills, particularly drawing from observation, memory and imagination.

The proportion of poor lessons fell from two in ten in 1994 to one in ten by 1996/97; this latter statistic has subsequently proved difficult to shift, and there remain about 10 per cent of art lessons in which the teaching is poor. Where the teaching is poor, it is usually because the subject is treated superficially and regarded as relatively less important than other subjects; the full potential of materials and equipment is never explored. Teachers fail to understand, for example, the importance of different sizes of brush and types of paper in changing and improving the outcome of a painting exercise. The requirement to cover Attainment Target 2 (Knowledge and Understanding) often produces work with too much emphasis on copying a picture rather than studying and adapting the technique employed by

the artist for the pupils' own use. Too often teachers focus on working from readily accessible reproductions of Impressionist paintings (which are often very sophisticated and complex works) while ignoring other more rewarding forms of art such as narrative painting.

Although there was an improvement in the overall quality of art teaching, this was not as rapid as it could have been. At the beginning of the inspection cycle, art was largely taught by class teachers, many of whom were still unfamiliar with the National Curriculum requirements and who often lacked experience in organising and using the materials involved. Most schools then appointed art co-ordinators; in some schools, but not all, they were given the support, time and resources to carry out their role effectively. However, many co-ordinators have not been provided with sufficient time or opportunity to disseminate specialist advice to colleagues. Further, in some schools, co-ordinators were appointed who knew little more about the subject than their colleagues. There was insufficient and, over the period, worsening provision of specialist in-service training courses to ensure teachers were developing the skills, knowledge and understanding required to teach and manage art effectively.

Nevertheless, co-ordinators and other teachers generally became more familiar with the National Curriculum requirements and were able to improve their command of the subject, helped in many cases by the experience of teaching the programmes of study.

Where an art co-ordinator had subject expertise or was able to develop it, and was given the opportunity to take a lead in setting standards, raising expectations and demonstrating how these could be achieved in practical terms, teachers became much more confident and standards rose accordingly. Similarly, teaching improved where teachers were able to attend practical in-service training sessions aimed specifically at enhancing their skills in the teaching of the two attainment targets of the National Curriculum, namely Investigating and Making, and Knowledge and Understanding.

Assessment in art improved over the review period, but there were still weaknesses which stemmed from the lack of a workable national assessment regime for the subject. At the start of the period, in too many schools teachers did not assess art systematically. Where a school has no systematic approach to assessment in art, it is difficult for teachers to judge and raise standards of achievement. The modification of statutory assessment requirements into end-of-key-stage descriptions following the Dearing Review led to some improvements, and teachers began to be aware – as they were in other subjects – of the importance of reaching judgements in art that were consistent with colleagues in their own and other schools. An SCAA document entitled "Expectations in Art at Key Stages 1 and 2", published in 1997, was useful in helping teachers to make these judgements, but had limited impact at such a late stage in the period under discussion.

The most effective developments in assessment were seen where a co-ordinator built up a profile of art in the school by collecting pieces of good work and used this as a guide for the whole staff to establish and raise expectations. Displays of pupils' work were used to help teachers assess accurately. Sketchbooks were used increasingly to provide individual records of pupils' work. Collecting portfolios of pupils' work, showing the development of, for example, their drawing and painting over a year, and showing a range of work at various levels of attainment, has helped in co-ordinating teachers' judgements and in planning work. In a small proportion of schools, teachers related achievement in art to the end-of-key-stage descriptions for the purposes of reporting to parents.

Curriculum and lesson planning

Good curriculum planning helps promote the progressive acquisition and reinforcement of skills. It should define the learning objectives for a series of art lessons, and not simply the art activities to be covered. Good lesson planning highlights the particular skill or knowledge to be developed, includes opportunities for the teacher to demonstrate techniques, and allows the teacher to check what pupils know or can do. Where art takes place alongside other activities – which is often the case in primary schools, particularly at Key Stage 1 – lesson planning can help to ensure that the focus remains on the quality of the experience and the outcome, and that classroom assistants and other helpers are well briefed about the work.

The coverage of craft and design within the art programmes of study has been very patchy. There is rarely reference to, for example, English textile or fashion designers; this work is not often seen in primary schools as relevant to the art curriculum and yet textiles and fashion are highly successful products of English art education. Too few teachers use work from different cultures, such as Indian or African art forms, as source material, and although this has improved over the four-year period, references are frequently superficial.

Resources

The National Curriculum has made a heavy demand on schools in terms of the range and quality of resources required by the programmes of study. In the period 1994 to 1998, most schools provided adequate resources for two-dimensional work but continued to be less well resourced for three-dimensional work. Although the provision of information and communication technology has improved over the period, its use within art lessons was generally underdeveloped as primary teachers lacked awareness of its potential as an art medium.

At the start of the period, books, posters and reproductions to support the teaching of Attainment Target 2 (Knowledge and Understanding) were being acquired ever more widely by schools, and by 1998 most had at least an adequate collection of books and reproductions of the work of famous artists. However, the focus has been largely on readily available images such as the paintings of the Impressionists, with a consequent narrowness to pupils' learning about the work of a variety of artists. Despite the availability of resources, many teachers, lacking effective guidance, are still not sure how to use them to best effect.

Well resourced lessons provide pupils with good-quality materials chosen carefully to match learning objectives. Where, for example, Year 6 pupils observe and record the effects of light and shade on natural forms, a selection of different grades of pencils used with good cartridge paper allows them to respond accurately and sensitively to what they see. The expressive potential of charcoal is only fully exploited where a teacher knows about, demonstrates and provides examples of the range of tonal effects which can be achieved by working on a rough-toothed, tinted sugar paper, holding the charcoal in different positions relative to the work surface. Without the teaching, pupils working with charcoal usually achieve little more than with pencil.

There is a small but significant proportion of primary schools where an insufficient range of basic equipment and materials restricts the variety and quality of art work. Accommodation is broadly satisfactory, although very few schools provide a specialist room or studio. In the majority of schools, accommodation is sufficient for National Curriculum art, although in some schools the limitations of working and storage space restricts art activities mainly to two dimensions. There are some relatively common weaknesses, however: not all classes have ready access to running water, enough space for pupils to work freely, or sufficient storage or display facilities.

Improving standards of art: the way forward

The period from 1994 to 1998 saw significant changes and some improvements in the teaching of art in English primary schools. The main improvements which schools should be seeking to achieve are:

- establishing greater progression in the teaching of art, particularly the skills of drawing;

- providing pupils with enough experience of two- and three-dimensional work for them to develop confidence in their ability to express their ideas in visual and tactile form;

- increasing the opportunities for teachers to refine judgements on standards in art, across individual schools and between schools.

12.5 Design and technology

Standards of achievement

Pupils' achievement in design and technology in primary schools has improved slowly but steadily since 1994. Although achievement remains more limited than for most other subjects, standards have improved more rapidly since the implementation of the revised National Curriculum Order in 1995. Pupils are better at the practical skills of making products than at designing them. Both making and designing skills are stronger than pupils' knowledge and understanding of technology.

Throughout the review period, pupils' designing skills have lagged behind their making skills because most teachers are unsure how best to structure and develop this aspect of design and technology. However, with improving teaching, pupils' designing is getting better. Teachers have increasingly realised the crucial role of discussion in helping pupils to improve their designing skills and that designing is more than just drawing ideas. At Key Stage 1, as pupils discuss their design ideas with each other and with their teacher, they realise the strengths and weaknesses of these ideas and make practical suggestions about how they might proceed. Through the answers to the teachers' questions they show that they have a clearer idea of what they are trying to do, that they understand how materials will function and how tools can be used to adapt them. While they are making and when talking about their finished products, they evaluate their work with an increasing understanding of the need to meet a specification of what the product has got to look like and to do.

At Key Stage 2, pupils now use an increasing range of strategies, especially where designing skills are good, in order to establish what they are expected to do. They understand that there is a need which requires a practical solution. They are guided to use interviews, questionnaires, books, magazines and information technology systems to find out more about the problem and potential solutions. In the very best lessons, pupils plan their work to help ensure they have the time and resources to complete the task on time. By the time they reach the end of Year 6, high-attaining pupils can use drawings and modelling techniques to good effect. These pupils also recognise the need to try several potential solutions to see how they work, before deciding on the most suitable proposal. They can, for instance, use sketches with notes alongside to explain their train of thinking, and cut-away drawings to explain the inside workings of their products. For example:

A Year 6 class was set a design task to work in groups to produce a model car which would travel two metres, cost less than £4, and be of attractive appearance. Pupils had to justify their designs against given criteria, produce an invoice for the materials, with penalty points for every 10p over £4, as well as design and make the car. They drew on a range of sources for ideas, but there was no direct copying. They used glue guns, drills, rasps, saws, craft knives, bench hooks and a vice efficiently and accurately; used correct terminology such as "chassis, aerodynamic, spoiler, body-shell" accurately and with confidence; could discriminate between different woods; made continuous reference to the design brief; and were able to comment knowledgeably on design faults brought to their notice by the teacher.

Pupils' competence in using materials and components has improved and more now use a wider range than four years ago. The technological use of resistant materials, paper and card has remained better than attainment with mouldable materials, textiles, food or electrical and mechanical components. Work with textiles, for example, is often concerned only with aesthetic appearance and not with function. Similarly, while most pupils understand how to mix and blend food ingredients and know that cooking changes the taste, texture and appearance of some ingredients, very few know how to improve these characteristics by adding another ingredient, altering the proportions of ingredients, or by using different preparation techniques.

At best, pupils build on their earlier experience and develop an increasing range of techniques so that, for example, they are able to choose when to use different types of glue and when best to use different fasteners such as staples, paper clips, split fasteners and sewing to join paper, card and fabrics successfully. They learn to be selective and use materials economically, with an eye to fitness for purpose.

Knowledge and understanding of mechanisms and control has steadily improved. More pupils now know how to use simple mechanisms to produce different types of movement and know how to use switched electrical circuits. For example, they often use switches and batteries to provide lights on model vehicles or buildings that they make. Overall, however, even by the end of Key Stage 2 most pupils' levels of knowledge and understanding of structures and of mechanical and electrical components remain low. Similarly, although teachers have increasingly realised the importance of the correct use of technological vocabulary and language, and pupils often enjoy using new and unfamiliar specialist words, this is

an underdeveloped aspect of the subject in many schools.

The National Curriculum Order for design and technology expects pupils to apply skills, knowledge and understanding from the programmes of study of other subjects, particularly from science, mathematics and art. Initially this occurred infrequently and incidentally. Now planning has improved, and pupils make more use of what they have learned in other subjects and make better progress as a result. But this is a two-way process; attainment in literacy and numeracy and in various subjects of the curriculum is enhanced as pupils engage is designing and making. For example, in one school pupils' understanding of life in wartime was heightened by analysing gas masks and selecting materials to model their own designs. Those pupils who are less interested in reading fiction are often motivated to read non-fiction books to find out about some aspect of their design and technology work. Measuring, marking and charting skills are often practised, and the concept of "fair testing" is frequently used as pupils select the best material for a particular task. For example:

A Year 2 class made products to "keep Teddy dry" in rainy weather. Pupils discussed the problem as a whole class and then suggested various solutions – coat, boots, hat, umbrella – and what materials would be most suitable. They "fair tested" a range of textiles and flexible plastic sheeting to see which were waterproof and experimented with each to find out how they might be shaped and joined. By carefully examining their own wet-weather wear they were able to see how each item was made. In groups they evolved their designs for different garments, developing paper patterns and choosing the best joining methods. They made the items before trying them out for fit and considering how they might be improved. The planning decisions, accounts of the work and evaluation of the results were all recorded using discussion, drawings, written notes and an excellent wall display. The account of this work in the SCAA exemplar material has encouraged other schools to develop their own versions of similar activities.

The quality of teaching

When compared with other subjects, there has

been a marked improvement in the quality of teaching in design and technology. The majority of teachers found the original Order for design and technology problematic: not only was it difficult to understand and open to wide differences in interpretation, but there was insufficient time for teachers to plan the required new approaches. The introduction of the revised National Curriculum for design and technology helped schools know what they should teach and was a major factor in the significant improvements in the quality of teaching.

Design and technology is still a comparatively new subject in the primary curriculum, although some of the elements of it were already well established. Initially, teachers tended to make the tasks that they set pupils either too prescriptive, little more than a "craft" experience with pupils making identical products, or excessively open-ended with pupils not equipped with the knowledge and skills required for the design task. As teachers improved their understanding of the objectives of the subject and expectations became clearer, they learned how best to structure the work and pitch it more appropriately. Consequently, standards of pupils' work have improved.

The establishment of an effective subject co-ordinator for design and technology has led to the greatest improvements in teaching. Building the expertise of subject co-ordinators has been an important objective of in-service training, especially through extended courses, and where teachers have opportunities to share the benefits of the training with their colleagues in the school. In these circumstances, all aspects of design and technology have improved: staff have become more confident; subject knowledge has become more secure; schemes of work, progression and lesson planning have become more focused; and resources have been used more efficiently and effectively. Importantly, teachers have lost their previous apprehension of design and technology and become more confident in teaching the subject.

Although most teachers have now gained a basic understanding of the materials, equipment, processes and pedagogy associated with design and technology, the more demanding aspects of the subject, especially for many of those teaching the older and the more able pupils, still need attention. Teachers' lack of subject knowledge and expertise remains a constraint to progress in many schools.

It is for this reason that the early good progress in Key Stage 1 is not maintained in Key Stage 2, where subject knowledge is more demanding.

The planning of units of work and of lessons has improved markedly, although overall planning of schemes of work is less satisfactory. Pupils' designing tends to be better when teachers plan units of work that link together the three types of activity identified in the National Curriculum: "design and make" assignments; focused practical tasks; and product analysis when pupils investigate, disassemble and evaluate existing products. This last activity develops pupils' understanding of why things are as they are and helps them design higher-quality products for themselves.

Teachers' familiarity with the revised Order, the sharing of experience between schools and the publication of examples of the high quality of work produced in some schools have contributed to much raised expectations of what pupils can do, although they remain poor in a quarter of schools.

Whereas previously teachers were not sure about asking pupils questions about their design ideas, good teachers now often use questioning to good effect, prompting pupils to question for themselves and look at problems afresh. At best, pupils are given responsibility for organising their work, but their plans are frequently questioned and checked by the teacher. Teachers have a clear idea of what pupils are doing, and know when to intervene. When evaluating the products that pupils have made, teachers look for and make sure that pupils understand the reasons why some things perform well and others do not. Teachers are more able to judge pupils' attainments in design and technology and give them constructive feedback about what they need to do to improve their work.

The curriculum

At the start of the inspection cycle there were few materials available for schools to use to support their planning, especially in those local education authorities where there was no specialist advisory support. The exemplar material provided by SCAA and *Guidance Materials for Key Stages 1 and 2*, published by the Design and Technology Association, provided much needed support and guidance and has led to an improvement in the quality of planning. The latter was purchased by over 15,000 schools, indicating the extent of perceived need.

There has been an increase in the use of longer blocks of time for design and technology projects, because teachers are finding this is a more efficient way for pupils to develop their skills. On the other hand, the amount of curriculum time given to design and technology has dropped slightly over the last four years.

Funding for design and technology has struggled to keep pace with the increasing costs of materials and equipment. Some schools have been hard-pressed to extend resources to cover the full expectations of the National Curriculum, resulting in a narrower range of work, especially in areas such as control technology.

Similarly, in some schools cramped classrooms have made it difficult to make effective use of equipment. A lack of sinks, often in temporary classrooms, restricts the range of materials that can be used. A lack of equipment and appropriate accommodation has meant that some pupils have had little opportunity to undertake work in food technology.

Improving standards of design and technology: the way forward

There is considerable scope for improving the quality of teaching and standards of design and technology in primary schools. Nevertheless, the impact of in-service training has done much to promote the subject in schools, improve the confidence and skills of teachers, and raise standards. The first priority for those schools which struggle to provide good-quality design and technology should be to increase the subject knowledge of the teachers, particularly the co-ordinator. Beyond this, there are three further areas for development which would help to improve standards. Schools should:

- ensure that design and technology work is progressively more demanding, building on pupils' previous experience by collecting and analysing samples of pupils' designing and making work from each year group;

- develop and make the most of the specialist expertise that co-ordinators and other teachers already have, by pooling knowledge and sharing ideas;

- ensure that pupils have access to an adequate range of materials and tools when they are designing and making.

12.6 Geography

Standards of achievement

Standards of achievement in geography in primary schools have improved steadily since 1994. At that time, and with the National Curriculum only just beginning to be implemented, the general quality of geography was particularly weak and a low baseline from which to start. Although standards have improved, there remains a substantial gap between successful and weaker schools. By 1998, pupils' progress was satisfactory in seven schools in ten and good in two in ten – significant improvements, although in comparison with most other subjects there was less good progress. There is now less unsatisfactory and more good work in geography than previously. There remains a great deal to do to improve standards and progress, but the evidence of the past four years indicates the benefits of the National Curriculum Order for geography and that continuing improvement is possible with sufficient support for schools and teachers.

The state of geography in primary schools was generally poor in 1994, typified by a great variety of practices ranging from excellent to non-existent. This pattern was long-established. The HMI survey of primary education in 1978[72] had noted that at least one-tenth of pupils in Years 4, 5 and 6 received no geographical education and that where it occurred there was often unnecessary repetition of content. Some ten years later the situation was found still to be poor:[73]

> *Overall standards of work in geography were very disappointing; in only one-quarter of both infant and junior schools and departments were they satisfactory or better... in a minority of schools there was either no or very little teaching of geography.*

This was the baseline to be built on when the National Curriculum for geography came into force in 1992, making geography an entitlement foundation subject for all primary school pupils.

The increasingly successful practice in geography starts from this relatively low point and is based

---

[72] *Primary Education in England: A Survey by HM Inspectors of Schools.* HMSO, 1978.

[73] *Aspects of Primary Education: The Teaching and Learning of History and Geography.* HMSO, 1989.

on much very good work by teachers, many of whom have had minimal initial and subsequent in-service education in geography. The general lack of teachers' subject expertise and experience of geography was not helped by the overcomplex and detailed initial Order for geography, which many schools found difficult to distil into a usable scheme of work. The revisions to this Order in 1995 have resulted in simpler and clearer programmes of study for Key Stage 1 and Key Stage 2, including a reduction from five attainment targets to one. Almost all schools have now made these programmes of study into schemes of work which can be used by teachers with their developing subject knowledge to plan units of geography based on places, themes and skills. They have been assisted in this by slowly improving resources and particularly by helpful guidance materials about geography – for example, from the SCAA and subsequently the QCA, and from the Geographical Association.

In one-third of lessons in Key Stage 1 and Key Stage 2 pupils now make good progress, and satisfactory progress in much of the rest. There is unsatisfactory progress in one lesson in ten in Key Stage 1, and in one in seven in Key Stage 2. The number of lessons in which good progress is made declines between Years 2 and 3, from one-third of lessons to one-quarter, but then climbs steadily to better than one-third in Year 6. There are more unsatisfactory lessons in Key Stage 2 than Key Stage 1, largely because of the poor progress in one lesson in six in Years 3 and 4. Progress in individual schools, as opposed to all lessons, is good in one-fifth of all schools in both key stages and unsatisfactory in one in ten schools in Key Stage 1 and one in eight in Key Stage 2.

Typically, pupils: develop a sense of direction with left and right and points of the compass; are able to follow routes and make plans of their journeys; create maps, analyse photographs and write about how places they have studied are similar or different from each other; undertake field visits and use instruments to measure the weather; investigate their local environment; learn enquiry skills; use specialist vocabulary in their discussions and writing; study contrasting places in the UK and abroad, identifying changes taking place; consider topical environmental issues, ranging from local concerns with transport and shopping to global ones about deforestation.

Strengths and weaknesses

Pupils in both key stages make good progress where their learning is based on practical experiences and activities. The positive impact of site visits, especially residential courses in Key Stage 2, is noticeable in the quality and quantity of work produced as well as the enthusiasm to learn. Some schools have arranged links with other schools, as examples of "contrasting localities", and these have had beneficial effects on geographical understanding and interest as well as social development. This type of work is frequently linked with investigative skills and the development of an enquiry-based approach in which, for example, local issues are successfully addressed through studying the effects of a new bypass or the change of use of a building or piece of land.

The strengths in primary geography lie in the suitable use of geographical terms and vocabulary; in the development of investigative and enquiry skills; and in the good quality of the practical and field study, which gives good understanding of the local area. In Key Stage 2, for example, the skills of observation, recording and mapping are well developed in studies of local streams and rivers, in places where pupils live and how these change; and in the regular recording of weather and seasons, which allows an understanding of how weather and climate affect people's lives. Many pupils have a good knowledge of some distant places, such as the nature of village life in India or China, and through the use of text, photos and films, and often with food and artefacts, develop a sense of what such places are like. Nevertheless, the quality of the study of distant places varies considerably.

Unsatisfactory standards arise for a variety of reasons. Too often, pupils are insufficiently challenged or stimulated by the tasks set (for example, repetition of four-figure map co-ordinates, colouring in rather than devising a key). Pupils have poorly developed enquiry skills because of overdirected tasks or a lack of opportunity to investigate geographical issues. They have a limited range of communication skills of a geographical nature, insufficiently using maps, plans, diagrams and field sketches. Attainment for some pupils is limited by the irregular teaching of geography, and in both key stages progress is also limited by insufficient opportunities to discuss geographical issues. In Key Stage 2 some pupils rarely undertake any extended writing in geography, being limited to short answers of a descriptive nature, and little exercise in analysis and explanation. For some pupils locational and factual knowledge is not retained because the contexts for learning were forgettable and practice infrequent.

The quality of teaching

In Key Stages 1 and 2 teaching is now good in one-third of schools and satisfactory in most of the rest: a steady improvement in recent years. There is still unsatisfactory teaching in Key Stage 2 in one in ten schools and lessons, but this is a significant improvement on the position four years ago, when one-fifth of lessons were unsatisfactory. Although much geography teaching is now satisfactory, there is less good teaching than in most of the other subjects taken by the same teacher. This situation is often the result of teachers with limited subject expertise still coming to terms with the new geography Order of 1995 and devising ways of organising a flexible curriculum content into suitable units of work and lessons. Teachers have become more successful when supported by an effective geography co-ordinator and suitable resources. Although the quality of teaching is improving steadily, it is often variable within schools (often between key stages) as well as between schools.

Good teaching is associated with a detailed scheme of work, offering clear guidance on learning outcomes, suitable teaching activities, resources and means of assessment. Weaker teaching often lacks this support, where there has been little or no in-service training for the co-ordinator or classroom teacher. Geography has had limited priority in many school development plans and is rarely a key issue for improvement. A fundamental feature of good geography teaching is good subject knowledge, which is particularly shown in some local work and in studies of more distant places in Key Stage 2. Using practical and field-based studies, skilled geography teachers use the school grounds and the local area effectively in ways in which geographical skills and knowledge develop progressively. In Years 5 and 6 the teaching and curriculum design often have a sharper focus on geographical topics than in other years, and it is in these years that much of the best teaching is seen. The following, from **Standlake CE Primary School**,

Oxfordshire, is an example of such teaching:

Pupils in Years 5 and 6 studied the effects of a new retail store on a nearby market town. (The school's long term planning had taken account of "topicality" and the new store offered a good opportunity for a geographical enquiry.) The school made contact with the store management and was given support for the project and access to the site. As a result of their work, over some ten hours, the pupils found out about the effects of the new store on existing provision by using interviews and questionnaires and by plotting changes in pedestrian and traffic patterns. They developed their mapping skills and entered data on suitable information technology software. The outcomes were some excellent written and cartographical analysis, presentation and evaluation of quantitative data and an assessment of understanding through the pupils' ability to vigorously debate the issue of change and its effects on their local area and families.

Many of the features of poor geography teaching stem from inadequate subject expertise or a lack of understanding of the requirements of the programmes of study. When the geographical principles and ideas are not fully understood, objectives for units of work and lessons are often poorly defined. Lack of confidence and competence about subject matter also leads to poor planning, inadequate sequencing of activities, and an undemanding and narrow range of tasks, resulting in boredom and underachievement.

Raising standards of geography: issues and some ways forward

When teachers have greater confidence in their subject knowledge and how to use it, the quality of teaching improves. Many primary teachers have had limited initial training in geography and little in-service training since. Where geography co-ordinators and teachers have attended the local education authority Grants for Education Support and Training (GEST) courses, or used other specialist consultants, there has been a noticeable, and at times substantial, improvement in planning and a better understanding of the National Curriculum requirements.

At the beginning of the review period many teachers were confused by the content and complexity of the initial geography Order, and this was visible in the quality of work. The revised Order, simpler in structure and reduced in content, has allowed many schools to devise a scheme of work with a clearer focus. The effects of this are still working their way through, with more schools working confidently, although with a few still having only an outline policy and sketchy guidelines for implementation.

Geography suffers from inadequate resourcing in one school in seven. Resourcing is weak in a number of areas: atlases suitable for different ages; globes; films which illustrate case material; wall maps; photographs, including aerial photographs related to base maps; instruments for field study, for example to measure weather; and texts, especially of more-distant places. Some schools have built up good resources to match their curriculum, but geography has rarely been a priority subject for in-service training or funds; and some of the early purchases to meet the requirements of the first Order have not been entirely suitable.

The role of the geography co-ordinator, backed by firm leadership from senior staff, has been critical in promoting higher-quality teaching. However, too often the postholder has had little specialist training and is given no time to work with other teachers. Although some schools and their geography co-ordinators are active in geographical curriculum development, a significant number are not; for instance, a report states that "there is no policy, no scheme of work and teachers refer directly to the programme of study". In these circumstances the quality of teaching is unlikely to improve, and the same applies to standards of pupils' work. Progression of skills is haphazard, there is little continuity of contexts and places and no detailed intentions for lessons which can be evaluated in pupils' work.

The picture presented in this review is of steady improvement but with great variability. In some schools, pupils make good progress and teachers have high expectations; in many others, progress could be improved with clearer leadership and a more systematic professional development for teachers.

Environmental education

Prior to the advent of the National Curriculum, a number of schools made environmental education a positive feature of their curriculum and for a few the environment was an important way of defining the school's ethos, through pupils' work in, for, about and through the environment. This was not commonplace, however, although the National Curriculum Council's Guidance[74] on environmental education had begun to move more schools to recognise the value of environmental education.

The curricular restructuring in the early years of the National Curriculum put environmental education under pressure in many primary schools as teachers grappled with teaching ten subjects. However, as schools have become more confident in managing the requirements of the National Curriculum, they have often seen aspects of environmental education as a valuable means of underpinning work in subjects such as science and mathematics as well as geography.

Increasingly, schools are valuing environmental education as an effective way of making links between subjects, as a major contributor to pupils' moral and social development, and as a way of promoting links between the school and its community. A growing number of schools are now supported in their initiatives by non-governmental organisations which provide human and material help. These initiatives often actively involve the pupils in improving their environment, to make it more sustainable, in making decisions which help them understand simple implications of democracy, and in being responsible for their own and other environments.

A number of schools have recognised that their school can be managed as a microcosm of the wider world, reflecting, for example, the need to be efficient in using resources. Pupils help design changes to their school grounds, often carried out with help from teachers and parents, to provide ponds, gardens, wild areas for butterflies, sculptures, playground markings, trees and artefacts to climb on. The organisation Learning through Landscapes has done much to help schools identify, provide and manage school grounds initiatives.

Some schools take part in the Eco-schools Award of the Tidy Britain Group, where they set up a school council of pupils, teachers, governors,

---

[74] *Curriculum Guidance No 7: Environmental Education.* National Curriculum Council, 1990.

parents and employees to review how energy and water can be used efficiently and how materials are purchased and recycled. This initiative has frequently brought about noticeable reductions in the running costs of schools, as well as involving pupils in a democratic process. Other programmes have, for example, made many pupils aware of responsibilities for sustainable energy consumption. Many schools have benefited from the guidance of the Royal Society for the Protection of Birds in its initiative for a whole-school approach to the environment.

Work in schools also shows concern for a world beyond the gate. Work in geography, particularly, has brought pupils into contact with the developing world – issues such as conservation of rainforests and the effects of tourism on fragile ecosystems. Many pupils are thoughtful and concerned about such matters, and fundraising for conservation projects, both local and overseas, is a feature of many schools' charitable work. Linking the message of far and near is not always translated into actions, however, as litter or graffiti round the school sometimes illustrate.

12.7 History

Before the introduction of the National Curriculum there was relatively little systematic teaching of history in primary schools. There were some very effective studies of history either in its own right or within history-led topics, but these were, as the HMI of the time put it, "rubies in porridge". A decade later, history is prospering in primary schools. A visitor walking round a primary school is now likely to see lively history displays on the walls of classrooms and corridors, as well as artefacts of all kinds and a range of attractive history books. In general, this reflects the fact that most teachers and pupils like history; and this includes many teachers who, for example, dreaded the prospect of teaching about the Greeks but who now relish the retelling of Homeric tales.

Standards of achievement

Over the past four years there has been a modest but steady improvement in standards achieved by pupils in both key stages, with an increase in the number of schools where pupils' progress is satisfactory from eight out of ten to nine out of ten. In 1997/98, history was good overall in two out of

ten schools at Key Stage 1 and in three out of ten schools at Key Stage 2. There is, therefore, considerable room for further improvement.

For history, the knowledge, understanding and skills are set out as "Key Elements", and developed in the context of a prescribed body of content. The Key Elements are: chronology; range and depth of historical knowledge and understanding; interpretations of history; historical enquiry; and organisation and communication.

In Key Stage 1 these Key Elements are taught through broadly defined "Areas of Study", which include family and local history as well as stories of the lives of famous people. In Key Stage 2 the content is set out in the form of six study units: Romans, Anglo-Saxons and Vikings; life in Tudor times; Victorian Britain or Britain since 1930; the Greeks; a past non-European society; and local history.

In Key Stage 1, many pupils gain a sense of time (Key Element 1), often related to their own home, family or school experience. In Key Stage 2, chronology is further developed, for example through increasingly sophisticated use of timelines and terminology. Where progress is weak, it is often for lack of sufficient reinforcement to enable pupils to make links and build up an overview of the past.

Pupils in Key Stage 1 develop their knowledge and understanding of history (Key Element 2) in a wide range of contexts. Much successful work which has meaning for pupils involves hearing about and discussing familiar material such as families, toys, schools and the local area, and comparing old and new. Additionally, some pupils make good progress in retelling stories of famous people and events, and in identifying reasons why people acted as they did. In Key Stage 2, pupils begin to develop an understanding of the organising concepts of history. For example, some pupils in Year 5 and Year 6 are able to account for change in Victorian times, and to explain why Britain went to war with Nazi Germany in 1939. At best, pupils acquire in outline a knowledge and understanding of the main events and characteristics of the period they are studying and additionally study particular aspects in depth. Pupils' knowledge and understanding is weak where they can offer only an overview or a narrow focus on the periods they have studied.

Progress in the Key Element 3, interpretations of history, lags behind that in other Key Elements, and it receives inadequate attention. Key Element 4, historical enquiry, is also weaker in many schools. Where progress is good in Key Stage 1, pupils find out from parents and grandparents about differences in their respective childhoods, or can ask questions of sources of evidence, such as photographs. In Key Stage 2 where progress is good pupils learn to be more discriminating in the selection of evidence; they become aware of the relative value to the historian of particular sources, for example by grasping the problems of bias, the purpose of propaganda, and the advantages and disadvantages of first-hand evidence; and they can combine information in order to produce clear accounts. Often, however, progress in historical enquiry is limited, with pupils taking limited evidence at face value.

In some schools pupils produce excellent individual work as a response to historical questions or open investigations, often illustrated accurately and sometimes using information technology (Key Element 5). On the other hand, some quite extensive written work is of little value because it does no more than transmit information.

The quality of teaching

There has been a steady improvement in the quality of teaching. In 1994/95 teaching was at least satisfactory in eight lessons out of ten; in 1997/98 teaching was at least satisfactory in nine out of ten lessons and good in half of lessons. This reflects both a growth in teachers' expertise and confidence and a growing enjoyment of the subject teaching. The problems identified in 1994/95, including a lack of clear purpose, overdirection, insufficient differentiation, lack of challenge and poor use of resources, can still be found, but to a considerably lesser degree.

Good history teachers are very effective in using stories to develop pupils' knowledge and understanding. For example:

> *In a Year 6 class working on Victorian railways the teacher used expert subject knowledge to tell a compelling story of the development of the railways. The teacher established a clear chronology enlivened with fascinating detail which aroused the pupils' curiosity. This, and a well managed discussion, provided the basis for subsequent tasks in which the pupils further*

> *investigated Victorian railways and produced their own reports.*

Many teachers successfully introduce pupils to sources of historical evidence through the use the local area or of artefacts:

> *In a Year 2 class the teacher made very good use of a favourite guessing game to promote investigative skills. In a well planned lesson, artefacts were used as a medium for discussion about time and evidence. The lesson was great fun, with all pupils involved and willing to use their imagination to identify the artefact and its use. In asking and answering questions, pupils developed their historical vocabulary and their understanding that information can be obtained from a variety of sources.*

Good examples can be found of teaching which, even with younger pupils, develops an understanding that interpretations of the past differ and that this can arise because of the limitations of the available evidence:

> *In a Year 2 class, pupils listened to the story of the wooden horse of Troy, and then quickly drew their own version of what the horse looked like. The teacher used the different versions to show that there are many possible interpretations of what the horse looked like. Pupils discussed why this was the case, establishing that it was impossible to be precise for lack of evidence. In turn, this was related to work already done on the difference between "facts" and "myths", including an appreciation that in telling a story people may exaggerate the truth.*

Conversely, weak teaching occurs where teachers' subject knowledge is insufficient to enable them to relate new work to prior learning, to grip pupils with a well-told story, or to select suitable material for a historical enquiry. Some teachers who succeed in these respects are nevertheless unclear about the sorts of tasks which will help achieve their learning objectives. Frequently teachers "play safe", asking questions which require location and transfer of knowledge rather than higher-level understanding and skills. As with many other subjects, the quality and use of day-to-day assessment is weak; and in too many schools the opportunities to write extensively in a "historical genre" are missed.

The curriculum

In 1991, Key Stage 1 history set out to develop an awareness of the past and how we find out about it, with particular reference to everyday life, famous people and events. This was generally successful, and fitted well with a topic-based approach to the curriculum. It was not, however, without difficulties. In some schools pupils experienced good individual lessons, but their overall programme was limited and incoherent, especially where teachers did not plan for the progressive development of pupils' knowledge, understanding and skills as defined in the Statements of Attainment. Even so, the revised National Curriculum retained the same broad approach in this key stage, and many schools have carried forward their successful practice with regard to content. Many schools, however, have not given due attention to the Key Elements or to issues of depth of study and progression. This is particularly the case where there is no policy or scheme of work for history. Indeed, planning for progression and continuity is good in less than one-quarter of schools and poor in nearly one in three.

The 1991 Key Stage 2 history National Curriculum, with nine study units, was a tall order for many schools. In particular, where history was taught as part of a broader topic, study units did not receive proper treatment and learning against historical objectives was often limited. Additionally, the particular nature of assessment in history caused great difficulty, in part because the attainment targets were ticked off as "covered" in a literal sense without due consideration of the necessary context of increasing quality as pupils moved through the levels.

The reduction in number of study units to six was generally welcomed, although some schools continued to offer more than the minimum. For most schools, fresh planning was required. Some schools, such as **St Gregory's RC School**, Preston, Lancashire, made this a priority:

The subject policy outlines five aims for history, expressed in more general terms than the Key Elements of the National Curriculum, which appear as specific aims for each key stage. Requirements for planning and assessment are common to all subjects, as is the role of the co-ordinator which includes to "review teacher

planning, develop a policy and scheme of work with the staff and contribute to the school development plan". The scheme of work outlines the study units to be covered and, for early years and each key stage, a full list of "Key Questions" that teachers should bear in mind when planning and teaching; these provide good support for teachers, albeit being stronger on chronology and historical knowledge than they are on interpretations of history and historical enquiry.

Many schools have not reached this stage, and have yet to gain confidence in using Key Elements to determine learning objectives and, via the level descriptors, to inform planning for progression. As in Key Stage 1, planning for progression and continuity in Key Stage 2 is good in less than one-quarter of schools and poor in one-third.

Subject leadership

Over the four years of the inspection cycle a common factor in the success of history in schools is the effectiveness of subject leadership. The example below, from **Spinfield County Combined School**, Marlow, Buckinghamshire, illustrates where subject leadership is good and its effects permeate all history lessons:

There is a common approach to timelines from the start of each study unit, giving pupils the opportunity to carry forward what they already know; clear objectives developing the Key Elements through the Areas of Study or the study units; teachers have a good understanding of the nature and use of historical evidence; they use tasks which are well matched to the capabilities of the pupils; the use of small "research projects" such as an investigation into Henry VIII, narratives such as the discovery of Tutankhamun's tomb, or empathetic writing such as "Boudicca's diary" or "the factory inspector's report"; teachers make good use of homework; there is regular marking of pupils' work, which helps pupils forward with comments such as "always try to give a reason to support your opinion"; and teachers use "quizzes" (in fact, tests) as end-of-unit assessments.

This situation is achieved and maintained by an active co-ordinator who, with staff, has considered the requirements of the National Curriculum within the broader contexts of the school's intentions for the subject and their particular strengths; has developed a school policy for history; has set targets for the development of the subject; has established a high expectation through a focus on standards, which includes the development of a benchmark portfolio of pupils' work standardised against level descriptions; has established a way of recording progression; and is in a position to monitor the work of colleagues in order to promote a further dialogue on teaching and standards.

However, subject leadership and management was judged at the end of the inspection cycle to be good in only three out of ten schools, and in one in six schools it is unsatisfactory. In this respect, and particularly with reference to monitoring and development planning, history is in a relatively poor position compared with other subjects. Typical weaknesses include the lack of a policy and scheme of work, and little influence on teaching quality. Very few subject leaders have the time necessary to undertake a productive programme of lesson observation. Some subject leaders continue to see their role as restricted to being providers of ideas on request, and of basic resources.

Neither has the subject fared well in terms of professional development, with less than one in five schools in 1997/98 being well provided for, and approaching the same number having unsatisfactory provision. Where, however, teachers have had the benefit of training courses, especially 10- and 20-day courses which have enabled them to develop expertise across key areas of work, there have been tangible benefits at individual and whole-school level.

Improving standards of history: the way forward

History now has a high profile in most schools, and there is much good practice to build on. In reviewing how well they are doing in history, schools need to ask of themselves the following questions:

- Does the planning do justice to the Areas of Study or study unit?

- In deciding on the objectives for lessons, is there sufficient focus on progression in the Key Elements?

- Are resources well chosen to support historical objectives?

- Are good ideas and dynamic practice in history teaching being shared?

- Is assessment being used to inform pupils of strengths and weaknesses, and move them forward?

- Are opportunities for mutual support of history and literacy being recognised and exploited?

12.8 Information technology

Standards of achievement

There is extraordinary variation in attainment in information technology capability, both within schools and across schools in the country. It is not uncommon for pupils in the same class to have significantly different backgrounds in terms of information technology use. Access to computers in the home greatly affects pupils' confidence and fluency in handling equipment and software from quite a young age. There is little difference in the attainments of boys and girls.

This uneven exposure to outside information technology-related activities is reinforced by pupils' uneven exposure to the programmes of study in information technology in schools, particularly in Key Stage 2. Few schools have good overall attainment in the subject even though, in a growing number of schools, many pupils may be producing work of great complexity or excellence.

Strengths and weaknesses

The strengths of pupils' attainment and progress in information technology are that:

- where information and communication technology tools are used to teach another subject, pupils are usually confident and fluent in their use; work, such as reinforcement of language skills or of facility with mental arithmetic, does not usually require high attainment in information technology, but it can reinforce good working habits, independence, concentration and co-operative working;

- overwhelmingly, pupils are adept at using aspects of word processing. During the last four years there has been an increase in the sophistication which pupils bring to this skill. It is now not unusual for pupils to manipulate and mix graphics and text in a way which was rare, and technically more complex, in 1994; the visual quality of some of the work produced with the aid of information and communication technology tools is uneven but improving;

- most pupils show little difficulty in transferring skills learnt on one computer system to other systems and menus; they quickly adapt to the idiosyncrasies of various systems and user interfaces; the availability in many modern items of software of templates, which offer some (temporary) security to novice users, benefited many pupils greatly, allowing them to achieve success where this would have been more difficult when hardware and software were more limited;

- the increased availability of useful CD-ROM materials in the period under review has given the great majority of pupils valuable experience of searching for data in textual or graphical form. In the best cases, pupils were critical of the materials they retrieved, selected only material relevant to their purpose within identified constraints, and showed awareness of the intended audience as they did so.

Some weaknesses in terms of attainment and progress are that:

- while pupils learn from the earliest years to manipulate peripherals, such as keyboard, mouse and even printer, their subsequent development in independent use seems to be arrested through lack of practice and rigour. Although progress has been made nationally in developing pupils' independent use of information and communication technology tools, a significant proportion of pupils still enter secondary schools without sufficient fluency in locating keys, with a tendency to use just one hand when working at a computer, or with no systematic approaches to securing valuable data, for example through regular saving of files and occasional printing;

- in one-third of schools in Key Stage 1 and one-half of schools in Key Stage 2, the greatest factor limiting overall high attainment and progress was not so much performance in the communicating and handling information strand of the 1995 National Curriculum, as the slender opportunities available for appropriate experiences in the controlling (monitoring) and modelling strand;

- even pupils who are apparently quick and confident in working with information technology, and have learnt, for example, how to use spreadsheets, or to adjust printer settings, or to retrieve material from CD-ROM, do not necessarily apply their information technology capability at a sufficiently high level. They often produce outcomes of modest quality, particularly when one considers the power, complexity and cost of the information and communication technology tools used for the purpose. In some schools, the work done in previous years, with the software and facilities available on older equipment, may have looked less impressive but offered at least comparable challenge and often higher levels of achievement in terms of National Curriculum level descriptions.

Pupils' attitudes towards information technology remain overwhelmingly positive, and modern equipment and software attract particular praise from them. It is rare to see irresponsible behaviour or lack of courtesy in sharing or employing equipment. Pupils are prepared to learn from their mistakes, to persevere, to take risks, to teach themselves new facilities and skills, to consult and to help others. In some lessons real pleasure can be sensed, for instance when in a Year 5 class a teacher showed how certain screen patterns could be produced by a sequence of Logo commands. If frustration sets in during an information technology-based task, it is usually because of equipment or software malfunction; accidental loss of data; slowness of hardware; or lack of sufficient attention from an expert helper.

The quality of teaching

In the majority of primary schools, information technology skills, knowledge and understanding are not systematically taught, and almost never systematically assessed. There is considerably less good teaching in information technology than in any other subject. In only one school in five is the overall teaching of information technology judged to be good. But of greater concern is that, while in all subjects the percentage of primary schools with unsatisfactory teaching is in single figures, the percentages of schools with unsatisfactory teaching in information technology are, typically, four times larger, ranging from 23 per cent for Key Stage 1 to 29 per cent for Key Stage 2.

The major reasons for the greater incidence of unsatisfactory teaching of information technology are teachers' lack of knowledge of the subject and inadequate planning and organisation of lessons and tasks. The management of pupils rarely presents a problem in information technology, and in fact improved in the last year of the review period; but the effective use of the curriculum and teaching resources challenges teachers.

While the subject was often marginalised and rarely taught systematically, especially in Key Stage 2, there has recently been an increase in the practice of teaching information technology to larger groups of pupils. This is often planned quite carefully, and where the resources function well and can be easily supervised, some fine lessons result. Not all teachers, however, are skilled in handling a whole class in a room with more than ten or twelve microcomputers, particularly in the early years of Key Stage 2. This can result in some difficulties when pupils, who have not understood instructions the first time, are unable to gain help when they need it.

While many teachers' knowledge of the subject continues to be unsatisfactory and expectations of pupils compare unfavourably with other subjects, some characteristics of good teaching seen in 1998 were:

- the attention given in Key Stage 1 by teachers and some classroom assistants to developing pupils' independence in using information technology;

- the careful use of mnemonics to help pupils remember functions and keys that access them;

- the use of exemplars of work across several classes to ascertain standards and co-ordinate expectations.

A primary pedagogy for information technology is thus developing, albeit very tentatively and patchily. Examples of good practice are emerging: teachers are using information technology skilfully and providing good role models for their pupils; and there is careful and systematic teaching of classes through tasks, avoiding misunderstanding and ensuring progress is made in the essential skills, with the minimum of backtracking.

Enterprising teachers have already taken advantage of the enhanced resources now becoming available to an increasing number of primary schools to experiment with whole-class teaching of information technology. Some of these resources were recently installed as part of the Government's drive for a National Grid for Learning, and facilitated the enhanced siting and linking of modern computers. While it is too early to comment on the wider impact of these initiatives, initial indications are that the grouping of information and communication technology resources into areas which can be readily supervised following a whole-group introduction eases lesson planning, delivery and appropriate intervention.

However, the vast majority of schools are still unaffected by these changes in pedagogy: even where information and communication technology tools are used to promote learning, the teaching of information technology is mostly an adjunct activity rather than a systematic part of lesson planning.

The curriculum

Although the DfEE's Survey of Information and Communication Technology in Schools (Issue 11/98) shows that computers are used by pupils in about half the lessons, the exposure of any one pupil to information technology is closer to 3–4 per cent of the timetable in a "good" week. There is no assurance that this time will be equitably distributed, consistently available or properly focused on the development of information technology skills, knowledge and understanding. According to the DfEE survey, one primary school teacher in five uses information technology less frequently than twice a week in lessons. The pupils in such classes thus experience limited teaching of information technology and little time to apply learnt skills to other work. This view is supported by inspection evidence: in Key Stage 1 the breadth and balance of the information technology curriculum was judged to be good in only about one in six schools and unsatisfactory in one-third. In Key Stage 2, breadth and balance for information technology was unsatisfactory in almost half of the schools. Thus almost half the schools with Key Stage 2 pupils are not yet offering them the full programmes of study in information technology.

The marginal place of information technology in the curriculum of some schools during the period under review meant that one school in five was not complying at all with the requirements of the National Curriculum in information technology. Schemes of work for information technology are often not specific enough or resourced, nor monitored sufficiently to allow progression. Many schemes exist on paper only and are not implemented.

In the primary schools which have made serious attempts to meet the requirements of the National Curriculum in information technology, the schemes of work for most subjects make reference to suitable information technology applications and mention specific information technology competences which have to be taught through such applications or separately from them. Such analysis often owes much to support from local education authority staff, and from the exemplification of expectations in Key Stages 1 and 2 published by SCAA in 1997. This provided helpful guidance on what progression of information technology skills and understanding needed to be developed and monitored. Some of the schemes of work are partial and do not span all programmes of study in information technology, but they contain helpful hints about such aspects as:

- what aspect of the programmes of study to stress in each year group;

- how to encourage pupils to be independent users of equipment;

- which hardware or software to use to teach, for example in data handling;

- how to organise the entitlement of pupils in data handling, and how to check that they have it;

- instances of useful retrieval from CD-ROM and (in a handful of cases) the sites on the World Wide Web to support school topics more generally;

- encouragement not to accept from pupils cut-and-pasted material on its own.

Staffing and resources

The rapid changes of the technology have posed a massive challenge to primary school teachers. Many are to be commended for readily adapting to the increasing demands of sophisticated facilities and some for grasping the new opportunities that these offered. Not surprisingly, for many teachers with little access to information and communication technology at home, the rapid pace of technological change has presented challenges that it was not easy to meet. Even those who are personally confident in the use of information and communication technology require much training to enable them to teach Information Technology Capability.

Although the average expenditure on information technology in primary schools rose from about £10 to £11 per pupil during the years under review, individual schools had very different priorities indeed in terms of information technology provision. A growing minority of schools have invested heavily in modern equipment, including networking, and some have added peripherals, such as digital cameras or electronic display facilities in selected classrooms. A significant minority have begun to receive Standards Fund grants for upgrading their provision and joining the National Grid for Learning.

Unfortunately, the expansion of physical provision, though very necessary, is not generally accompanied by sufficient investment of time and expertise in the development of staff competences with information and communication technology and in the methodology of teaching the skills, knowledge and understanding of information technology as a subject. For every £8 spent on hardware, less than £1 was spent on staff training in information technology. The non-teaching time available to curriculum co-ordinators was insufficient in most schools to provide adequate support to other members of staff.

Many schools, however, continue to believe – mistakenly – that once information technology has been given priority in the school development plan during one year, it can be left alone in the following year. Given the rapid technological developments and varying personal attitudes to information and communication, the monitoring of work in information technology remains crucial to its success.

12.9 Modern foreign languages

The rationale for the teaching of a modern foreign language in primary schools

A modern foreign language is included in the curriculum at Key Stage 2 in about one primary school in five,[75] although it is not a National Curriculum subject until Key Stage 3. The rationale for providing modern foreign languages for pupils under the age of eleven varies considerably from one school to another. In some schools, the aim of modern foreign language provision is to teach the language skills of listening, speaking, reading and writing, usually with the emphasis on the first two; in others, the aim is to raise the "language awareness" of pupils in order to arouse their interest in foreign languages at an early stage. In the latter case, the development of positive attitudes to, and enjoyment of, language may be seen initially as more important than the levels of competence reached. Some schools seek to combine these aims; others may be confused as to which they are pursuing. It also appears that some schools, especially those in areas with easy transport links to continental Europe, feel obliged to include a modern foreign language in their curriculum in order to encourage parents to choose a particular school for their children.

Schools organise the teaching of modern foreign languages in a range of ways. Some introduce a foreign language as a "taster" prior to pupils' transfer to secondary education. Others provide a brief introduction in preparation for a school visit abroad. Others hold voluntary, after-school, language clubs. More significantly, many include modern foreign languages as a regularly timetabled subject alongside the foundation and core subjects, especially towards the end of Key Stage 2.

With very few exceptions, primary schools offer only one modern foreign language and French continues to be predominant; for every 30 primary schools offering a modern foreign language, only one is likely to offer another language (usually German, occasionally Spanish, rarely any other

language). This situation can create tensions on transfer to secondary school in some areas where the diversification of the first modern foreign language, encouraged by successive governments, is well established in the secondary phase. Parents may resist the idea of their children switching from French to study, for example, German or Spanish on arriving at their secondary school. There is a concern in some areas that diversification in secondary schools may be undermined by the promotion of French in primary schools.

Standards of achievement

The motivation of pupils in the first year of study is usually good and their response positive. However, the attainment of pupils in using foreign language skills is very uneven and reflects the variation in the quality of both the teaching and the planning. Young learners usually make a good start, but progress often slows later. They normally imitate speech well and, provided they regularly hear a good model of the foreign language, they develop good pronunciation. With appropriate visual support, they can comprehend the spoken language in familiar contexts. They may be less inhibited than older pupils and use basic greetings more spontaneously or adjust more quickly to classroom routines in the foreign language. If they have an authentic model to imitate, they show a capacity for memorising and repeating accurately rhymes and songs, particularly where the singing or chanting is supported by actions or mime. In the early stages of study, they often acquire quite quickly vocabulary such as numbers, colours and nouns referring, for example, to classroom objects and toys.

Unless the momentum is maintained and pupils have the opportunity to consolidate and recycle the language acquired, progress slows, with the result that it is sometimes difficult, for example among Year 6 pupils compared with the pupils in Year 5, to identify an increased communicative capacity as opposed to a larger vocabulary. Where the work is well planned, pupils progress to more demanding tasks, involving the active use of structures and phrases, and not simply the acquisition of vocabulary.

The quality of teaching

Many classes are taken by non-specialist teachers, who are more likely to offer an unacceptable

---

[75] *Modern Foreign Languages in Primary Schools*. Centre for Information on Language Teaching, 1995.

(Anglicised) model of the foreign language. Where teachers do not speak the foreign language well, the pupils may be imitating inaccuracies in pronunciation and intonation or be exposed to too much English instead of the target language. For example:

The excessive amount of English used does not encourage pupils to use the language other than in a very limited manner. While the pace is good, there is too little practice of structures before tasks are set for pupils, and this constrains their use of the target language. Opportunities for the use of the target language for the purposes of classroom management are also overlooked.

Teaching styles and their effectiveness vary greatly, often reflecting the varied backgrounds of the teachers and any other adults involved: for example, the class teacher, French co-ordinator, specialist, foreign language assistant or a parent. The main consequence of this variety is the very uneven extent and quality of use of the target language. This presents a significant in-service training issue.

Pupils are likely to be confused if they hear predominantly English in French lessons or constant switching between the two languages. They are unlikely to be equipped with the attitudes or strategies to cope later with the consistent stream of the target language in secondary school foreign language lessons.

The following extract from an inspection report illustrates many of the features of successful teaching:

Teachers' objectives and planning are clear. Methods, resources and classroom organisation are carefully prepared to promote pupils' learning. Teachers vary activities very effectively to hold pupils' attention and reinforce their understanding. Teachers are skilful at conducting lessons in the target language using vocabulary which pupils can understand. Generally they manage oral sessions well and maintain a brisk pace. As pupils advance, teachers place an appropriate emphasis on reading material that stimulates their interest in language and culture. In both oral and written work, teachers correct pupils' work regularly and encourage good levels of attainment through their guidance and comments.

Reinforcement for oral and aural work in some schools is provided by other means outside the limited timetable slots available for modern foreign language teaching. For example, routine business, such as greeting the class and taking the register, is done in the foreign language. Songs in a foreign language can provide a medium for developing pupils' linguistic and musical skills at the same time. Practice in simple arithmetic can be provided by simple addition and subtraction in the foreign language or pupils reciting their tables through that medium.

Such reinforcement is usually more effective when the class teacher is also the modern foreign languages teacher for the class, provided the teacher has adequate linguistic expertise to support their generic classroom skills and wider curricular experience. Unfortunately, this dual expertise is rarely found.

Curriculum and assessment

Schemes of work often provide insufficient guidance for teachers. Better guidelines for assessment are needed if progression within Key Stage 2 and continuity with secondary education are to be reinforced. A few local education authorities have set up local schemes (including advisory support) for teaching modern foreign languages in all their primary schools; others have set out common principles for provision and guidelines for methodology for those schools which have chosen to introduce modern foreign languages. Although guidelines are sometimes not consistently followed – for example on the use of the target language – schools usually benefit from this support. The teachers in them are more likely to teach an integrated programme of language skills than to present a disconnected series of partial linguistic experiences to their pupils. They are also more likely to be aware of the nature of the studies that the pupils will be expected to undertake under the National Curriculum when they move into Key Stage 3. The need for progression and continuity is therefore more likely to be taken into account, although liaison remains a weak point. Too often, secondary schools discount pupils' prior learning in modern foreign languages, although this is partly understandable where, for example, a secondary school receives pupils from several primary schools, the majority of whom may not have studied modern foreign languages before.

The amount of time for which modern foreign languages is studied varies considerably. The most common starting point is Year 5, but some schools start in Year 4 or earlier. Pupils starting before Year 4 may have only a few minutes of modern foreign languages per week, and not necessarily every week. In Year 5 and Year 6 it is more usual for pupils to have about an hour per week, split where possible into two short sessions. Given the pupils' need for constant reinforcement through regular exposure to the foreign language, primary schools might usefully consider concentrating the available time into more intensive teaching of modern foreign languages over a shorter period of time. Since in secondary schools infrequent contacts with the foreign language often lead to lower standards, there is no reason to assume that primary school pupils can benefit from a more diluted approach. Moreover, the sensible emphasis on listening and speaking in the early stages of study means that homework based on reading and writing is not available to provide reinforcement between lessons.

There is little formal assessment, recording and reporting of progress in modern foreign languages. Partly because it is not a National Curriculum subject and partly because in many schools only one teacher is involved in teaching modern foreign languages, an informal approach is usually considered adequate. There are cases, especially when there is a change of teacher, where progress is adversely affected because teaching is not able to take prior attainment into account. If pupils' progress is not efficiently recorded within the primary school, it is improbable that liaison in the subject will be effective when pupils transfer to secondary school.

Improving standards of modern foreign languages: the way forward

The aims and objectives of teaching modern foreign languages in Key Stage 2 need to be set out clearly in each primary school which includes the subject in its curriculum. These aims and objectives should be shared with partner secondary schools so that issues such as progression, continuity and diversification can be addressed.

The modern foreign languages policy in the school should be implemented through clear schemes of work consistently applied in the teaching and

supported by a coherent approach to assessment, recording and reporting.

The implications of using non-specialist teachers should be considered carefully and appropriate staff development measures taken, particularly where the teacher's linguistic knowledge and fluency are insufficient to teach effectively using the target language.

12.10 Music

Standards of achievement

Standards of achievement in music rose sharply during the period 1994–98. The high standards in singing, playing instruments, composing, listening and appraising that were found in a few schools in 1994 are now found more frequently. The proportion of schools that provide very little music for some of their pupils has decreased. Fewer pupils leave primary school with low attainment in music; they enter secondary school as confident users of the raw materials of music, namely voices, instruments, timing and, above all, sound.

Although the improved standards apply in all the National Curriculum programmes of study for music, they are observed most clearly in composing because this is where practice was previously most uneven. In 1994 many teachers were still familiarising themselves with the programmes of study, and taught them mechanistically and without necessarily building on pupils' prior learning. It was not uncommon for teachers to think that composing had to take place within the conventions and limitations of staff notation, and that compositions had always to be written down. Pupils were rarely taught to reflect on the aural quality of their compositions, and to propose and try out ways of improving them. Too much composing consisted of brief clapped rhythms that made no use of voices or instruments. Pupils often found their compositions boring. Greater experience of teaching composing has brought greater confidence. Now teachers recognise that many pupils come to school with experience of working imaginatively with sound, and are seeking to develop and build on this ability through the ways that they teach composing. For example:

Pupils in Year 2 experimented with several percussion instruments to find the best sound for expressing a particular mood. They tried different ways of producing sounds from the instruments – tapping with their fingers and different types of beaters, scraping...

In some work linked with history, pupils in Year 6 composed music to portray an air raid during World War Two. They recorded their compositions using a range of symbols and notations. Some of the compositions made imaginative use of dynamics and texture, for instance building up layers of sound "as the planes approach".

Pupils' compositions are now examples of creative work that can be evaluated in terms of their aural effect rather than, for example, the number of crotchets they contain. Pupils have become more proud of their compositions. This has had an impact on pupils' standards in other areas of the National Curriculum in music. Composing has helped pupils to listen with concentration and attention to detail, talk about and discuss the structure and effect of pieces of music, and develop their memory for music. For example:

Pupils in Key Stage 1 make suggestions about the mood of music being listened to: that it is sad, has a strange ending or that it is unusual in that it feels as if it has finished but it hasn't.

Pupils usually have positive attitudes to music, but become frustrated when teaching lacks pace. They can lose concentration and become restless when they have to wait unduly long for their turn to play a musical instrument. They become bored by teacher-dominated activities that only allow them one or two taps on an instrument before passing it to someone else, and that do not give them the chance to gain knowledge and understanding of the instrument and the range of sounds it can produce. In schools where musical instruments are used too infrequently, pupils may react to their occasional appearances by wanting to play all the instruments continuously and very loudly.

The quality of teaching

Teaching in class music has improved sharply during 1994–98, and is now satisfactory or better in nine lessons out of ten. It is good or better in over a half of lessons in Key Stage 1 and three-fifths of lessons in Key Stage 2. In contrast to other subjects, there is no evidence of a general dip in the quality of teaching during Year 3 and Year 4.

Music is usually planned as a discrete subject, but many teachers have become adept at building on pupils' experience in other subjects when they need to be certain that a stimulus for a composition has been understood. For example:

Pupils in Year 5 developed their appraisal of a painting of El Greco by trying to capture its mood in group compositions that lasted exactly 30 seconds and were recorded on a time grid. The teacher helped pupils to find ways of talking about the mood of the painting, and then allowed them to be creative within the framework of the grid, and within the time allowed. She supported groups while they worked, and tried to help them move on their thinking. Some well-chosen performances of work in progress were used, midway through the lesson, to make various teaching points. The pupils responded enthusiastically to this lesson, and took pride in refining their compositions to achieve the effect that they sought.

Since 1996, OFSTED has collected data for peripatetic instrumental lessons separately from class music lessons. In 1997/98 the teaching was good or better in three-quarters of lessons, and rarely unsatisfactory. Good instrumental teaching builds on pupils' prior learning, including their learning in class music lessons, and helps them to develop the practical and aural skills needed to perform accurately and expressively on a particular instrument. Many pupils learn to read staff notation during instrumental lessons, but good teaching ensures that they do not become too dependent on written music and encourages them to play by ear, apply and extend their memory for music, and improvise and compose on their instrument.

In 1994 there were many primary schools where teachers believed that class music lessons taught by class teachers were necessarily inferior to those taught by music specialists. The meaning of the term 'specialist' varied between schools, but usually denoted a teacher who visited the school only to teach music, or a teacher on the full-time staff of the school who co-ordinated the music curriculum and had taken music as a main subject during initial teacher training. Since 1994 more schools have become aware that good class teaching and poor specialist teaching both exist, and that what matters is whether a teacher has the professional competence, including subject knowledge, to teach music effectively.

Teachers who lacked confidence in their own expertise as composers and performers have worked hard, often with the support of music co-ordinators and in-service training, to learn to teach music effectively. They have developed sufficient confidence in their planning and subject knowledge to allow pupils to contribute to the content and flow of their lessons. They show determination to teach all aspects of the music curriculum, and not just those activities that they find easier. Specialists are now expected to be as accountable as class teachers, and to demonstrate – for example through documentation of the curriculum and assessment records – that they are building on pupils' prior learning and giving them a balanced experience of singing, playing instruments, composing, listening and appraising. However, some problems remain. For example:

> *At Key Stage 2 the specialist teacher delivers lessons that are pitched at an appropriate level for the age of pupils but takes insufficient account of previous learning. The lessons do not excite or enthuse pupils and lessons are a chore rather than a rewarding experience. Relationships between the teacher and class are barely satisfactory and not helped by the teacher not knowing the pupils' names... opportunities for composition are few and pupils have unsatisfactory understanding of musical vocabulary.*

The curriculum

The provision that schools make for the creative development of under-fives often gives pupils opportunities to sing, echo rhythms, and listen to music, but it underplays creative work in music. However, some schools encourage under-fives to make imaginative use of sound. For example:

> *Pupils developed their language and literacy by suggesting alternative words (big, huge, enormous) to describe one of the three bears, developed their understanding of volume and capacity by making porridge for the bears, and finally composed a piece of music for each of the bears.*

Most schools have improved their music curriculum since 1994. Many now place more emphasis on the class music that they offer to all

pupils, which is one of the main reasons why standards have risen. Extracurricular activities and peripatetic instrument lessons still take place; indeed, they have expanded in some schools, but are seen increasingly as a means of enhancing the music curriculum for pupils with a particular interest in music, and a way of further raising their attainment, rather than being the *raison d'être* of the curriculum leader for music. Schools have become better at evaluating the opportunities that they offer to different groups of pupils, including boys and girls, through their curricular and extracurricular work. Reports written by peripatetic teachers feed into the assessment systems of the school. There is greater coherence to the music that many schools offer: pupils may compose on their orchestral instrument during their class lessons, or during a peripatetic instrumental lesson they may try to play by ear the melody of a song that they know from their class lessons. The repertoire of recorded music that pupils hear has expanded beyond the light classics to include music with a broad cultural base and music from the twentieth-century avant-garde movements. In the best examples, pupils can apply some of the knowledge and understanding that they gain from listening to and discussing this music when they perform and compose.

Not all schools have followed this trend: there remain some where the music curriculum is unduly narrow and standards are low. Some of these schools feel overburdened by other priorities; others think of music as one of their strengths, but have not evaluated their music curriculum adequately since the introduction of the National Curriculum. Many of these schools neglect composing, or introduce it only in Key Stage 2, when pupils' enthusiasm for working imaginatively and experimentally with sound has already atrophied. These schools often spend too much time on specialist activities not required by the National Curriculum, for example teaching all of the pupils the early stages of playing the descant recorder from staff notation. Clearly, the descant recorder does have a role in primary music, particularly among pupils who like the sound of a descant recorder played well, and when pupils are encouraged to play by ear or from memory and improvise. However, schools need to consider whether their massed recorder lessons are an efficient way of using pupils' time, in terms of raising standards and sustaining or increasing motivation. It is not uncommon to find pupils, often mainly boys, who are still only playing the note B at the end of Year 2, B, A and G at the end of Year 3, and B, A, G and E at the end of Year 6 – and who have become very confused about staff notation. They are rarely motivated by this.

Improving standards of music: the way forward

This brief review has drawn largely on evidence from Section 9 and 10 inspection reports, but also includes evidence from *The Arts Inspected*.[76] Both these sources indicate that in order to improve further standards in music, schools should:

- recognise that many pupils arrive at school with experience of moving and listening to music, working imaginatively with sound and singing, and should develop a music curriculum that develops these abilities in all pupils;

- ensure that the time which pupils give to music is used efficiently; check that all music lessons are planned to promote learning in music; and avoid musical activities that simply occupy pupils, for example massed singsongs;

- organise the time that the school makes available for music in a manner appropriate to the pupils' age; give younger pupils frequent, preferably daily, opportunities to make music; and allocate to older pupils lessons that are long enough for them to develop thoroughly and that give an opportunity to appraise their performances and compositions;

- judge the effectiveness of a school's provision in music by its effect on pupils who do not participate in music outside class lessons, for example by taking peripatetic instrumental lessons or attending voluntary choir rehearsals;

- take opportunities in music lessons to reinforce pupils' prior learning in literacy and numeracy, for example by singing number songs or, drawing attention to rhyme or alliteration in the lyrics of songs that pupils have composed;

- teach pupils music-learning skills that they can apply also to other subjects; help them to develop and have confidence in their memory; expect them to listen with concentration and attention to detail; encourage them to talk

about and discuss the structure and effect of pieces of music; and provide them with strategies for improving the quality and standard of their work.

12.11 Physical education

Standards of achievement

Over the four years since 1994, standards of achievement in physical education at Key Stage 1 and Key Stage 2 have remained consistently satisfactory in a large majority of schools and good in one-quarter to one-third of schools; by 1998 they were poor in only about one school in 20. Good progress is often made at pre-Key Stage 1 and at least satisfactory progress is achieved overall from then to the end of Key Stage 2. Where progress is restricted, it is often due to weak teaching that pursues repetitive practice of known skills rather than challenging pupils with tasks to develop these further.

The main focus of the work is on the development of skills in the activity areas of gymnastics, dance and games, though strongly positive comment is often made in reports about attainment in swimming. Most pupils are competent in running, jumping, turning, rolling, balancing and linking of actions in sequences in gymnastics, interpreting mood and expression in music and dance, and mastering skills of throwing, catching, hitting and kicking in games. Developing the ability to work well in pairs or groups as pupils move from Key Stage 1 through Key Stage 2 is essential. By the end of Key Stage 2, most pupils can co-operate well with others and compete fiercely but fairly. Many show good understanding of the rules and basic principles of play in adapted or mini versions of the traditional team games. In swimming, the majority of pupils are able to meet the minimum requirements of the National Curriculum and can swim at least 25 metres with confidence; some reach standards well beyond this.

Outdoor and adventurous activities (OAA) is a neglected area of the National Curriculum, but a recent survey of good practice in OAA showed that there are good examples of high attainment in primary schools. For example, interesting approaches to the teaching of early orienteering skills, often by teachers who were not specialists, had given the pupils confidence to make map-

---

[76] OFSTED (1998) *The Arts Inspected*. Oxford: Heinemann.

reading decisions and to demonstrate skills in pairs in competitive events. One rural school linked well with its area secondary school to provide elements of the OAA curriculum. Pupils hiked to the secondary school, took part in practical problem-solving challenges, camped overnight, and journeyed home the following day by a different route that allowed for environmental work.

A consistent weakness is the lack of development of the central and essential skills of planning, performing and evaluating in the context of physical activities that underpin the National Curriculum in physical education. In most schools the concentration is on attainment in terms of performing; consequently planning and evaluation skills are too often neglected. There has been little change in this position over the four years of the review period.

The quality of teaching

Over the four-year cycle there has been an impressive and steady improvement in teaching; in 1997/98 fewer than one in ten lessons were judged to be unsatisfactory compared with one in five in 1994/95. Conversely, the percentage of good or better lessons has increased consistently throughout the period and now stands at between one-half and three-fifths of all lessons at pre-Key Stage 1, Key Stage 1 and Key Stage 2. Nearly all lessons in physical education are taught by the class teacher; use of any specialist expertise in a school to teach across classes is rare.

Good teachers demonstrate most of the following characteristics in their teaching. They have a good knowledge of the subject and this is well used to promote learning. Lessons are very well planned, linking into National Curriculum programmes of study and allowing for the clear development of a theme. Teachers have high expectations of pupils. Appropriate resources are well prepared, often by the pupils themselves, and the lesson begins at the changing stage in the classroom. These teachers manage pupils well and give clear instructions, with a good pace maintained. With younger pupils, appropriate activities are selected to encourage confidence and early skills; with Key Stage 2 pupils, an increasing complexity of activity and task is used to maintain challenge. Emphasis is given to the development of quality in the work, and the teachers encourage the improvement of

skills. They judge effectively when to intervene and they help pupils to make judgements about the quality of the work for themselves. Careful selection and appropriate use of pupils to demonstrate good performance is made, and the pupils are encouraged to define what was good about the work and what might be improved. They ensure that pupils receive immediate feedback to enhance future performance. Teacher assessment of pupils' work is ongoing and is used to inform future planning.

Assessment and recording of pupil achievement in primary schools have developed little over the four years of the inspection cycle. Although teachers provide good formative feedback to pupils during lessons, few schools have developed a system for recording progress over time. Many teachers know their pupils well, and too many schools are heavily reliant on the teachers' memory when writing reports for parents.

In the best practice, records are structured but might be kept informally in a notebook. The teachers follow common prompts – for example to make reference to a pupil's movement quality, to an ability to manage and control the body in different activities, to handle apparatus and equipment, to meet significant new challenges and to work well with others. Such recording should demonstrate improvement over time, the pupils' developing understanding of the body, the acquisition of skills, social maturity in competitive and co-operative situations, and the ability to sustain activity. It should be informal and simple, but highly informative.

The curriculum

The revised National Curriculum for physical education reduced the range of activities for pupils at Key Stage 1 and this was welcomed by teachers, most of whom are confident in teaching gymnastics, dance and games skills. At Key Stage 2, however, the six areas of activity required were retained, and in many schools only lip service is paid to OAA and athletic activities, while the other areas are generally covered well. Despite this, the problem lies less with coverage of the activities than with the balance achieved between them. Games still dominates the programme at Key Stage 2 and some of the traditional and less desirable features of games lessons – such as single-gender football and netball lessons, mixed year groups and a strong focus on invasion games – linger on in too many cases. Where dance is taught, it is often taught very well by some teachers in the school. As a result, pupils have intermittent experiences across the key stage, depending on whose class they happen to be in. Most schools are able to include the compulsory swimming element in their programme, but some are prevented by lack of an accessible swimming pool.

A central and underpinning principle of the National Curriculum is the continuous cycle of planning, performing and evaluating in movement, yet it is the least well understood or developed element and there have been few signs of improvement over the four years under review.

New developments

Extracurricular physical activity and sport is a feature of many primary schools and provides an extension to the physical education curriculum for many pupils, especially in Key Stage 2. The use of outside expertise – coaches and other volunteers – is increasing in both curriculum and extra-curricular time. These people may bring valuable knowledge and skills in specific activities to share with pupils, but not always the teaching expertise or understanding of how young pupils learn. It is essential that schools follow the guidance of the local authority when selecting adults other than teachers to work with pupils, and that outside helpers work under the supervision of qualified teachers when working with pupils.

The work of the Youth Sport Trust, through the development of in-service training and materials for the Top Play and BT Top Sport schemes, is impacting on a very large number of primary schools across the country. The schemes are designed to support rather than replace the National Curriculum. Evaluation reports are beginning to show that the schemes are having a positive effect on teacher knowledge and understanding, and on their confidence in teaching games in particular. Further evaluation studies will be required to judge their effect on other aspects of the physical education programme in schools.

The designation of 26 secondary specialist sports colleges in different regions is making a significant contribution to the development of primary physical education and after-school physical activity. Each sports college has a remit to work with the wider community to increase opportunity

in its area; this includes primary schools. Each sports college is unique and is approaching its work with primary schools in a different way; some are supporting the teaching of curriculum physical education, others are focusing on extended curriculum opportunities for primary pupils using their specialist facilities, and some are doing both. Early indications suggest that the links are positive and are welcomed by primary schools. If successful, the models will be shared with other secondary schools to help them to build stronger links with feeder primary schools and to extend opportunity for participation in physical activity.

Improving standards of physical education: the way forward

Progress is assisted or constrained by the teachers' subject knowledge, by planning and by awareness of the requirements of the National Curriculum. The good practice described in an earlier paragraph is far from universal. Where achievement is restricted and progress is unsatisfactory, there is a lack of challenge and too many pupils are physically inactive for substantial parts of the lesson. Often the teacher's focus is on the level of activity rather than the quality of the work. Failure by the teacher to intervene in the learning inhibits progress over time, as does the introduction of too many new activities without allowing time for consolidation of existing skills.

Balancing repetition and consolidation of prior learning against the pace of moving learning forward is an essential teaching skill which demands good observation, sound knowledge and understanding of the subject, and well timed intervention in the learning process. Progress is best supported by an effective subject co-ordinator and planning within a well designed scheme of work, which clearly outlines progression towards the National Curriculum end-of-key-stage descriptors in physical education.

A healthy lifestyle

The promotion of physical activity and a healthy lifestyle is an important aspect of physical education, but it is often neglected in the planning and delivery in schools. Pupils develop an understanding of the effects of exercise on the body in only a few schools and, even here, this is limited to an awareness of the need to warm up before exercise and to noting increased heart rate and body temperature. The National Curriculum requires much more than this. Over the two key stages a positive attitude to physical activity should be developed. At an appropriate level, increasing attention should be given to the benefits of physical activity for good health; to posture and the safe use of the body; to simple understanding of cardiovascular function, flexibility, muscular strength and endurance; and, by the end of Key Stage 2, to the need for personal hygiene in relation to vigorous physical activity. This approach will also make a significant contribution to science and health education.

12.12 Religious education

This section applies only to LEA maintained schools teaching non-denominational religious education according to a locally agreed syllabus.

Standards of achievement

There is no national data for standards in religious education since there are no tests, no statutory teacher assessment and no nationally determined standards. Inspection offers the only evidence for standards and shows that, judged against the expectations of a locally agreed syllabus in use, pupils' attainment and their progress in religious education is satisfactory or better in more than nine out of ten schools at Key Stage 1 and just less than nine out of ten schools at Key Stage 2.

Pupils' progress in religious education has improved significantly, particularly over the last three years. However, these improvements have been largely from "unsatisfactory or poor" to "satisfactory". Progress at both Key Stage 1 and Key Stage 2 is good or better in one-third of lessons. At Key Stage 2 the rate of pupils' progress in religious education falls slightly short of that in other subjects. Progress is weakest in Year 3 and strongest in Year 6.

Strengths and weaknesses in religious education

Four years ago it was unusual to find pupils leaving primary school with much more than rudimentary knowledge of popular Bible stories, and many had had no religious education at all. Now, most pupils arrive in secondary school with at least sound knowledge about Christianity and often of other religions as well. Typically, they know a range of stories from religious traditions,

know the life stories of founders and exemplars of the faiths, and can describe some of the significant places and events of the religious traditions studied.

However, it is less usual to find pupils whose understanding and skills extend to other objectives in the agreed syllabus, such as the application of religion to life, the ability to consider and come to an opinion on religious questions, or insight into the common questions and concerns of humanity so often explored in religious texts and teachings. This is why progress is only on the whole satisfactory rather than good.

Where progress is good, pupils make gains across the range of agreed syllabus objectives. In particular, they understand why religion is important in some people's lives and can see a connection between many of the issues in religious education and their own lives. They ask and respond to questions such as "Why?", "What does this mean?" and "What do I think about this?" rather than simply "Who/what is this?". For example, Year 5 pupils writing about the life of Muhammad considered what it meant to submit to the will of God, and after learning about Gurus Nanak and Gobind Singh discussed what their lives taught them about relationships, leadership and peace. Year 6 pupils learnt the story of Rama and Sita and understood from the story the qualities of character valued in the Hindu community.

Where pupils have made good progress across a key stage, the contrast with recent years is evident in both the breadth and depth of their attainment. For example, from an HMI survey:

Key Stage 1 pupils have deepened their understanding of community by considering the themes of relationships (being friends) and responsibility (caring and helping) in stories from the Bible and other literature. They have developed a good knowledge of the key features of Judaism, eg Shabbat, wine, candles and Hanukkah, and many of them can use the correct terminology. They are aware of festivals in the Christian calendar such as Christmas and Easter and the key events in the life of a Christian; baptism, confirmation and marriage. They have some understanding of stories in the Bible, eg Moses, Joseph, the Creation and events in Jesus' life. They can express their own feelings and responses to artefacts, stories and pictures.

The progress made across Key Stage 2 in the next school illustrates how, over the last four years, primary pupils are increasingly reaching standards formerly associated with Key Stage 3.

Pupils demonstrate very good knowledge and understanding of Christianity, Judaism and Hinduism. They understand the key events in these religions and their significance (eg worship, celebrations, rites of passage). They can very clearly articulate their views on issues such as faith and worship and understand that religion involves belief as well as practices. They are aware of the richness and diversity of different religions expressed through their celebrations, symbols and places of worship and can use technical terminology such as "covenant", "Pesach" and "Exodus". They can debate to a very high level the meaning and interpretation of events, such as the Exodus, and consider the feelings of the groups and individuals involved. Older pupils are able to relate some of the concepts they encounter (eg freedom, forgiveness, repentance) to their own experiences.

These examples illustrate the best that pupils can achieve; but they represent the minority. In spite of recent improvements, there are some typical weaknesses in religious education, regardless of which agreed syllabus is followed, which could and should be rectified in the near future. These include:

- weak knowledge and understanding of Christianity;

- weak knowledge and understanding of faiths other than Christianity;

- knowledge which is limited to stories and festivals;

- confusion between religions (eg the ability to describe a festival but an inability to name the religion to which it belongs);

- little or no understanding of concepts, and hence an inability to make any links between the teachings of religions and their own experiences;

- little or no understanding of the spiritual and moral messages contained in stories and

events, and a general lack of understanding that religious stories can be approached at different levels apart from the literal.

The quality of teaching

The recent improvement in standards in religious education is a direct result of a similar improvement in the teaching of it. Although religious education has been statutory since 1994, only in recent years have most teachers come to understand what it involves. Following the adoption of a new range of content-specific agreed syllabuses from 1994 onwards, many teachers became aware for the first time of the scope of religious education. It is not uncommon now to find teachers teaching with enjoyment and interest a subject they once feared, largely through not knowing what it was about. During the last 12 months of the review period, there was a significant increase in the proportion of schools where teaching was judged good or better.

Standards in religious education are largely determined by teachers' understanding of those elements that constitute progress in the subject and the methods most likely to achieve them. This was particularly clear in one school using an agreed syllabus with levels of attainment, where Year 3 pupils, whatever their ability, were consistently attaining at Level 2, which requires pupils to "describe" features of religions. No pupils had progressed to Level 3, which demanded "explanation" because the teacher had never set a task which required them to explain anything.

Conversely, the following infant school illustrates clearly what happens when a teacher designs tasks with progression in mind:

Pupils were making good progress in their knowledge and understanding of Christianity through an extensive study of their local church. They studied the gravestones and the interior of the building, and used evidence from newspaper cuttings and interviews with parishioners to produce their own accounts of the church, its activities and its importance to worshippers and the community generally.

Teachers' subject knowledge is good in one-third of schools, and unsatisfactory in less than one in ten. There is a sharp contrast between teachers whose knowledge, largely gained from pupils' books and worksheets, is just adequate, and those whose knowledge is good. These are the minority, who have read more widely or have visited places of worship and spoken to adherents in the furtherance of their own understanding. Confidence accompanies knowledge and, where both are lacking, teachers avoid opportunities to ask or receive questions or encourage discussion. For example, a teacher of a Year 1 class, confident of her own ability to cope with challenging questions, taught the story of Jonah in relation to concepts of obedience, salvation and forgiveness in the pupils' own experience. It is unusual to find a primary teacher with this degree of conceptual understanding. Most draw a moral from a story at best and at worst simply tell the story and ask questions about what happened. However, the indications are that teachers are gradually building up their knowledge base of a subject in which most of them have no qualifications or training.

Whole-class teaching is favoured in religious education and, typically, teachers make an input (eg story, video, visit) and engage with pupils in question-and-answer sessions. When there is no variation from this style, pupils lack opportunities for independent learning or working with others. The style can be used effectively when teachers have a clear plan for the progression of the discussion and focus questions in relation to the objectives of the agreed syllabus. For example:

Pupils in a Year 4 class knew that the New Testament was about Jesus and that a parable was a story with a meaning. The teacher tells the class the lawyer's question, "Who is my neighbour?" and gives background information about Jews and Samaritans. Questions are well focused to get pupils to respond to the story in depth. For example, questions about the motivation and response of the different characters take pupils' understanding forward and encourage them to make comparisons to situations today: "People often drive past when there's an accident because they don't want to get involved"; "If you saw someone you didn't like who was hurt, you might not want to help them". The teacher builds effectively on pupils' responses, eg "Do you think that is what Jesus would want us to do?", "No, he meant us to be kind and help everyone that needs help". By the end of the lesson pupils understood why this story is so central in the Christian tradition

and could relate it to their own relationships and events in modern times.

Good religious education teachers make full use of the wide range of resources available today and are aware of which resources and strategies are best suited to developing different aspects of religious education. So, visits to places of worship, artefacts, games, CD-ROMs and posters are used to explore religious practices and traditions, while drama, dance, role-play and circle time are used to explore ideas and feelings.

In spite of the increase in good practice, there are still too many teachers who do not challenge pupils sufficiently. Features of these lessons include an emphasis on drawing, colouring in, word searches and other low-level tasks, and an exclusive reliance on lesson preparation by the co-ordinator. In such cases, lessons are perceived as something to be delivered without personal involvement.

In most schools, religious education is taught by the class teacher. Where class teachers are prepared to improve their own subject knowledge and are committed to high standards, this can succeed. However, there are cases of religious education being taught by teachers who have no interest in, or sympathy with, the subject. This is an important factor in lowering the quality of religious education in the school as a whole, even where some teaching is very good.

In contrast to the start of the inspection cycle, most schools now have a co-ordinator or teacher with responsibility for religious education. The effectiveness of the co-ordinator often determines the quality of religious education in the school. The co-ordinator is usually responsible for planning across the key stage from the agreed syllabus, for resourcing religious education and for suggesting activities. During the last four years many co-ordinators have benefited from 10-day in-service training financed by GEST. The following profile gives a detailed insight into the work of a co-ordinator who is seeking ways of improving religious education in a school where it is already good:

There was careful planning at school level, and provision of helpful resources and interesting pupil activities. In the past year, the co-ordinator has rewritten the policy document and redrafted the scheme of work to include Judaism and other religions. A two year rolling programme is in place for Years 5 and 6, and another is being trialled for Years 3 and 4. The co-ordinator has introduced a scheme for monitoring progression in pupils' development of concepts, initially in relation to Christmas. She has established links with religious bodies in the community and is introducing visits to places of worship. So far, pupils have visited the local church and Hindu temple. Visits to the mosque are at planning stage. The co-ordinator is acquiring books and other resources for teaching world religions, and provided assistance to staff on request. The religious education curriculum has been planned to make explicit contributions to pupils' spiritual, moral, social and cultural development through the inclusion of stories with spiritual and moral messages and through the expectations on pupils to consider respectfully beliefs, practices and experiences different from their own.

The curriculum

In 1994 an estimated half of primary schools failed to teach religious education to all their pupils. In 1998 only one school in ten failed to do so. This partly explains the increase in satisfactory standards and teaching and indicates that for some schools, despite previous legislation, religious education is a comparatively new subject.

Another significant change during the last four years has been the move to discrete religious education lessons rather then religious education being "bolted on" to topic work. This development has increased the necessity for distinct religious education schemes of work dictated by the agreed syllabus rather then by the subjects forming the focus of topics. As teachers' subject knowledge improves, so do sensible links with other subject areas. For example, instances of Noah's Ark unsuitably linked with other teaching on animals, water, buildings and weather are now rare compared with helpful links between religious education (Islam) and geography (Pakistan).

Assessment

At both key stages, assessment is weaker in religious education than in any other subject. Schools rarely have a policy on assessment in religious education, and even where an agreed syllabus does include clear expectations, these are rarely used for assessment purposes.

Improving standards of religious education: the way forward

In order to build on already substantial improvements in religious education, schools should:

- encourage teachers to extend their subject knowledge;

- develop and implement an assessment policy;

- make full use of expertise within the school in improving the knowledge, understanding, teaching strategies and task setting of all teachers;

- ensure that teaching and progress relate to all the objectives of the agreed syllabus, not just those concerned with the acquisition of knowledge.

13 SCHOOLS WITH SERIOUS WEAKNESSES AND THOSE REQUIRING SPECIAL MEASURES

13.1 Introduction

Since the first inspection of schools according to the Framework for the Inspection of Schools, about 3 per cent (474 to the end of 1997/98) have been put into special measures and about 8 per cent have been found to have serious weaknesses. As a result of being put into special measures the schools have, in almost all cases, made good progress and very significantly improved the quality of the education that they provide for their pupils.

Primary schools subject to special measures are found in the full range of types and contexts of primary schools. Just over one-third are in urban areas where there is an obvious degree of social and economic disadvantage. But schools in suburban and rural areas are also found to be underperforming and when judged against the stated criteria they too are found to require special measures. Small rural schools in some counties form a large proportion of failing schools.

13.2 Standards of achievement

The characteristics of failing primary schools encompass all the criteria published in the annex of the Framework for the Inspection of Schools,[77] but low attainment and slow progress of pupils, together with unsatisfactory teaching and leadership, feature more prominently than the rest. In the reports of almost all schools in special

---

[77] *Guidance on the Inspection of Nursery and Primary Schools.* OFSTED, 1995.

measures, there is a reference to low standards of achievement. Most frequently the core subjects of English, mathematics and science are mentioned and, within those, attainment in literacy and numeracy are increasingly quoted. Low standards at Key Stage 2 are cited more often than low standards at Key Stage 1 or in early years classes.

The pupils' progress is judged by the gains in knowledge and skills that they make over time, as indicated in written work or records of progress or in the lessons observed during the inspection. In primary schools in special measures, the percentage of lessons where satisfactory progress is made is frequently less than 75 per cent. The criteria for consideration of failure include reference to the progress of distinct groups of pupils. The two groups most commonly quoted are pupils who have special educational needs and boys. Judgements about the progress of pupils who have special needs encompass the accuracy of the diagnosis of need and the appropriateness of the provision. A common cause of failure is the very slow progress made by pupils whose needs and provision are left entirely to the class teacher. In this respect, they often have too low expectations of progress.

13.3 Attitudes and behaviour

Negative attitudes to learning and poor levels of behaviour are often associated with pupils making insufficient progress. Obvious signs of poor discipline may well be in the form of unruly and disruptive behaviour, but there may also be considerable quiet restlessness in class, where concentration is difficult and engagement in work is low. Quantitative evidence of poor behaviour and attitudes is increasingly expressed in the numbers of exclusions, unauthorised absence and unexplained lateness.

13.4 The quality of teaching

Invariably in primary schools made subject to special measures there is criticism of the quality of teaching. This is the touchstone of the acceptability of a school's provision. The proportion of unsatisfactory teaching in failing schools can reach very high levels. The great majority of the weaknesses in the teaching include: inappropriate pitch of work; inefficient use of time; poor assessment of the pupils' progress; and weak lesson planning. These factors are often related to weak subject knowledge, particularly in English, mathematics and science. Poor presentational and organisational skills result in low engagement and poor progress of the pupils. In some schools, difficulties in recruitment and retention of teachers lead to discontinuity and fragmentation of learning.

13.5 Management and leadership

Ineffective leadership frequently features in reports of failing primary schools. Inadequate direction, unclear delegation, vague task and target setting, low levels of monitoring, weak analysis of the school's position, and a passive involvement by governors are the most commonly cited descriptions of weak leadership and management. This is manifest in low morale and poor motivation of staff, lack of teamwork and commitment, and inadequate implementation of the National Curriculum.

13.6 The improvement process

The improvement process starts with the recognition of weakness and the willingness to act urgently and vigorously to improve the school. The progress of some schools has been hindered by a reluctance to accept the inspection findings and a continued denial of failure. The positive attitude of the staff, led by the headteacher, is critical to restoration.

13.7 The action plan

The next important step is the preparation of the action plan. This provides a school with an opportunity to involve the staff in a review of the school's position and to set new shared goals. Clear, practical and manageable strategies for the achievement of those goals are at the heart of a good action plan. Schools where improvement is readily marked have action plans where priorities

are clear, responsibilities for parts of the plan are assigned, targets and success criteria are set, and there is effective monitoring and evaluation. Clarity is often reflected in the link between the action proposed and the intended outcome. Occasionally, priorities can be muddled and objectives blurred in the welter of information contained in the plan. It has been important that teachers, governors, local education authority personnel and headteachers all recognise where their contribution fits into the whole plan and how their effectiveness can be recognised and valued.

The setting of quantitative targets is an important yet difficult aspect of action plans. Many schools are rightly keen to set high targets for improved attainment, but they do not want either to be overambitious or to set their sights too low. Target setting has been given added significance with the advent of local education authority and school targets for improved attainment. Where the targets are firmly rooted in the actual performance of pupils, teachers have been able to relate more closely to the objectives and pupils have been more likely to reach the target levels. Teachers also find that targets set as stages of the improvement process are helpful. The coverage and learning of key scientific knowledge or a particular reading skill at certain points of the year, for example, provide the teacher with a clear map for improvement and the recognition of work successfully completed.

13.8 Improving management

The progress of a school in special measures is firmly linked to the quality of leadership and management. Strong leadership by the headteacher is the most prominent feature of primary schools that make good progress while in special measures. Questions are asked at an early stage about the capacity of the incumbent headteacher to lead the school's required improvement. In many cases new headteachers are quickly appointed to failing schools. In some instances this is undertaken with the temporary appointment or the secondment of another headteacher from within the local education authority; these are frequently experienced and successful headteachers. A new appointment often helps in the gaining of a fresh and unprejudiced perception and in generating increased impetus for change. This, in turn, leads to changes in staff and the revision of roles and responsibilities.

Incumbent headteachers can also improve. Where clear and detailed guidance and support have been given to the headteacher – for example by the local education authority or other external agencies – effective leadership has ensued. This has taken the form of additional training focused on managerial and organisational skills, close monitoring by the local education authority, in-school support in the form of a consultant headteacher, and a personal action plan specifying tasks and targets for improvement in the headteacher's work.

A key feature in developing the management of the school is the extent to which systems and procedures are built to ensure continued and lasting effectiveness. In this respect, self-evaluation of the school's performance can make a significant contribution. Where this is undertaken rigorously and honestly, clear gains have been made. The key ingredient is the knowledge and drive of the headteacher in setting appropriate expectations of teaching and attainment.

Just as the school's reaction to the initial inspection report is crucial to the improvement process, so too is its response to subsequent monitoring visits. Where careful note is made of the evaluations of progress on each key issue and action is geared to address specific points, success generally follows. This occasionally entails altering the emphasis or focus of the school's work.

13.9 Improving behaviour

Even if it is not a key issue in the inspection report, many primary schools choose to improve behaviour as a matter of priority. They recognise that the gaining of a calm and studious classroom is a necessary prerequisite to improving learning and achievement. Frequently, behaviour policies are developed or revised and more consistent application of new rules is sought. In some schools the enforcement of a new code of behaviour has led to a sharp increase in the number of pupils excluded for short periods of time before they learn what is expected of them and settle down to improve their behaviour. In many schools the improved behaviour of pupils is the first and most tangible achievement identified, and this is

important at a time when teachers are anxious to see early signs of success.

13.10 Improving teaching

Improving the quality of teaching can take longer. Planning is often the first aspect to be worked on in order to specify in some detail what needs to be taught at the varying stages. From this the teachers are encouraged to write detailed lesson plans with particular emphasis given to framing learning intentions more precisely. In some cases, the objectives, content and approaches are prescribed by the school and are implemented rigorously by the teachers. This, with some schools, is based on the structure and planning formats developed by the National Literacy and Numeracy Projects. When this is accompanied by effective training and support, there has been marked improvement in the quality of teaching. This is related to increased understanding of what is to be taught and what outcomes can reasonably be expected from the majority of pupils in the class. This in turn is related to more confident teaching, in which more time and attention can be given to listening to, and building on, the responses of the pupils.

13.11 Raising standards of achievement

Improving the pupils' attainment is the prime aim of schools requiring special measures and this is the crucial measure against which they are ultimately judged. Raising standards, however, can be a slow and difficult process.

Time and again schools – some in the most difficult of contexts – have demonstrated that achievement from a very low base can be improved significantly. Many headteachers and teachers have been heard to say in the initial stages of special measures that many aspects of the school's work can be changed but they doubt whether standards can be lifted. Yet, often the pupils' achievements have overtaken national averages and expectations. This progress has been gained through much detailed work in planning, monitoring and assessment. Particular attention has been given to the key skills of literacy, oracy, numeracy and information technology. This has frequently entailed a change of culture in the school to focusing on the direct and explicit teaching of knowledge, understanding and skills. This does not imply a narrowing or impoverishment of the primary curriculum. On the contrary, this focus has given a large number of pupils the chance to have greater access to a wider range of activities and a clear sense of success.

13.12 The contribution of governors

Governors have helped schools in special measures by contributing to and supporting the plans for change. Strong, well-organised governing bodies are a common feature of schools that make good progress. As with headteachers, changes of chairmanship quite often follow the designation of special measures and this may precede a revision of the whole membership of the governing body. The local education authority often appoints additional governors who have experience and skill in management and finance. Most governing bodies have developed effective committees for planning developments in the curriculum, personnel, finance and buildings. This is often accompanied by the delegation of subject responsibility to individual governors, who then visit and report on the subject to the governing body. Governors are generally slower, however, in developing effective procedures for monitoring and evaluating the school's overall progress.

13.13 The work of the local education authority

Most local education authorities provide sound support for their schools which are subject to special measures, but there is considerable variation in the manner and effect of this support. In almost all schools, much help is given with the preparation of the school's action plan. The local education authorities, through their statements of action, say what they will do to help the school. In this they may commit personnel, money and training to the school. Relatively few schools have their delegated budget withdrawn following the designation of special measures, but some local education authorities do this as a matter of policy. In future, local education authorities will be required to have regard to the Code of Practice on LEA–School Relations, which does not allow them to withdraw budgets as a matter of policy but only on a case-by-case basis. Depending on a school's needs, local education authorities often provide subject-specific help in the form of training, which is followed up by practical school-based work from advisory teachers. This help is usually highly valued by the teachers.

The monitoring and evaluation of a school's progress is a major responsibility of the local education authority. It is carried out with varying degrees of success. The best practice is found where a knowledgeable and skilful inspector relates closely to the role of the headteacher, visits regularly and provides detailed, practical advice for sustained improvement. Success is also achieved when the managerial advice is accompanied by support for teachers, mostly through the provision of practical advice from advisory teachers. A major challenge to the local education authority is in its ability to give support without encouraging dependence. The local education authority is rigorously held to account for the commitments made in the initial planning for the school's improvement.

13.14 Coming out of special measures

The work that many headteachers, staff, governors, parents, pupils and others have put into their schools to turn them from failure to success must not be underestimated. It has been those primary schools that have been determined to act quickly and decisively to bring about improvement that have made the best progress. Looking for excuses and someone to blame only hinder progress and limit improvement. Most primary schools have improved and have been removed from special measures within two years; indeed, some have reached this goal significantly more quickly.

The transformation in some schools has been quite remarkable, with provision that was poor changing to become good, unsatisfactory teaching replaced by teaching that is all sound or good, and weak leadership replaced by strong and visionary educational direction. If there has been poor behaviour, the new attitudes, enthusiasm for learning and self-discipline have made the schools pleasant places in which to learn rather than ones to avoid.

14
INITIAL TEACHER TRAINING

14.1 The context of initial teacher training and recent legislation

The Government determines policy for all aspects of teacher training – for example, defining the ceiling of expenditure for initial teacher training and continuing professional development, the overall size of the teaching force and the numbers of training places required. All initial teacher training providers must have been accredited for this purpose by the Teacher Training Agency, which also has operational responsibility for allocating trainee numbers to providers.

There are 115 initial teacher training providers in England. Most of these are universities or colleges of higher education, which are required to work in partnership with schools to deliver training courses in line with the Secretary of State's requirements set out in DfEE Circular 4/98.[78] Alongside the higher education institutions, there are 17 school-centred initial teacher training (SCITT) courses, provided by consortia of schools which work together to provide primary training, sometimes in co-operation with a higher education institution.

Under current legislation, universities and colleges are required to work in partnership with schools in the training of students, or "trainees" as initial teacher training students have been described formally by legislation since 1998.

In 1998 there were approximately 33,000 primary trainees; the numbers of primary trainees recruited for the 1997/98 academic year were 7,600 undergraduates and 4,860 Post Graduate Certificate of Education (PGCE) trainees. In general, recruitment for primary courses is good. For some of the higher education institutions the

main focus of their training is on undergraduate courses. Other institutions focus entirely on training PGCE trainees and have no undergraduate programmes.

Legislation in recent years has been focused on improving standards in initial teacher training by laying down requirements, outlined in successive Circulars, about the length, structure, management and outcomes of training courses. These have given particular prominence to the part that schools, whether in SCITTs or in partnership with higher education institutions, are expected to play and, as a result of their training, what trainees are expected to do and know and the standards they should achieve. Circular 4/98 sets out current requirements.

There have been three general principles behind recent developments in initial teacher training. First, schools and higher education institutions should work closely together in partnership in the design and delivery of courses. Second, there should be a sharp focus on subject knowledge, practical teaching and assessment, recording and reporting, defined as **standards** which all trainees have to achieve. Third, there should be a greater variety of high-quality routes to Qualified Teacher Status, reflecting the different backgrounds and qualifications of candidates and responding to the increasingly diverse needs of schools.

Circular 4/98 is the most comprehensive Circular for initial teacher training to date. It covers most aspects of training, including the content and form of the Initial Teacher Training National Curriculum for English, mathematics, science and information and communication technology. The implementation of the initial teacher training curriculum for primary English, mathematics and science is seen as a key element in the Government's plans for raising attainment in literacy and numeracy, and making progress towards the targets. The curriculum specifies the essential core of knowledge, understanding and skills which all primary trainees, on all courses of initial teacher training, must be taught and be able to use in relation to English, mathematics and science. In addition, trainees on 3–8 and 3–11 courses must demonstrate they have particular knowledge of appropriate ways of working with early years pupils, including a detailed knowledge of the Desirable Outcomes for Children's Learning.

[78] *Circular 4/98. Teaching: High Status, High Standards. Requirements for Courses of Initial Teacher Training.* DfEE, 1998.

All providers must have procedures for assuring quality, including arrangements for course validation, and course monitoring. In addition, all courses must meet the criteria specified by the Secretary of State. The Teacher Training Agency uses OFSTED inspection evidence as the basis for withdrawing accreditation from providers who do not comply. OFSTED's remit to inspect initial teacher training was first established through the Education (Schools) Act 1992, which explicitly provided for the Secretary of State to assign functions to Her Majesty's Chief Inspector of Schools in relation to the inspection of the training of teachers. Subsequently, the Teaching and Higher Education Act 1998 made explicit HMI's right of access to higher education institutions. The following sections of this chapter report and comment on the evidence from the inspection of initial teacher training, largely conducted by HMI.

14.2 Partnership between schools and higher education institutions

As was reported above, a principle of recent developments in initial teacher training has been that schools and higher education institutions should work closely together in partnership in the design and delivery of courses. The sufficiency and quality of "partner schools" vary; in some areas, especially those with several higher education institutions, providers report that there are barely sufficient partner schools and that in consequence they cannot always select their partner schools solely on the basis of quality; although most have quality criteria for selection, compromises are not uncommon. Deselection of schools in partnership is rare, although several schools have withdrawn temporarily from a partnership because of particular pressures on the school in a year: staffing changes or a forthcoming OFSTED inspection have been reasons cited for such a withdrawal.

Many schools have a strong commitment to sustaining a partnership; headteachers recognise, for example, that trainees can strengthen a school's provision or its staffing flexibility.

Among those in schools who are involved in initial teacher training, the understanding of their training role varies. In schools with more

established experience of partnership arrangements and a co-ordinating mentor on the staff, there is a greater clarity of role. Even so, not all staff are fully comfortable with the assessment of trainees, especially where a trainee is likely to fail. Several aspects of the training role often need further clarification; these include, in particular, the role of subject co-ordinators in the training process and the role of the school in the development of a trainee's subject expertise. Both these aspects are sometimes seen by schools as adding to the training costs.

Much depends on the perception that an institution and a school hold of their relative responsibilities. A minority of schools appear to look on the training role partly as an income-generating opportunity. There are also some schools which prefer professional support to money; one school, for example, received no money but took advantage of at least four visits from tutors in response to requests for in-service training. However, some schools take only limited responsibility because they do not see initial teacher training as a core activity. The perception of training as an "add-on" to a school's business reinforces the notion that the institution has the main responsibility for the training, impeding the sense of real partnership.

Many partnerships face a high turnover of mentors; 25–30 per cent is not uncommon. This puts considerable pressure on the training programme for mentors, and some institutions involve teachers other than the designated mentor in the training.

The main issues facing partnerships relate to quality assurance: how to ensure consistency in assessing the trainees against the standards established by the Teacher Training Agency; and how to ensure that trainees receive comparable training experiences of a sufficiently high quality.

14.3 Primary initial teacher training, 1995/96

In 1995 and 1996, OFSTED undertook the inspection of primary initial teacher training in 67 higher education institutions. Provision was inspected in English, mathematics, assessment, recording and reporting, and quality assurance. The inspections, which became known as the

"Primary Sweep", took place at a time of considerable change in initial teacher training, as providers adapted to the demands of the revised National Curriculum and assessment arrangements, to changing regulations relating to teacher training, and to the OFSTED inspection process itself. No formal publication of the overview of the sweep occurred because of the decision to embark on the follow-up survey, but some of the issues to which the sweep reports on institutions drew attention were the following.

English

While much of the training to teach English was good, and sometimes outstanding, the overall picture was one of too much variation in the quality of the training. Too many trainees had insufficient knowledge of the structures of the English language to teach the language requirements of the National Curriculum, and they were often insecure about how to teach reading.

For providers, the needs were to structure their courses more coherently, to ensure trainees had experience and training across the full primary age range, and to ensure consistency in training and practical classroom experience. There was a need to audit trainees' own subject knowledge, and to support and monitor this throughout the course.

The teaching of reading was the least secure element of the training. While trainees often received very good training in using a range of strategies for teaching reading, and had a good knowledge of children's literature, they were not well prepared to teach phonics and were uncertain of how to structure a reading programme for a class of pupils.

Mathematics

The content of courses reflected the balance of the National Curriculum, but the time allocated to the teaching areas of mathematics did not relate sufficiently to the relative difficulty that trainees experienced in understanding and teaching them. The monitoring of trainees' subject knowledge was insufficiently rigorous on most courses. It was uncommon for training to recognise the different needs of trainees whose subject knowledge was particularly weak, or of trainees with substantial subject expertise.

In many courses the teaching of mental methods was not given enough emphasis. Trainees often restricted their mental methods to the testing of the recall of number facts; they need more guidance on how to encourage pupils to perform mental calculations more efficiently.

The principal challenges for the higher education institutions and the partnerships were: how to ensure that the time allocated to the training to teach mathematics is used effectively; how to ensure that the national concerns about standards of numeracy are reflected in the balance of the courses provided; and how to give trainees more confidence in teaching numeracy, especially mental calculations, to pupils in Years 5 and 6.

Assessment, recording and reporting

In the best courses, training in assessment, recording and reporting was coherently planned across the range of educational and curriculum studies, and was well integrated with practical work in schools. Most courses introduced trainees at an early stage to the basic principles of assessment, the statutory requirements, and the links between planning, teaching and assessing learning.

There was, however, too much variation in the quality and effectiveness of the school-based links; much depended on the quality of the schools' own practice in assessment, recording and reporting. Furthermore, Section 10 inspections indicate that this is frequently one of the weakest aspects of primary school practice.

Many trainees found the links between planning, teaching and assessment to be tenuous and needed more help with this. Trainees' competence in assessment, recording and reporting was directly related to the quality and effectiveness of the training; and weak practice in assessment had a depressing impact on the quality of teaching and the pupils' learning. Record keeping was the aspect of practice that varied most; and few trainees had experience of reporting to parents.

Issues for the providers included: the need to be clear about the level of competence required by trainees at the end of their training; and the need to provide opportunities for trainees to accumulate experience which develops confidence and competence in assessment as an integral strand of teaching.

Quality assurance

The overwhelming majority of higher education institutions had well-established quality assurance procedures in place governing the validation and review of courses of initial teacher training approved under Circular 24/89. Quality assurance procedures for courses approved under Circular 14/93 were more varied, reflecting the recency of the initiatives. Establishing the new quality assurance arrangements in partnership schools was more successful where the institution and partner school had a long tradition of collaborative working.

Controlling the quality of provision was the major challenge facing partnerships, and much remained to be done to ensure consistency. This was not easy; for example, some partnerships were attempting to establish effective working relationships with as many as 350 schools, while placing trainees in schools as far as 100 miles from the institution.

Where consistency was a prime consideration, time was allocated to common planning; regular "cluster" meetings were held; collaborative practice and issues of moderation were addressed; and agreed guidelines for the marking of assignments were developed. Such features were not universal, however, and there were too many examples of work in schools which was insufficiently monitored and where criteria for assessment lacked consistency.

Conclusion

The main findings were that, while primary phase initial teacher training provision was generally at least satisfactory, it varied considerably in quality. One of the main generic problems was the failure of many courses to prepare trainees properly to teach English and mathematics across the full primary age; another was the absence of, or hit-and-miss approach to, the auditing of trainees' subject knowledge. However, the most worrying and striking findings of the Primary Sweep concerned the training to teach reading and arithmetic. Trainees were often very insecure about how to teach reading; in particular, they were not well prepared to teach phonics and were uncertain of how to structure a reading programme for a class of pupils. Similarly, trainees were often found to be unsure of how to teach mental calculation and often lacked competence in teaching arithmetic, particularly to pupils in Key Stage 2.

14.4 The training of trainee teachers to teach number and reading, 1996–98

The findings of the Primary Sweep emerged at a period when there was already some disquiet about the basic skills of reading and number within primary education, as well as an active debate about methods of teaching: particularly the teaching of reading and arithmetic, and the relative merits of whole-class teaching and other methods. It was in this context that HMCI decided to institute the follow-up to the Primary Sweep, with the specific purpose of following up the findings about the training to teach reading and number. The focus was in virtually every case on the training of trainees to teach reading and number in PGCE courses.

In **reading**, there was in general a marked improvement in the attention that courses gave to phonics. Most courses recognised the importance of phonics in the teaching of reading and included some training on phonics as a decoding strategy, although this was an area of weakness in a few courses.

In **number**, providers were generally showing trainees how to teach accurate, rapid, mental calculation as well as efficient standard and non-standard written and part-written methods of computation. A small minority of courses still did not teach trainees how to recognise and remedy pupils' errors and misconceptions in number.

Most trainees had at least an adequate subject knowledge of reading and number, but some common weaknesses persisted. The national literacy and numeracy initiatives had improved substantially trainees' teaching methods and classroom organisation. The time trainees spent teaching reading and number to whole classes had increased, but a few trainees still had had too little experience of teaching reading to whole classes over a sustained period. There had also been improvements in the assessment of trainees since the survey began. However, assessment was not always sufficiently rigorous or accurate and did not always cover fully the standards for qualified teacher status.

Training and assessment

Most courses ensured that trainees worked in both key stages, but the extent and quality of their experience across the full age range were a cause for concern. The majority of trainees on both early years and later years courses had insufficient opportunities to teach and assess pupils outside their specialist age range, and school-based time was sometimes used ineffectively. Trainees often carried out observations, but did not do enough teaching and assessment to put into practice what they had learnt. A substantial minority of trainees on courses for the age range 3–8 had very limited experience of teaching in nursery settings.

Class teachers generally provided good support for trainees but did not offer sufficient training in subject knowledge, planning and assessment. This was a widespread weakness in the school-based training. Trainees had insufficient opportunities to work with good teachers of reading or number. Although trainees benefited from working with co-ordinators of English, mathematics and special educational needs, these opportunities were not widespread or planned systematically within training.

Trainees received regular oral and written feedback from class teachers, mentors and higher education tutors on their teaching, but feedback from school-based staff often focused too much on class management and pupils' behaviour rather than on trainees' teaching and pupils' learning of number and reading. As a result, target setting often did not pinpoint how trainees could improve their subject knowledge, teaching and assessment.

Subject knowledge

Providers were fully aware of the need to audit trainees' subject knowledge. However, a significant minority did so ineffectively – for example by relying too much on self-assessment, by not monitoring improvements in subject knowledge or by failing to assess subject knowledge sufficiently rigorously at the end of the course.

Trainees generally had a good knowledge of the National Curriculum in reading and number and of the relevant level descriptions for their specialist key stage. However, most had too limited a knowledge of the other key stage. Trainees'

understanding of how pupils learn reading and number over the primary age range was limited by their lack of practical experience across both key stages.

In English, trainees often had limited knowledge of linguistic terms, including those relating to the teaching of reading. A minority of trainees still had significant weaknesses in their own spelling and punctuation. In mathematics, trainees often did not see the links between related aspects of number such as fractions, decimals and percentages, and sometimes could not identify and apply the properties of number.

Teaching and class management

The majority of trainees taught effectively, managed classes well, established very good relationships with pupils and seldom experienced problems with discipline. A minority still exhibited shortcomings in aspects of their class management.

Most trainees planned well-structured lessons. However, a significant minority did not define learning objectives clearly, often concentrating too much on what pupils were doing rather than on what they were learning. Many trainees had difficulty in planning and pacing a structured sequence of lessons for reading and number.

Most trainees were at least adequately trained to use information and communication technology, but such training was rarely good. Trainees often had very limited opportunity in schools to observe information and communication technology being used well or to use it themselves in teaching. A significant minority of courses did not show trainees how to make efficient and effective use of calculators.

Assessment, recording and reporting

The quality of trainees' monitoring, assessment, recording, reporting and accountability remained the weakest aspect of their work in number and reading. Over a third of providers needed to make significant improvements to their trainees' standards in this area.

Almost all trainees kept records of pupils' performance in reading and number, but the quality of those records was very variable, ranging from excellent to barely adequate. Of course, the quality of schools' systems varied and trainees were often required to use these even where they were not particularly good. Providers did not always offer sufficiently strong guidance about what records trainees should keep.

Trainees were familiar with the statutory assessment requirements. Schools, however, often missed opportunities to introduce trainees directly to the national tests, even when the trainees were in schools when these took place.

School experience often does not coincide with parents' meetings and hence often does not allow trainees to take part in or observe such meetings. However, many providers attempted to compensate for this by setting up mock parental interviews, and some partnership schools (especially in SCITT courses) offered trainees the experience of reporting to parents.

Improving standards: key issues and some ways forward[79]

In reviewing their courses in the light of future requirements, partnerships should look closely at the need to:

- strengthen further all trainees' practical ability to teach reading and number systematically and their knowledge and understanding of pupils' development in these areas, by making the best use of the time they spend in schools;

- ensure that all trainees:
  - ◆ cover the curriculum in reading and number for the full primary age range;
  - ◆ have effective practical experience of teaching and assessment in each key stage;

- enable high standards of subject knowledge to be met, in accordance with the new requirements of the National Curriculum for initial teacher training, by ensuring that:
  - ◆ in reading, all trainees, including those specialising in the later years, are knowledgeable about phonics and have a confident understanding of linguistic terminology, particularly at word and sentence level, to support their teaching;

  - ◆ all trainees can plan and implement a structured programme of phonics teaching in order to develop systematically pupils' ability to read;

  - ◆ in number, trainees know and understand the conceptual links between related aspects of number (such as fractions, decimals and percentages) and have deeper understanding of the number system, number operations and relationships;

  - ◆ all trainees can plan and implement a clearly structured sequence of number lessons;

- ensure that the assessment of all trainees against the standards for qualified teacher status is comprehensive, rigorous and accurate;

- build into school-based training more opportunities for trainees to observe and work with teachers who are expert in the teaching of reading and number;

- assess trainees' subject knowledge in number and reading rigorously and systematically, monitor their progress during the course, teach subject knowledge directly in training sessions, and have secure systems for assessing trainees' knowledge by the end of the course;

- improve the oral and written feedback to trainees, so that it focuses on the quality of their teaching of number and reading and on the pupils' learning, and also provides explicit targets for trainees which will develop their subject knowledge and their planning, teaching and assessment skills;

- improve the standard of trainees' assessment, recording and reporting through:
  - ◆ providing strong guidance on defining and assessing learning objectives;
  - ◆ clarifying the purpose and extent of the records that need to be kept;
  - ◆ extending trainees' knowledge and use of level descriptions beyond their specialist key stage;
  - ◆ increasing their practical experience and knowledge of national tests;
  - ◆ improving their involvement in reporting to parents;

---

[79] These issues are largely taken from *The Inspection of Initial Teacher Training: Primary Follow-Up Survey 1996 to 1998*. OFSTED, 1998. The full report is published as *Primary Follow-up Survey of the Training of Trainee Teachers to Teach Numbers and Reading*. OFSTED, 1999.

- provide opportunities for trainees to try out in school what they have learned about information and communication technology to support the teaching of reading and number, including the effective use of calculators as a tool for pupils' learning about number.

ANNEX 1: THE STATUTORY BASIS FOR EDUCATION[80]

The education system in England is to a large extent governed by Acts of Parliament and related Statutory Instruments. The years before the first full inspection cycle brought an unprecedented amount of reforming legislation, largely enshrined in the Education Reform Act 1988. This Act established the subjects of the National Curriculum and the local management of schools. Issues of accountability were taken further than before through the publication of national test results, the publication of performance tables, and published inspection reports on every maintained primary school in England. The principles and frameworks laid down in successive Acts from 1944 onwards are consolidated in two recent Acts: the Education Act 1996 and the School Inspections Act 1996.

The Department for Education and Employment (DfEE) administers the statutory framework that governs the education system, establishes national education policies and works with other central and local government bodies in the implement-ation of those policies. Advice is provided by Government departments and also by non-departmental public bodies such as the Qualifications and Curriculum Authority (formerly SCAA and NCVQ).

Central Government provides the bulk of the finance for the education system, but it is largely administered by local education authorities and the governing bodies of individual schools and colleges. The Funding Agency for Schools is responsible for administering the payment of grants to grant maintained schools; however, by 1998 there were only 502 grant maintained schools, serving 3 per cent of the pupil population.

OFSTED is a non-ministerial government department established in September 1992 by the Education (Schools) Act 1992, now consolidated into the School Inspections Act 1996. OFSTED is headed by Her Majesty's Chief Inspector (HMCI), the first of whom was Professor Stewart Sutherland; after Professor Sutherland's return to Scotland, the post of HMCI has been held by Chris Woodhead. HMCI is responsible for securing the inspection of schools; for the registration of inspectors; and for advising the Secretary of State on all aspects of the quality of education and school standards.

The secular curriculum of all maintained schools is inspected by registered inspectors under contract to OFSTED. However, in schools in which denominational religious education takes place, this, and in some circumstances collective worship, must be inspected by a person chosen by the governing body rather than OFSTED.

Much of the evidence in this report is drawn from the substantial database constructed from the first cycle of inspections carried out under the legislation of 1992 and 1996; such inspections are usually referred to as "Section 9" (now Section 10) inspections. Denominational education, inspected separately and not reported on here, comes under "Section 13" (now Section 23).

Much of what happens in schools has been influenced by recent legislation. This legislation inevitably forms the backdrop to much of this report. The principal influences have been on the following.

The characteristics of the school

- **Admissions:** parents have the right to express a preference as to the school at which they wish their children to attend, and local education authorities and governing bodies must try to meet these preferences.

- **Charging** for admission and education in all maintained schools is prohibited, but there are some exceptions such as individual musical tuition and board and lodging on residential visits.

- **Special educational need provision:** schools must pay regard to the Code of Practice on the identification and assessment of special educational needs. Where a child has been assessed as needing special provision determined by a statement, the local education authority must make and maintain a statement for that child and review it annually.

---

[80] This chapter draws principally on *School Inspection: a guide to the law,* OFSTED, November 1997, and *School Governors: A guide to the law,* DfEE, 1997.

Aspects of the school

- **Results of pupils' attainments**. Schools must publish the school and national results of the National Curriculum assessments in the core subjects of English, mathematics and science of seven-year-olds and eleven-year-olds. Schools must also provide at least annually a **written report to parents**, giving details of progress in all subjects and of attainment in nationally assessed subjects.

- **The National Curriculum** applies only to pupils of statutory school age. Maintained schools must teach the subjects of the National Curriculum and religious education, and the curriculum must be broad and balanced.

- The overall number of **lesson hours** per week is not prescribed, although guidance is given. Good practice is taken to be 21 hours for pupils aged 5–7 and 23.5 hours for pupils aged 8–11.

- **Religious education** in LEA maintained schools (and generally in controlled schools) must be taught in accordance with a locally agreed syllabus. Parents can withdraw their child from all or part of religious education.

- Schools must provide for all pupils to attend a daily act of **collective worship**, which over a term must be broadly Christian in character. Parents may withdraw their child from collective worship. Schools may apply to the local Standing Advisory Council on Religious Education for a determination that the requirement for Christian collective worship should not apply in the case of the school or any class or description of pupils.

The management and efficiency of the school

Governors have a general responsibility for the effective management of the school within the framework of national legislation and, in the case of local education authority maintained schools, of local education authority policies. Detailed decisions about the day-to-day running of the school are the responsibility of the headteacher.

The duties of governors now include:

- establishing, with the headteacher, the aims and policies of the school and how standards can be improved;

- helping to draw up the school development plan;

- advising on spending the budget;

- ensuring that the National Curriculum and religious education are taught;

- selecting the headteacher, and appointing, promoting, supporting and disciplining other staff;

- acting as a link between the school and the community;

- drawing up the post-inspection action plan and monitoring how that plan is put into practice.

Local education authorities must maintain schemes under which delegated budgets apply to all LEA maintained schools.

The role and duties of local education authorities

The period 1994–98 was one in which the roles of local education authorities changed, were increasingly defined and came under public scrutiny. Local education authorities must maintain schemes under which all county and maintained schools have delegated budgets. The Funding Agency for Schools is responsible for administering the payment of grants to grant maintained schools. The accounts of schools with delegated budgets are subject to regular internal audit and must be available for inspection as necessary by local education authorities' external auditors.

Towards the end of the inspection cycle the role of the local education authority was more closely defined in terms of intervention, which should be "in inverse proportion to success" and has been established as a primary role for local education authorities. These responsibilities are now set out in education development plans which include, for example, their progress towards meeting performance targets in their schools, targets for reducing exclusions and unauthorised absences, approaches to tackling schools causing concern, and their plans for implementing national strategies such as that for literacy.

Index

Note. Page references for main entries are printed in **bold**.

Index compiled by Indexing Specialists, Hove.

Printed in the United Kingdom for the Stationery Office
J85243 C220 7/99 19585 436856